D0923435

THE RISE AND FALL
OF
HERMANN GOERING

By the same author

TWILIGHT IN VIENNA

THE RISE AND FALL
OF HERMANN GOERING

Lieutenant Hermann Goering, appointed to the command of the famous Richthofen Squadron at the age of twenty-five, poses proudly with the heavy stick without which his great predecessor, Manfred von Richthofen, the "Red Knight," had rarely been seen. Goering, in 1918, had earned the Pour le Mérite, and been credited with shooting down twenty-two Allied planes.

THE RISE AND FALL OF HERMANN GOERING

BY WILLI FRISCHAUER

ILLUSTRATED

19  51

The Riverside Press Cambridge

HOUGHTON MIFFLIN COMPANY BOSTON

The Riverside Press
CAMBRIDGE · MASSACHUSETTS
PRINTED IN THE U.S.A.

CONTENTS

ILLUSTRATIONS

INTRODUCTION

IT WOULD have been extremely difficult to write this biography of Hermann Goering without the assistance of his widow, Frau Emmy Goering, to whom I am indebted for invaluable information. But a few words are necessary to explain her position to the reader. Frau Goering was arrested by the American authorities in 1945, was held as a potential witness at the Nuremberg trial, and released in March, 1946. She was again arrested in 1947, this time by order of the Bavarian Minister, Alfred Loritz, and held in various prison camps until 1948, when she was indicted before a German de-Nazification court in Garmisch-Partenkirchen. By verdict of this court, she was classified in Category II of Nazi offenders (profiteers from Nazism). The court sentenced her to one year's imprisonment, but, as she had been held for fourteen months, ordered her immediate release. Thirty per cent of her property was declared forfeit and she was deprived of all civil rights for five years; under Article 65, paragraph 1b, of the de-Nazification Law, she was barred for the same period from carrying on the profession of writer, teacher, preacher, editor, or radio commentator.

Soon after her release, an inquiry reached the Minister for Political Liberation in Bavaria with regard to the provisions of the sentence which barred her from writing her memoirs. The interest in her story, particularly in America, was great and she received many offers to write about her life with Hermann Goering. On behalf of Ministerial Director Camil Sachs, in charge of the Bavarian Ministry for Political Liberation, Senate President Braun explained in reply to this inquiry that violation of the provisions of the verdict was a punishable offence: "Any activity in which formulated expressions of thought are transmitted to a third person," Senate President Braun wrote, "can be regarded as prohibited. The law cannot and does not want to restrict the mental activity of those affected; it aims at excluding them from influencing the political or cultural life. Accordingly [Frau Goering] is not allowed to publish or circulate her writings before the end of the period [of five years]."

Ministerial Director Sachs, on July 8, 1950, at my request, handed me a copy of this interpretation of the verdict which emanated from his office. When I realised that Frau Goering was under the impression that she was also forbidden to give interviews, I consulted the Ministerial Director, who is the highest authority on de-Nazification affairs in Bavaria. As a result of our conversation, he wrote to Frau Goering. Here is a literal translation of his letter: "I have received the visit of Mr. Willi Frischauer . . . who would like to interview you. At his visit at Etzelwang [where Frau Goering was living at the time], he gathered that you were apprehensive about giving an interview because the verdict has forbidden you to engage in any writing activities. Mr. Frischauer has asked me to relieve you of your fear. . . . You are in no way forbidden to give information. . . ."

Frau Goering also had to consider the possible reaction of the Bavarian Office of Restitution which is dealing with the financial provisions of the verdict and still held the whole of her property. To allay Frau Goering's fears in this respect, the President of the Office of Restitution, Dr. Philip Auerbach, at my request, wrote to her as follows: "I have received the visit of Willi Frischauer . . . who intends to publish a book on Hermann Goering. I believe that nobody can give better information about the positive sides of your late husband than you. . . . Frischauer is known to me as a reliable, serious person who would not in any way publish sensational accounts. . . . I believe that you need have no hesitation to discuss this matter with Frischauer. It would be of vital importance, also for you, if the world public, apart from much negative, would also hear something positive, about Hermann Goering's life and work. . . ."

These two letters reassured Frau Goering, who had hitherto refused all requests to co-operate on stories about Hermann Goering. I first met her at Wenningstedt on the island of Sylt, where she owns a little house, which was at the time occupied by a high ranking British Air Force officer. Although it was a painful experience for her to speak about her husband, she patiently replied to a thousand questions. I did not, of course, offer her any financial reward; neither, I am convinced, would she have accepted it. I have made much use of the information which she supplied, although I was reluctantly unable to accept some of her statements and was forced in several instances to modify her accounts in the light of information from other sources. Hermann Goering, in the memory of his widow, lives as a knight in shining armour without a blemish on his character. At her own trial, she said that she shared his Weltanschauung — his ideological view of the world.

Frau Goering gave me an introduction to Robert Kropp and I made no excuse for including in this book much of "what the valet saw." Herr Robert Kropp was with Goering from 1933 to 1945 and was one of my most important and reliable informants. I am grateful to the former General Karl Bodenschatz, chief of Goering's Ministerial Office, for the information which he was able to give me. A de-Nazification court verdict, similar to the one passed on Frau Goering, prevents him, for the time being, from writing his own story. Former General Karl Koller, the last Chief of Staff of the Luftwaffe, also assisted me with lucid and extensive accounts of his work and meetings with Goering.

Many other erstwhile associates of Hermann Goering talked willingly — under the proviso that I should not mention them as sources of information. I have respected their requests. Only very few members of Goering's own entourage refused to co-operate — among them his secretary, Fraeulein Gisele Limberger. Dr. Erich Gritzbach, one of his closest collaborators, told me that he planned to write about his experiences in the Goering period at a later date: "I want to retain my material for my own use," he wrote. It should be an interesting book, although the crop of autobiographies of the innumerable satellites in the Nazi firmament has already induced German humourists to produce parodies under such titles as "I was Hitler's moustache" or "I was Goering's medal."

I want to make it clear that my observation post for over twenty-five years was on the other side of the fence. If occasionally it may seem that I have fallen under the spell of Hermann Goering's posthumous charm, this is in spite of the fact that my parents perished in a Nazi concentration camp. If certain passages of this book bear the stamp of a lifelong anti-Nazi, this is also in spite of the fact that I have spared no effort to discover and use information coming from Hermann Goering's numerous surviving friends and admirers.

Much use has been made of the extensive literature dealing with the hectic historical events through which Goering lived. I have had the assistance of many librarians, both in Great Britain and in Germany. I should like to thank them all for their help, but I must specially mention the Wiener Library in London, where I found many gems which are not now available anywhere else. The American Army authorities in Germany, the Air Ministry and the War Office in London, among other official bodies, have also supplied me with facts and figures, but they are, of course, in no way responsible for the use which I have made of their information. Among others, I am grateful to Sir Archibald Sinclair, Bart., to Sir David Maxwell-Fyfe, to Lord Douglas of Kirtleside, for the estimates of Goering which they have given me. My thanks also to Joan Peskett for her patient work on the manuscript and to my wife, who kept the home fires burning while I worked.

WILLI FRISCHAUER

MUNICH — LONDON, 1950

PRELUDE

THE AFTERNOON of October 7, 1946, was frosty and miserable. A sharp wind whirled the dust around the ruins of Nuremberg and seemed even to penetrate the thick walls of the old Palace of Justice. Through a creaking door Frau Emmy Goering was shown into Room 57, reserved for visitors to the condemned Nazi war criminals. Waiting on the far side of a partition, handcuffed to a sergeant of the American Military Police, was her husband, pale and quiet, an eerie picture with his head and shoulders framed in the wooden crossbars.

For a few seconds the silence was heavy, oppressive. Then Hermann Goering spoke. The voice was clear, the words sounded firm and strong, perhaps a little too loud — in the effort to hide an overwhelming emotion: "God bless you," he said slowly, " — and the child. God protect all those who are good to you. . . . God protect Germany."

As he took leave forever from his wife and child, Hermann Goering tried to raise his right hand. His move jerked the arm of the American sergeant. It startled the man, who brought his arm down violently and Goering's hand with it. "He thought," Emmy Goering told me, with tears in her eyes recalling the scene, "that my husband was going to give the Nazi salute — the Nazi salute — at this moment — Good God! He wanted to touch me, to grip my hand, to kiss me for the last time . . ."

Abruptly the sergeant swung his prisoner round. Emmy's own hand groped after him as if to hold on to him, to bring him back to herself, to little Edda and to life. Hermann Goering did not turn his head — did not see her gesture. Tears blurred Emmy's view as he was led away. For a long time it was as if the sound of his footsteps beat a rhythm in her head, though she is not sure whether she ever really heard them.

Frau Emmy does not remember her husband as he looked just then — his weight reduced from over two hundred pounds to a mere hundred and fifty, the old grey-blue Luftwaffe uniform, stripped of all insignia, dangling loosely around his body, deep shadows under his eyes which matched the colour of his tunic, the muscles of his jaw contracting and relaxing in nervous tension, his lips quivering. Death, above all, the French say, means parting, leaving those one loves. This, then, was the hour of Hermann Goering's death.

Emmy Goering, they whisper in Germany, will not believe that her husband has gone, that he is really dead. I told her of this story and she smiled sadly. Quietly she explained that there was just a grain of truth in it. Yes, she can still feel his presence. It is often difficult to believe that he is no more. Yes, Hermann, in a sense, is still with her; but it is not the Hermann Goering of the grey October afternoon in the Nuremberg Jail. It is Hermann Goering the Prussian Prime Minister, speaking from a platform draped with flags; Hermann Goering the Reichsmarschall, swinging his ivory, diamond-studded baton; Hermann Goering her husband as she knew him at home — a big, busy, bustling, agile man, too agile for his size. She can still hear his ready laugh, his booming, sonorous voice, the fun, the stories about himself and others which he told with gusto. How he enjoyed being Hermann Goering! In Emmy Goering's mind he survives as I expected this extraordinary character to be mirrored in the eyes of the woman who loved him.

He was the type to provoke an immediate reaction to his personality. The first impression counted and often remained. Opinion about him however, is by no means unanimous. Goebbels called him "the upright soldier with a child's heart"; Konrad Heiden, the anti-Nazi writer, added, " — and with a child's brain." The American Ambassador, William E. Dodd, saw in him "a fat, ridiculous-looking man," and someone else said that when he entered a room he created the impression of the presence of "an old dowager." Sir Nevile Henderson, the British Ambassador, found "certain attractive qualities" in him, and added, "I must frankly say that I had a real personal liking for him." The epithets which have been linked with his name range widely. To some of his friends he was "the last real Renaissance figure." I have heard him described as "the modern version of a Roman proconsul." He liked to think of himself as a "German Maecenas." His enemies say that he was "the greatest thief of contemporary history." He has been called a Falstaff, a buccanneer, a hero, a playboy, a great diplomat, a ruthless adventurer, a likeable bully, an able administrator, a cunning politician, at once simple, vain, and brutal.

I asked Sir David Maxwell Fyfe, the King's Counsel and former British Attorney-General, what he thought of Goering, whom he mercilessly and skilfully cross-examined in the Nuremberg trial. His reply was: "He had a quick brain, an excellent memory, a complete mastery of political approach to mass German opinion, courage, and a power to get himself liked by the great majority of people that he met. When these qualities are coupled with complete ruthlessness, vanity, and greed," Sir David elaborated, "you have a figure that could not be laughed off."

No, you could not easily laugh off Hermann Goering. My own thoughts went back to Berlin, to the evening of Monday, February 27, 1933. With a great number of other journalists I had come to Germany to report final stages of the Reichstag election campaign. The election was due the following Sunday, when a decisive vote was to test the country's reaction to the somewhat unexpected appointment, barely a month before, of Adolf Hitler as Chancellor. The political atmosphere was tense. Every hour brought rumours of revolution and counter-revolution.

It was about 9.25 P.M. when a shout was heard above the din of voices at the Café Hessler, behind the Kurfuerstendamm: "The Reichstag is on fire!" We jumped into our car and rushed to the Reichstag, to arrive just before a police cordon had closed around the building. There was a glow in one of the cupolas, a column of smoke rose to the sky. A minute later a cavalcade of fast cars came to a sudden halt at the side door to which we had made our way. Uniformed men jumped from the cars. Surrounded by a big entourage, Hermann Goering moved quickly towards the entrance. As he passed us, I saw that his face was a purple red. He looked as if he were clenching his fists deep down in the big pockets of his greatcoat. An official emerged from the door to meet the Minister. The noise of cars and fire engines, of excited shouts and clipped police commands, could not drown Hermann Goering's voice: "A crime!" he thundered — "an unheard-of crime!" The men around him echoed his words. Once more, as he entered the Reichstag building, I heard him, every word cutting sharply through the air which was thick with dust and smoke: "An den Galgen mit ihnen!" he screamed — To the gallows with them!

Two hours later, our messages were on the wires to the four corners of the world. My own report said: "There can be little doubt that the fire which is consuming the Reichstag was the work of hirelings of the Hitler Government. It seems that the incendiaries have made their way to the Reichstag through an underground passage which connects the building with the palace of the Reichstag President, Cabinet Minister and Reich Commissioner for the Prussian Police, Captain Hermann Goering. . . ."

Within a few days this version of the origin of the fire had been almost universally accepted. A German newspaper reported the arrest of two persons who had asserted that Goering was the instigator of the incendiarism. The front pages of the world press displayed pictures of the burning Reichstag and of Goering. The reports coincided with the publication in Berlin of a government decree virtually suspending the German Constitution and abolishing the liberty of the individual German. It was signed by Goering. Thus, from the sea of flames which destroyed the Reichstag — and German democracy — Hermann Goering emerged to international notoriety.

1

AN EARLY INSTINCT

ON THE MORNING of May 28, 1885, two hansom cabs were ordered by a middle-aged German, who was staying at the Charing Cross Hotel in the Strand of London. One was to take him and his fiancée to the German Chapel Royal, St. James's where they had arranged to be married that day. Another German couple, their friends, followed in the second carriage to act as witnesses. There was a simple, hurried ceremony. The bridegroom signed the register with an anglicised version of his name — Henry Ernest Goering, widower, aged forty-five years, civil service officer at Berlin. His bride was Fanny Tiefenbrunn, aged twenty-six, a spinster, and a daughter of a merchant. The witnesses were Franz and Marie Weber.

Thus Hermann Goering's father was married in London, in a part of the city against which his son was later to direct the Luftwaffe in the fiercest assault from the air ever known. The children of the late Heinrich Ernst Goering and Franziska Tiefenbrunn, even now, know very little about the circumstances of this wedding in the faraway British capital. Why should a patriotic Prussian civil servant have chosen London for the ceremony?

Fifty years later there appeared in Leipzig the fourth volume in the series of *Family Trees of Famous Germans* edited by Professor Baron Otto Dungern, whose subject was the Prussian Prime Minister, Air Minister, Colonel-General Hermann Goering. The racial laws were in operation in Germany, and research into the antecedents of the famous and infamous, even of the insignificant, developed into a profitable industry. Everybody was anxious to prove at least sixteen Aryan ancestors. Hermann Goering's family tree was an imposing plant: the diligent Professor Dungern was able to trace his ancestors back to the twelfth century. Though the

Goerings had always been proud of their family history, it was new to Hermann Goering that the blood of the ancient royal houses of Hohenzollern and Wittelsbach flowed in his veins. It appeared that he was also, however distantly, related to the family of Germany's greatest poet and thinker, Johann Wolfgang von Goethe, with the decendants of Bismarck, the "Iron Chancellor," and, appropriately, with Count Zeppelin, who had given his name to the erstwhile pride of German aviation. Through the Hohenzollerns Hermann Goering was even a kinsman of Kaiser Wilhelm II and — of Queen Victoria. Kings, dukes, princes, and counts figure prominently in many branches of his family tree.

Pride in such venerable family connections was a little damped by other revelations in Professor Dungern's scientific study. Heinrich Ernst Goering had been married before and was the father of five children, four of whom survived. Ida, his first wife, had died in 1879, after ten years of marriage. As a widower, Heinrich had led an independent life, unburdened by the care of his children, whom relatives had taken off his hands. Then he met Fanny Tiefenbrunn, a lively, buxom Bavarian girl of Austrian origin — "a remarkable woman," as all agree who knew her. These were difficult days for Heinrich Goering. He had just abandoned his career as a district judge and joined the consular service of the Berlin Foreign Office. Restless, anxious to get away from the humdrum petit bourgeois existence in the provincial towns to which his appointments had taken him, he had applied for a job abroad and had been lucky to attract the attention of Chancellor Bismarck. His son Hermann later missed few opportunities to recall the personal association of the two men.

Bismarck himself suggested that Heinrich Goering should go to London to acquaint himself with the famed British technique of colonial organization and administration. For Goering this was a unique opportunity, also a way out of an embarrassing situation. Fanny Tiefenbrunn was carrying his child under her heart and he was anxious to take her away from Germany. Together they crossed the Channel. In London Heinrich Goering was soon immersed in the study of colonial problems. It was not long before he could honestly report to Bismarck that he now felt qualified for

Karin Goering, née Baroness Fock, as she appeared in 1930. Hitler used to describe her as the "mascot" of the German National Socialist movement.

Hermann Goering as Commander of the S.A. (storm troopers) at week-end exercises near Munich early in 1923. (On his left, hatless, Adolf Hitler.)

On a ceremonial occasion Hermann Goering, as Prussian Prime Minister, is photographed with his closest personal friend and A.D.C., General Karl Bodenschatz. Bodenschatz was Adjutant of the Richthofen Squadron in the First World War; he joined Goering's staff again in 1933.

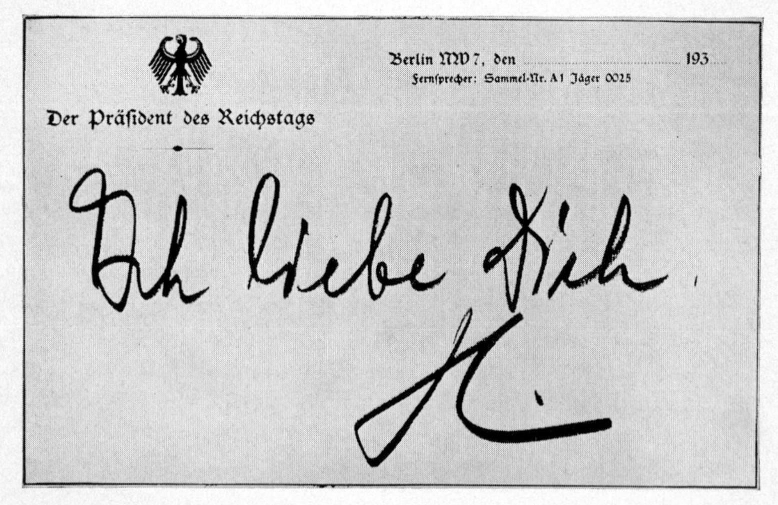

Berlin NW 7, den .... 193...
Fernsprecher: Sammel-Nr. A 1 Jäger 0025

Der Präsident des Reichstags

Ich liebe Dich

H

Goering's first note on Presidential-headed notepaper.

an overseas appointment. The German Chancellor decided to send him to Southwest Africa. Here Germany had acquired her first trading interests. It would be Goering's job to strengthen and to expand the German hold on this territory. The appointment enabled him also to solemnise his union with Fanny — whom he now married according to the rites of the German Lutherans. There was no time for a honeymoon. Heinrich Goering was off to Africa, but his wife was unable to accompany him. Hurriedly she returned to Germany, where her first boy, Karl Ernst, was born at the beginning of August.

Heinrich Goering's title was "Reich Commissar for Southwest Africa," but the Reich was not really in control. Modest branches of trading companies, however, bravely showed the German flag. They did not as yet add up to a colony. The new Reich Commissar went to work and proved himself an able administrator and an even better businessman. Unlike many of his successors, whose clumsy, dictatorial approach to the natives roused resentment in Africa, he handled the native chiefs cleverly, was diplomatic, considerate, always anxious to allay their suspicions. His agreements with the tribes enhanced German prestige, and enabled the traders to venture even farther inland. Goering was never too proud to learn. When he met Cecil Rhodes and sensed the greatness of the man, he tried to model himself and his work on the example of the British empire-builder. The two men became friends.

As soon as Hermann Goering rose to prominence in the Third Reich, the sycophants of the National Socialist Party were determined to build up a myth of achievement around his name. His Pomeranian great-great-grandfather, a ruthless tax collector in the service of the Prussian Kings, they turned into a "sponsor of trade and manufacture," until in the eyes of uninitiated Germans he appeared as the virtual founder of the Ruhr industry. His great-grandfather, a modest country judge, was described as a "fountain of German justice." There is little evidence to support these extravagant assumptions, but Hermann Goering's father deserves credit for the expansion and consolidation of German Southwest Africa. On his advice Bismarck's successor, Caprivi, abandoned a plan to barter the territory away to the British. The history books of

Nazi Germany called Heinrich Goering the founder of the colony. He certainly was a powerful protector of German commerce and a faithful servant of the German Government.

Fanny Goering, with her firstborn, soon followed her husband to Africa. She was a strong, tough, young woman of simple tastes and her energy and endurance were ideally suited to the arduous, primitive, sometimes dangerous, conditions under which the Reich Commissar was forced to carry on his work. Herero tribes, the Bergdamaras and Ramaquas, harassed the German traders and more than once in fierce raids attacked the Commissar and his wife, who were forced to flee and abandon their home on many occasions. Patiently Fanny built up a new home every time. She never gave up. When a daughter, Olga, was born to her, she was attended by a young Austrian doctor, Hermann Eppenstein, member of a wealthy Jewish family who had gone to Africa in search of adventure and was one of the few close friends of the family.

After five years the Goerings decided to return to the Fatherland. German traders and colonists now felt secure. The territory, safely under German rule, stretched five hundred miles inland. The administration which the Reich Commissar had established was functioning smoothly, but Germany, now that Bismarck was gone, held out few attractions for Heinrich Goering. After an extended holiday, he once more volunteered for an overseas appointment— this time for the vacant post of German consul-general in Haiti. After Fanny Goering had given birth to her third child, she cheerfully followed her husband once more into the wilderness. Her boy was five years old, little Olga was only one, and the youngest, Paula, barely three months, when she set out for Haiti, undeterred by the prospect of a bleak existence in another barely civilised part of the world.

It was Africa all over again. The natives were difficult, earthquakes shook the ramshackle abode of the consul, giant ants and scorpions invaded the house and threatened the children. Fanny Goering weathered all storms. Governing unruly servants, looking after the three infants, she still found time to accompany her husband on extensive hunting expeditions, was as adept a horsewoman as she was a cook. But Haiti was not a place where a European woman would gladly risk bringing a baby into the world. When a fourth child was on the way, Fanny decided that it should be born in Germany. In October, 1892, she undertook the long voyage home. In the Marienbad Sanatorium at Rosenheim in Bavaria, in the small hours of January 12, 1893, she gave birth to her fourth child, the second son. She named him Hermann Wilhelm Goering. Although his paternal ancestors hailed from Prussia, Hermann Goering liked to regard himself as a Bavarian. As a member of the "Bavarian Group" of the Nazi Party, he rose to prominence and many, even his closest friends, were later surprised to discover so many Prussian traits in his character.

In 1938 Hermann Goering forced the Anschluss of Austria. Among the refugees who fled from Vienna before the brown flood was Sigmund Freud, who has taught the world to trace the effect of infant experiences on adult life. Hermann Goering was a classic example of many of Freud's findings. Had Goering submitted himself to examination by a psychoanalyst, he would have been told that he suffered a severe shock when he was forcefully parted from his mother only six weeks after his birth. The tireless Fanny Goering left her son to return to her husband in Haiti. In later life Hermann Goering developed many characteristics of a child who was weaned too soon from his mother's breast. Subconsciously he was always trying to recapture the mother love which he had missed in his infancy. There is also other evidence to show how much he resented the separation. As a youngster he was jealous of his brother and sisters who had known the strange, mysterious lands across the seas. To his little friends he boasted that he had been born in Haiti. They repeated the stories at home and the tales persisted and spread. With Adolf Hitler a native of Austria and German only by a dubious process of naturalisation, Rudolf Hess, born in Alexandria, Egypt, and Ernst Bohle in Bradford, Yorkshire, England, the Nazi Propaganda Ministry had to work overtime to convince the Germans that Hermann Goering, at least, was a true son of Germany. He never saw Haiti.

He was left in the care of Frau Graf, a friend of the family, whom he called "Mother" as soon as he learned to speak. Not until six years later was he to be reunited with his real mother. The time had come for Heinrich Goering to return to Berlin. Aged and mellowed, a typical patriotic civil servant, he worked for a few more months at the Foreign Office. Then he retired. His friends were drawn from his own class and colleagues, civil servants and officers of the Prussian Army. Hermann Goering always traced his own love of soldiering to the atmosphere in his father's home. There the talk was of 1866 and 1870, of the "French enemy"; of Prussia's greatness and the power of her arms. He often told a story to show that "Prussian arms" in these days did not mean something vague or abstract to him. Frequently as a boy he persuaded Johann, the family servant, to take up to his bedroom the glittering helmets and shining sabres which his father's guests deposited in the lobby. On Sundays Father Goering would take the children to Potsdam to watch the military parades. This atmosphere of national grandeur was in regrettable contrast to the straitened financial circumstances of Goering senior, who was now dependent on a meagre pension. Berlin was expensive and he was living and entertaining on a standard far beyond his means.

The old friend of the family, Dr. Hermann Eppenstein, who had already acted as godfather to Hermann Goering, came to the rescue. A few years previously he had embraced the Christian faith and, like many Austrians of wealth and distinction, had been knighted by Emperor Franz Josef. Now he owned two castles, one in Mauterndorf near Salzburg in the Lungau district of Austria; another, Burg (Fortress) Veldenstein on the river Pegnitz near Nuremberg. The rich, retired gentleman's only interest in life were historical studies and his friends — foremost among the last the Goerings. Now he offered Veldenstein to his old comrade from Southwest Africa. Was it the offer of a temporary home? Was it a gift? The two friends never defined the transaction. Sufficient that it enabled Heinrich Goering — his wife had, in the meantime, presented him with a fifth child, Albert — to spend the rest of his days with his family at this imposing, if old-fashioned, castle in a beautiful part of Franconia. The upkeep was not cheap, but Hermann von Eppenstein did not mind making a contribution towards it. He also undertook to make the education of his godchild Hermann his own personal concern.

Official Nazi biographers of Hermann Goering have devoted much care and attention to research into his childhood. If we are to believe them, the boy must have led an unusually full and adventurous life, crowded with dramatic incidents, even before he had reached the age of ten. He was sent to Fuerth, sister town of Nuremberg, and entrusted to the care of a tutor. It appears that young Hermann did not enjoy the separation from his family and from Veldenstein, his new home, which — with towers and turrets, with ditches and bridges — lent itself admirably to war games in the true mediaeval style. Little Hermann played at soldiers most of the time. His father's accounts of the Boer War had impressed him deeply and the English represented the enemy in his games. He, of course, was a "General of the Boers." There is an inn in the district with a visitors' book in which the ten-year-old Hermann had signed his name with a proud "Burengeneral" underneath. He was already a general in the Third Reich when he told King Boris of Bulgaria something about his own strategic genius of these early days. Whenever he deployed his tin soldiers he used a big mirror: "In that way," he explained, "I could double my forces." In the final stages of the recent war Adolf Hitler frequently accused him of doubling the Luftwaffe forces on paper.

Erich Gritzbach, who became one of Goering's chief administrative officers, thought it opportune to record an incident which described the boy Hermann at the age of eight, setting his little dachshund on the Jews of Fuerth. Today members of Hermann Goering's family ridicule the suggestion. With the Jewish Dr. von Eppenstein as godfather and financial supporter of the family, that would never have done. But in a Goering biography, published in the Germany of 1935, it sounded well to draw attention to "his healthy instinct and early racial consciousness, which, in its clear conception, is rare in one so young." Whether it was his private war against the Jews of Fuerth or his generally unruly conduct, his teachers had frequently reason to complain. He, in turn, hated school. Gritzbach also quotes little Hermann's favourite expression whenever he had to go back to school after the holidays: "If only Fuerth would burn down . . . !" Was it an early instinct — to burn down what he hated?

Punishment for breach of discipline in those days was swift and hard. Young Goering did not take to it any more kindly than other boys. Years later, when he was at the peak of his power, Goering could not hide his amusement at the thought that there was a time when he could be punished. But he used to recall that not even at the age of eight, nine, or ten did he accept such punishment without most effective counter-measures. He was always a rebel, he explained. And when the cup of his suffering was full, his own story goes, he simply went to bed and demanded to be removed to his home in Veldenstein. For four weeks, as the tutor sent letters of protest to his parents and doctors examined him in vain, Hermann continued his sitdown strike, an act of heroism in the face of a superior enemy, an example of perseverance and an early sign of a strong character. That was how he himself interpreted his rebellion, but it seems more likely that the boy was affected by the first symptoms of a gland disease which a country doctor, at the turn of the century, would not be able to diagnose, and which later caused him considerable and repeated trouble. He emerged from his bed, limping but apparently fully recovered, as soon as it was time to return home for the holidays.

The family spent most summers at Dr. von Eppenstein's other and bigger castle at Mauterndorf. It was an imposing mediaeval burgh, a former residence of the powerful, wealthy Salzburg bishops. Precious antiques, old masters, Gobelins, valuable silver filled the house. To move among such treasures made a deep impression on young Goering. The Austrian mountains lured, and the boy soon ventured out on daring expeditions towards the high, snow-covered peaks. Here he felt in his element. "Adolf Hitler," Emmy Goering told me, "could live anywhere. He liked the Bavarian Alps, but he was equally happy in Munich or Berlin or in his field headquarters. My husband needed nature — Karinhall, Mauterndorf, the mountains were his world. Only in the mountains or among trees could he really 'tank-up,' as he called it."

Hermann came to regard Mauterndorf as his second home, himself as "almost an Austrian." While Hitler resented the land of his birth which had failed to recognize his genius, Hermann Goering loved Austria all his life. Once in Mauterndorf it was difficult to convince him that he would have to go back to school. Fuerth was out of the question now, and Goering senior chose a boarding school in Ansbach in the hope that the masters would succeed in taming his little nature boy. This hope was not fulfilled. Hermann found the atmosphere at Ansbach "stuffy," the masters "too bookish." After a few weeks, he gave his own schoolbooks to wandering gypsies: "You can pawn them and keep the money!" he told them. Then he set out for home.

Passing through Ansbach in 1935, Hermann Goering decided, on the spur of the moment, to visit his old school. A flustered headmaster hurriedly prepared a speech to greet the Prussian Prime Minister. How was he to know what young Goering had thought and said about the school, or of the circumstances under which he had left it? In glowing words he told him that Ansbach was proud to count the Premier among its old boys; he asked nothing of his present pupils except that they should model themselves on the great man who was a product of their school. Goering burst into laughter: "My friend," he said, "I only hope that none of your pupils feels about the school the way I did. . . ."

Young Hermann's unexpected return from the Ansbach school created consternation in Veldenstein. Father Goering called a family conference and asked Dr. von Eppenstein to help decide the boy's future. All agreed that Hermann needed the stern discipline of a military college. The boy was jubilant when he was eventually enrolled in the Cadet School at Karlsruhe. "Emphasis in Karlsruhe," a former German officer, a contemporary of Goering, told me, "was on military training. Book learning took second place." It was exactly what Hermann wanted. He was a good cadet, and he made quick progress. There were no more complaints. The stormy petrel of Fuerth, Ansbach, and Veldenstein was flattened by the steamroller of a German Army education which brooked no individualism. After a final year at the school of the Prussian Cadet Corps at Lichterfelde, and just a month after the death of his father in 1913, Hermann Goering was gazetted as a lieutenant in the 112th Prinz Wilhelm Infantry Regiment, with headquarters in Muelhausen, ready to fight and to die, according to the accepted formula, "for God, Kaiser, and Fatherland." A present of two thousand marks from Eppenstein was his reward.

2

YOUNG GOERING GOES TO WAR

MUELHAUSEN, in the German Alsace, was a typical garrison town. Social life was dominated by the young gentlemen of the 112th Prinz Wilhelm Infantry Regiment. Military duties, however, in this frontier region were more arduous than in other parts of the Reich. The proximity of France, the "traditional enemy," instilled a sense of urgency into the routine of drill and manoeuvres. The "military objective" seemed so close at hand. War in these parts was always more than a possibility.

In January, 1914, a slender, young, blue-eyed, and eager lieutenant presented himself to his new commanding officer. This first critical interview between the colonel and the newcomer proceeded along familiar lines until the colonel asked the obvious question touching on a point as important to a young Prussian officer as his physical fitness or his mental alertness, "Your allowance — how much?" Lieutenant Goering's reply came back swift and proud, "I have money of my own, sir!" Yes, he had two thousand marks. Two thousand marks was sufficient capital to enable a junior officer to become a popular member of the social set of Muelhausen. Goering performed his military duties to the satisfaction of his superior officers. The ladies of Muelhausen came to know him as an entertaining partner on the dance floor. He could drink with the best of his fellow officers. It seemed fun to be a lieutenant in the famous frontier regiment.

At first neither Lieutenant Goering nor the other officers of the garrison were unduly perturbed when they heard that Gavrilo Princip, a Serbian had shot the Austrian heir to the throne, Archduke Franz Ferdinand, and his Archduchess in Sarajevo on June 29, 1914. There had been trouble in the Balkans before; there always would be. But as the days went on, the spectre of war began to appear over the garrison of Muelhausen. On exercises blind ammunition was discarded and the men of the Prinz Wilhelm Regiment were issued the real thing — just to get familiar with the noise of war. Hermann Goering now remembered how he had happily told his comrades at the Cadet School: "Once I am an officer, there's got to be a war!" Now he was filled with foreboding. On July 27 he wrote a long sentimental letter to his mother: he wrote about Veldenstein and Mauterndorf, about the happy days of his boyhood, about the mountains. He poured his whole young heart into this letter.

Two days later Germany mobilized. Lieutenant Goering had his war. It was not the kind of war of which he had dreamed in the Cadet School or in his billet in Muelhausen. The order to march arrived, but his regiment did not march in the direction of France. The first trumpets Goering heard in the war sounded a real retreat. Before he knew what had happened, the Prinz Wilhelm Infantry Regiment had evacuated Muelhausen and had been withdrawn behind the Rhine. Lieutenant Goering was put in charge of a platoon, but it was weeks before he was able to go into action.

The front was stabilised with the French Army deep in German territory. The German High Command, contemplating a major attack across the Rhine, was anxious to have details about the disposition of the enemy troops. Goering's platoon was one of the small formations sent out to reconnoitre the French positions. An armoured train took them across the Rhine. Goering disembarked and, with his men, edged forward toward his old garrison town which was in French hands. On the way they conveniently "requisitioned" a few bicycles and, thus mechanised, went on their way.

In the suburbs of Muelhausen, Lieutenant Goering seemed to forget the task with which he had been entrusted. Right there, near enough to hear their voices, was a group of French officers, a senior officer, a general among them. Here was an opportunity to strike a blow at the "Red Pants," as the German soldiers called the French. Gathering his men around him, Goering explained his plan. They would take the French by surprise and snatch the general from their midst to take him back to the train in triumph. It sounded wonderful, but before Goering could give the signal for action, a nervous

N.C.O. fired his rifle. The startled French returned the fire. The great plan collapsed in confusion. A hasty retreat only just saved Goering and his platoon. They reached their train in the nick of time. Many years later Lieutenant Goering's first exploit in the First World War was described as an act of heroism. His superior officers at the time were less enthusiastic. The move, far from yielding any results, had endangered the invaluable armoured train and the whole reconnaissance operation.

In the many frontier skirmishes which followed, Lieutenant Goering, now an adjutant, in the 2nd Battalion, conformed more rigorously to regimental orders. Under the guidance of Corporal Tschersich, an experienced regular soldier, he developed into a conscientious officer, courageous but cautious. He was in the battles of Muelhausen, Saarburg, and Baccarat, a reliable observer officer, sometimes moving forward to bring back information, or again directing artillery fire from exposed positions hard on the fringe of enemy-held territory. His closest friend in these days was Lieutenant Bruno Loerzer, a happy-go-lucky regular, a little older than Goering, just as anxious to earn his spurs in this war. Neither of them had any doubt that it was only a matter of months before they would be in Paris with the enemy prostrate at their feet.

But the battle of Baccarat, for the time being, put an end to Goering's ambitious military projects. A swelling in his knees developed, which the medical officer soon diagnosed as rheumatism of the joints. Goering was removed to a hospital in Freiburg. Crippled with pain, helpless, he was forced to follow the fortune of his beloved regiment from a distance. Now and again one of his fellow officers visited him to bring a breath of the front line into the dreary hospital ward. One of them told him that his friend Bruno Loerzer had been sent to the Air Training School in the very town in which Goering was tied to his bed. That day Bruno Loerzer received an urgent appeal, "Come and see me at once, please," signed Hermann. Loerzer's accounts of his experiences in the Flying School opened up a new world for Lieutenant Goering. These knees would never allow him to be a good infantry officer again. From his sickbed he wrote an application for transfer to the Flying School. But long before the application had gone "through the proper channels" and reached the commander of the reserve battalion, Goering had made up his mind, come hell or high water, to join his friend Loerzer. He could now leave his bed and hobble around in the ward. On the day on which Loerzer came with the news that he was now a qualified pilot and due to go to the front, Goering received the reply to his own application. It was in the negative.

Years later, on his trial in Nuremberg, Hermann Goering discoursed one day at length about the rights and duties of an army officer. Obviously, he said, it would be impossible to conduct a war if a soldier, an officer, even a general were allowed to do as he pleased, to move forward or backward according to his own inclination, to attack or retreat or take up the position which suited him best. Goering as a young officer, however, had not acted as he preached later on. Disregarding the ruling of the Army authorities, he persuaded Loerzer to take him to the Darmstadt depot of the Air Force where pilots were allocated to the fighting formations. Loerzer agreed to have his friend as an observer. For a few weeks Lieutenant Goering was "lost" to the Army. A military court had sentenced him to be confined to barracks for three weeks, but the verdict never caught up with him.

The German Air Force was as yet short of planes and it looked as if Goering and Loerzer would have to wait some time for transfer to the front. They soon found, however, a way to expedite matters. On the Darmstadt Aerodrome they discovered a brand-new machine. A few hours later they were airborne and on their way to the West, Loerzer piloting and Goering in the observer's seat. The machine which was carrying the two hopefuls had originally been intended for a certain Sergeant Ziegler. They were lucky that Ziegler did not mind the trick which they had played on him. Twenty years later he received his reward. Goering appointed him Commander of the National Socialist Flying Corps — the S.A. of the air. Within a few days of arriving at the front, the Loerzer-Goering combination joined the 25th Field Air Detachment of the Fifth Army, which was under the high command of the German Crown Prince.

War in the air in these days was a haphazard affair. The small German air detachments were moved up and down the line and set new tasks every day. The Loerzer-Goering team, pilot and observer, was not expected to seek out the enemy in aerial combat. They were attached to artillery units and sent on reconnaissance flights to locate and photograph targets and, as Goering had done during his few months in the infantry, to bring back information about the disposition of the Allied troops. To obtain his photographs Goering had to lean far over the side of his observer's seat, holding on precariously to his camera. He was armed against all eventualities with the new Mauser gun, from which he could fire twenty-five shots, and with a revolver. When it was impossible to use the camera, Goering drew sketches of the heavy-gun emplacements and, flying back over the German lines, dropped them near the observation posts of his own batteries.

The objectives of these air expeditions were the fortifications of Verdun, against which the German armies were now massing. Taking back the photographic plates to headquarters at Stenay, twenty miles northeast from Rheims, the two young airmen were frequently called into conference with senior officers to explain and elucidate details of their photographs and to give eye-witness accounts of their observations. Sometimes, from a quiet corner, the Commander-in-Chief, the Crown Prince — "Little Willie" to the English — would listen to the animated reports of the young men, often amused at Lieutenant Goering's strong and unorthodox language.

One day in the spring of 1915, Goering and Loerzer were in conference at Stenay when the alarm sounded. A French air group had been observed flying in the direction of Stenay, obviously planning an attack on the headquarters of the heir to the throne of the Kaiser. Rushing to their aircraft to take off, it flashed through their minds that the Crown Princess had arrived at Headquarters the previous day on a visit to her husband. Bombs were already dropping as they engaged the French in the air. In a short battle the enemy was forced to turn tail. The house of the Crown Prince had narrowly escaped a direct hit, but many of the Headquarters buildings had been severely damaged.

That evening Loerzer and Goering were asked to report to their Commander-in-Chief. Personally, he decorated them with the Iron Cross First Class. He shook hands with Goering and engaged him in a long conversation. It was the beginning of a friendship which was to last many years and, while of doubtful value to the Crown

Prince, became extremely useful to Hermann Goering. From this day he received frequent invitations to join the dinner table of his supreme commander. In this elevated company he met many members of the wealthy and influential German aristocracy, whom he was later able to convince that the Nazi Party was by no means a collection of low-born riff-raff, but included many an "officer and gentleman" — like himself. One of the regular guests at these gatherings was Prince Philip of Hessen who eventually married Princess Mafalda of Savoy, the King of Italy's daughter, and became Goering's "social pacemaker" in Berlin.

In the autumn of 1915, Goering was at last sent to Freiburg Aviation School to be trained as a pilot. Courses were short and intense, but he passed his final tests easily, returned quickly to the front and rejoined his unit, this time on equal terms with his old friend Loerzer. At first they both still flew the big new A.E.G. type of plane, but they soon "organised" the coveted transfer to a fighter detachment — Squadron 5. Side by side, the two lieutenants threw themselves into the fight, Goering still a little uncertain, always overambitious, often incautious, sometimes not only risking his life, but his valuable aircraft, quite unnecessarily. The older and more experienced Loerzer, a man with a calmer temperament, was often forced to dash to the rescue of his young comrade.

Many prominent air officers of the Second World War who worshipped Goering were highly critical of his decision to appoint Loerzer to a key post in the Luftwaffe. That Goering would not have become an airman without Loerzer's help was an open secret. But few of his critics realised that the Reichsmarschall and Commander-in-Chief of the Luftwaffe owed his very life to Loerzer. Hermann Goering would not have survived his first air battles in the French skies had it not been for his faithful friend.

Loerzer was there again on a foggy November morning of 1916 when Lieutenant Goering, flying an Albatross, D.V. spotted a big British aircraft and at once dived to attack the powerful but cumbersome opponent. With his machine gun blazing, he was triumphantly moving in for the kill. But his friend was too late to warn him against a dozen British fighters which, in turn, were closing in on the reckless German. The battle was short, the outcome a foregone conclusion. One British bullet grazed Goering's leg, a hail of fire riddled his plane. He only just managed to escape his pursuers. More dead than alive, he reached the German lines for a last-minute crash landing. Unconscious, his hip ripped by the back of his broken seat, he was dragged from the aircraft. Confined to hospital with a deep wound, stretching ten inches across his side, Goering had six months to contemplate the tactics of aerial combat.

In the development of these tactics the British Flying Corps was far ahead of their German adversaries. British airmen had introduced formation flying and changed the whole technique of fighting in the air. Whenever the small German groups went up, they found themselves confronted with an overwhelming force. Before another group had come to join in the battle, there were heavy casualties. Hurriedly the German High Command reorganised along similar lines. Staffeln (squadrons) of twelve aircraft each were formed. While Hermann Goering was still convalescing, Lieutenant Loerzer was given command of one of them, Jasta (short for "Jagdstaffel" — Fighter Squadron) 26, which was stationed at Kolmar in Alsace. Soon Jasta 26 was moved to Muelhausen. Here Hermann Goering reported again for duty. He was back at his old garrison town — and with Bruno Loerzer.

The British Royal Flying Corps in these days had a great reputation, but the German enemy offered a spirited resistance. Mercilessly the British air forces pounded the German infantry. As the German Jastas were getting into their stride, they met even larger British formations. Few aerodromes were safe from their attack. The battle swayed back and forth and Jasta 26 was constantly on the move. By the spring of 1917, the big British offensive in Flanders was getting under way when Goering received his appointment as Commander of Jasta 27. He had caught up with Loerzer again. The two Jastas shared the aerodrome of Iseghem near Ypres and were in daily combat with the combined Anglo-French air forces.

Both sides fought cleanly. Chivalry and personal respect for a brave opponent were matters of course in both camps. Though there were great improvements in the types of aircraft employed, it was still chiefly a fight of man against man with pilots pulling the trigger only when they were able to see the white of their enemy's eye. Lieutenant Goering quickly distinguished himself in these battles. He was now a crack airman with six victims to his credit.

The scores of individual fighter pilots mounted fast. Many of them were making three or four sorties every day. The details of one encounter, at least, remained deeply ingrained in Hermann Goering's memory. As long as he lived, he would never forget the occasion. It started very much like any other dog-fight in the air. Goering's opponent was an Englishman, a fine airman who, in the middle of an involved air battle, had deliberately sought out the leader of the German formation.

Turning and looping, diving and again climbing, the two combatants strained every nerve to get each other into their sights. Away from their formations, they cut through the sky, twisting to get an advantage over the other. It was a battle of life and death. Those who watched from the ground knew that this engagement would not be broken off without a decision. After an exhausting ten minutes, the decision went to Goering, but almost miraculously the English pilot, his aircraft shot to ribbons, managed to glide out of a steep dive and to land behind the German lines. A few minutes later, Goering was by his side; "My name is Hermann Goering!" said the victorious German. "I think he said that his name was Slee," Goering mused as he told the story at the German Airmen's Club in Berlin twenty years later. "He was a famous English pilot who had brought down a number of our comrades." They shook hands and congratulated each other on their skill. Goering's narrow escape in this battle left him with a healthy respect for the British Royal Flying Corps.

Following the British lead, the Germans had again increased the size of their formations. Out of the Jastas grew Geschwader (wings) of fifty aircraft. Loerzer and Goering were attached to Geschwader 3, but, though their individual scores mounted, they looked up in awe to the Commodore of Geschwader 1, the death-defying, glorious, sheer invincible record-killer of the German Air Force, the twenty-five-year-old Manfred Freiherr (Baron) von Richthofen. Fighting a hopeless battle against the Allied forces, Richthofen, the "Red Knight," who had given his name to the Geschwade, still took a heavy toll of the enemy. On April 21, 1918, having brought down eighty Allied planes, Baron Richthofen failed to return from an air battle against a British formation. Despair descended on the German aerodrome at Cappy from which he had taken off; it spread to every other German unit. Germany had lost her greatest war hero. Every effort was made to find out how he had met his end. A few days later a lonely British Royal Flying Corps fighter dropped a message over the German lines. It was a photograph showing the grave in which the British had buried Manfred von Richthofen. Attached was a message: "To The German Flying Corps: Rittmeister Baron MANFRED VON RICHTHOFEN was killed in aerial combat on 21 April, 1918. He was buried with full military honours. From British Royal Air Force."

Now Lieutenant Karl Bodenschatz, the adjutant of the Richthofen Squadron, opened his commander's last will. It said: "Should I fail to return, Lt. Reinhard (Jasta 6) shall take over the leadership of the squadron." Richthofen's recommendation was implemented. Reinhard, with the rank of captain, became the successor of the "Red Knight." Every airman in the German Air Force now hoped to approach the achievement of the late great hero. Lieutenant Ernst Udet was well in the running as the most successful surviving fighter pilot. Hermann Goering steadily increased his scores. In May, 1918, he achieved his twentieth "victory in the air" and with it the ambition of every German soldier — the award of the Order Pour le Mérite, the German Victoria Cross, which is worn on a ribbon round the neck. It was one of the three decorations — the Iron Cross First Class and the Golden Airman's Medal were the others — without which Goering was rarely seen. He had joined the ranks of Germany's leading airmen. His pictures began to appear in the German papers. French and British "Intelligence" noted his name as one of their most dangerous opponents.

The German High Command had made a practice of calling on their most successful and experienced airmen to test the new types of aircraft with which they were constantly experimenting. Towards the end of June, 1918, both Captain Reinhard and Lieutenant Goering received a call to report at the Adlershorst Aerodrome on the outskirts of Berlin to take up an improved version of the old Albatross. On July 3, the demonstration took place in the presence of technical experts and Air Force officers. Goering was the first to take to the air and the machine responded perfectly to his gentle touch. His trial flight passed off without incident. When he had landed, it was the turn of the Commander of the Richthofen Geschwader to take off for a final check. His seemed just a routine flight. There was little doubt that the machine would pass its test. Flying at two thousand feet, Captain Reinhard was about to descend when, almost noiselessly, a wing broke and the plane crashed to the ground. Captain Reinhard was killed.

In the Headquarters of the German High Command expectation was rising to fever pitch as the finishing touches were put on an ambitious plan for a new big throw to reverse the fortunes of war. It was a venture similar in many ways to the last big coup of the Wehrmacht in World War II when, in December, 1944, von Rundstedt launched the Ardennes offensive by which Hitler hoped to snatch victory from the jaws of defeat. In 1918 the aim was to capture Rheims, to break through across the Marne and to reach Epernay and Châlons. Somewhere along the extended German front Adolf Hitler was serving as a dispatch orderly — his company commander was a young officer by the name of Rudolf Hess. At Heidelberg, where he attended university, a crippled student reported for medical examination at the recruiting office, hoping against hope that he would be accepted for military service. His name was Joseph Paul Goebbels. At the headquarters of the Richthofen Squadron, Germany's air aces were wondering on whom the mantle of Richthofen and Reinhard would fall. On July 7, the adjutant, Lieutenant Bodenschatz, emerged from his office, waving a message from the High Command. To his pilots, who crowded around him in anticipation, he read out the orders: "No. 178,654, 8.7.18. Lieutenant Hermann Goering has been appointed Commander of the Geschwader No. 1 (Manfred Freiherr von Richthofen)."

A few days later the new commander arrived at Beugneux Aerodrome to join his formation. In a few clipped sentences he told them how proud he was about his appointment and the honour to lead Germany's finest airmen. A little plumper than when he first joined the Army, a little shorter than most of the lanky airmen under his command, his blue eyes hard and steady, Hermann Goering had reached the peak of a fighting pilot's war career. But no outward sign betrayed his emotion when Adjutant Bodenschatz handed him the famous thick walking stick of the squadron, which Richthofen had always carried and which had become a symbol in the German Air Force. Three days later, a calamitous start to his new assignment, the squadron lost two of its crack pilots. It was a grave blow to the new commander. Almost his first duty was to write a report about the Fokker D. VII 309/18 aircraft which the two men had flown. The petroltanks had been pierced by British bullets and burst into flames causing the loss of the aircraft and the pilots. With this report Goering went to Berlin to discuss the technical problems of his unit's equipment personally with the highest Air Force authorities.

Goering always took a great interest in technical details and problems of equipment. Already in these early days it was suggested that he did so for reasons which were not entirely unselfish. He combined a keen business sense with concern for his men and machines and freely offered his advice on engines and material to be used not only by his own unit, but by the German Air Force as a whole. The technicians, of course, were always ready to listen to the advice of an outstanding fighter pilot and it was due to his influence that the new B.M.W. (Bayrische Motoren Werke) engine was adopted by the High Command. Herr von Gehrlich, a famous Bavarian Catholic writer, later accused Goering in a series of articles of having abused his privileged position to influence the Army authorities, of having accepted golden cigarette cases and other presents from his industrialist friends whom he thus helped to vast profits. There is no authentic proof for the suggestion that Goering accepted bribes while he was a serving officer. His association with Fokker, the aircraft constructor, and the Bavarian Motor Works, however, became very close after the end of the war and provided him with the only opportunity for a career and an income.

Towards the end of August, 1918, just as Lieutenant Udet had shot down his sixtieth opponent, Goering returned to the front, to devote himself to rather melancholy duties. The British Royal Air Force were playing havoc with his crack pilots and tearing yawning gaps in the ranks of the Richthofen group until it was reduced to less than half its strength. It was not easy to keep up the fighting spirit of his men, to regroup day after day and to send effective formations into the air. But some of Germany's greatest airmen were members of his squadron and ready to fly with Goering into death. Among his closest friends was Lieutenant Gehrt, who also held the Pour le Mérite.

The Richthofen "Circus" as it was called by friend and foe, was moved up and down the line to intervene wherever the weakening front showed signs of breaking. Reeling back the German forces, the British Fifth Army was on the offensive supported by the crack No. 84 Fighter Squadron, equipped with S.E. 5A's, the best fighter aircraft of the day. Commanding Squadron 84 was Captain William Sholto-Douglas, one of Britain's outstanding young airmen. Wherever the Richthofen Circus appeared, Squadron 84 was there to match its strength with that of the Germans. Today William Sholto-Douglas is Lord Douglas of Kirtleside, who earned even greater fame as an Air-Marshal in the last war. "We knew Goering's aircraft," Lord Douglas told me when we discussed the fateful battles of his youth. The German planes were painted in bright colours — the British thought it was done to terrify them, but the practice was actually adopted for the purpose of easy recognition. "I have once or twice 'revved around' in a dog-fight with a purple and yellow German aircraft which I took to be Goering's," Lord Douglas said, "but as we were both at this time highly experienced fighter pilots, we never succeeded in getting our sights on each other."

Hermann Goering did not altogether escape his formidable opponent. Though the two men never met face to face, that was not the end of their struggle. In a sense it was continued under different circumstances. "My only other contact with Goering," Lord Douglas continued, "was when I was Commander-in-Chief and Military Governor in Germany. The Control Council in Berlin, on which I was the British representative, was the Court of Appeal against the sentences passed at Nuremberg. Thus, with the other three Allied Commanders-in-Chief (Marshal Sokolovsky of Russia, General Koenig of France, and General McNarney of the United States), I had to consider the appeals made on behalf of Goering in mitigation of the death sentence passed on him by the Nuremberg Court. We decided not to interfere with the carrying out of the sentence. . . ." Lord Douglas wrote "finis" under the life story of Hermann Goering, even though the German made the end one of his own choosing.

As Commander, Goering was only able to bring down two more opponents. During sleepless nights he studied information about the enemy forces which were driving his unit from aerodrome to aerodrome. Reports from one of his squadron leaders sadly admitted that the British Sopwith aircraft were technically superior to the Albatross D. It was the same with the S.E. 5's and the Spad 140 P's and 200 P's, which both beat the Albatross in climbing power and manoeuvrability. Along the whole line the British superiority in quality and numbers was telling. One after another of the air aces who had been the pillars of the Richthofen Squadron went up — never to return. "There is little conversation in the Mess," noted Bodenschatz in his war diary. Finally the inevitable order arrived. It was signed by the Crown Prince: "Owing to the great losses which the group has suffered, I order the reorganisation of the group into a squadron. It is to co-operate with Group No. 3 under the command of Greim." Twenty-six years later, Hitler appointed Greim to succeed Hermann Goering as Commander-in-Chief of the Luftwaffe.

On September 1, 1918, Goering himself wrote a report about the situation: " . . . the enemy bi-planes are strongly armed and operate very well in close formation, even when attacked by several German single-seaters. They are equipped with armoured or fireproof fuel tanks. . . . On the fronts of the Seventh and Second Armies, enemy balloons have been attacked on several occasions without catching fire. . . . "

"Actually nothing can be done any more," Bodenschatz wrote. "The features of Lieutenant Goering are getting harder." The spirits of the young commander dropped. He knew little of conditions at home or on other sectors of the front. He was hoping for the winter to stem the tide of enemy squadrons which were darkening the skies over him. Casualties were so great that a doctor had been attached to the squadron for the first time. By the end of October, 1918, Lieutenant Goering's unit had dwindled to 63 officers and 484 other ranks, including administrative staff and cooks. The Americans were now greatly in evidence, fighting heroically against the stubborn remnants of the once great German Army. The weather deteriorated and Goering's men were earthbound. Only now did they begin to reflect on what was happening all around them — retreat on all fronts, revolution in Kiel, unrest in Berlin, the Kaiser to abdicate. It seemed as if the world had come to an end.

About that time Adolf Hitler, who had been almost blinded in a gas attack, was lying in an army hospital in the small Pomeranian town of Pesewalk contemplating the fate of Germany and working up resentment against the Marxists, the Jews, and the Kaiser, all of whom he blamed for the defeat of the German armies in the field. And so, he wrote in *Mein Kampf*, "I decided to become a politician." Hermann Goering never made such a decision, but his political awareness was aroused as soon as the fighting died down and he found time to discuss the causes of defeat with his comrades. They, too, were looking for a scapegoat and were convinced that the home front had let them down. Not enough aircraft, not enough recruits had been sent to enable them to carry on the fight. The revolution capped their argument. In their eyes it was not the outcome of defeat. Defeat had been sealed by the revolution. The fighting soldier had been stabbed in the back.

By November 9, 1918, it was obvious that the end had come. Goering made an heroic gesture. Bodenschatz told me how he called his officers together and asked them to be prepared for every eventuality, for a last death-and-glory battle. It was a vain gesture. Germany's fighting days were over. There were rumours that the armistice about to be signed would provide for their aircraft to be handed over to the Americans, but Goering from a welter of orders and counter-orders hurriedly chose an instruction to fly his unit to Darmstadt. Ordering Bodenschatz to take the ground staff and the equipment by road, the Commander and his men took off for the last time to fly towards the Fatherland. In Darmstadt it appeared that some of his pilots had lost their way and landed in Mannheim, where a revolutionary "Soldiers' Council" was already in control of the aerodrome. The airmen had been deprived of their arms. As soon as Goering received the news, he sent a peremptory message: "Let my men join me with their weapons or I'll come and bomb you all to bits!" The ultimatum was effective, the stragglers were allowed to join their unit fully armed.

The final battle came with an order to surrender the machines to the French in Strasbourg. "I am afraid you will have to comply," Goering told the air crews grimly, "but make sure that the French shall not get what they expect . . . !" The men understood his hint. The Richthofen Circus virtually crashed down on Strasbourg. Many of the planes were almost completely wrecked on landing. Goering always thought of the incident as a "successful operation," his final act of defiance. Now he wrote his last official report: "Since its inception the squadron has gained 644 victories in the air. Losses inflicted by the enemy amounted to 56 officers and pilots and six other ranks killed; 52 officers and seven other ranks wounded." Signed, "Hermann Goering, Lieutenant and Geschwader Commander."

Goering did not fly to Strasbourg himself, but arranged to meet the officers a few days later at a farewell party in a beer cellar at Aschaffenburg. In his capacity as a commander, Goering had made a number of speeches in the typical style of a Prussian officer — short sentences, every word to the point, a few harsh barks to drive home his meaning. At the beer cellar in Aschaffenburg, as he took leave from his comrades, he hit the note of a real orator for the first time. In flowery phrases which he was to repeat a thousand times from the political platform, he spoke of his glowing love for Germany, of his faith in the future of the Fatherland, of Germany's soul and undying strength, of the struggle to follow the battles of the war when morale and character would be the test . . .

His eyes were filled with tears. Like most of the men around him, he was confused, uncertain, trying to whip up his own courage as well as theirs. Defeat to these men was a very personal matter. What had they done to deserve it? A feeling of injustice gripped them. Surely, they had not failed their country? Day after day they had gladly staked their very lives. And the reward? That evening in Aschaffenburg Hermann Goering and his friends lost the only world they had ever known.

The British and the Americans have only tasted the bitter medicine of defeat in small doses, but they know that it stimulates the desire for revenge. After Dunkirk and Pearl Harbour they were dominated by one thought — to carry the Union Jack and the Stars and Stripes to Berlin and to Tokyo. Hermann Goering lost his flag together with the war. The colours of the Republic were a meaningless symbol to him. Arriving in Munich he also nearly lost his medals. Roving revolutionaries in German towns set upon returning soldiers to strip them of their decorations. This violent reaction against four years of futile war enthusiasm caused tremendous resentment among men like Hermann Goering, who felt that personal insult was added to national disaster. The whole of his adult life had been spent in an officer's mess or at the front. War was his chosen career. He had been proud of his profession, prouder still of the distinction with which he had performed his military duty. He could not imagine that millions of people by now abhorred the very idea of war and hated the officers who had forced them to fight.

Arriving in Munich in full uniform, he had to defend himself against one of these street attacks and was only just able to save his decorations. He vowed that one day he would earn many more medals — and nobody ever was going to take them from him.

3

KARIN

OVER the corpse of Imperial Germany, revolution and reaction were locked in a bitter struggle. Now that the clash of arms had died down on the battlefields, the returning soldiers flocked to the new organisations of the Right and the Left to fight each other. Communist cadres and militarist organisations armed themselves with the remaining weapons of war to reinforce their own often confused, always violent, policies. Assailed from both sides a moderate Socialist President and his government tried in vain to pacify minds and to restore real peace to the country. Impatient ex-officers organised "Free Corps" to continue the war off their own bat, persuaded disillusioned, jobless, hopeless soldiers to join them in attempts to recapture frontier territories lost to the enemy. Others, still disciplined in the old military tradition, accepting more far-sighted counsel, held themselves in readiness for a call to the colours of the Reichswehr, the new army of one hundred thousand men, which the victors conceded to the Republic.

Hermann Goering chose neither of these two courses. The arduous, unrewarding life of an unpaid legionaire in a force without aeroplanes did not attract him. His rugged individualism had gained a new impetus in the Air Force where a pilot was his own master, dependent for survival on his own effort and skill. Once or twice he attended one of the officers' meetings which were the order of the day. From Munich he went to Berlin, where friends took him to the inauguration of yet another Association of German Officers. First point on the agenda was a protest against an order of the War Ministry which made it illegal for officers to show the insignia of their ranks on the uniforms which they wore for lack of civilian clothes. War Minister General Reinhard, an active soldier of the war, attended. In a speech he asked the officers to maintain discipline, to obey the orders of the new Government. He had hardly finished when an officer in the audience jumped up and rushed to the platform. There was applause as the gathering noticed the Order Pour le Mérite below his collar: "General Reinhard," he shouted, "I knew you would be here today, but I expected to see you in mourning about the fate of the German Army. Instead . . ."

This was Goering speaking, the Goering of Aschaffenburg. There was silence in the hall as he continued: "We officers have done our duty for four years. . . . Now that we are home again — what happens? They spit on us, they want to take from us what we treasure, what represents our honour. And I am telling you . . . it is not the fault of the people for whom we fought. It is the fault of those who have incited the people to stab us in the back. Therefore, I preach hatred, deep hatred of those criminals. . . . The day will come when we shall drive them out of Germany. . . . Let us prepare for that day and work for it. It will surely come!"

This speech was his chief contribution to the political controversy which raged in Germany. In later years Goering explained that he had refused an invitation to join the Reichswehr because he could not reconcile service for the Republic with his political convictions. It is true that he was contemptuous of Republican Germany, but there were other reasons why he preferred to branch out on his own. Aircraft manufacturers, anxious to conquer new markets, were looking for airmen of Goering's calibre as salesmen. One of them, Fokker, had met the Commander of the Richthofen Squadron during the war and had often consulted him on technical questions. Now Fokker suggested that Goering should work for him to popularise his machines in Scandinavia. He offered him an aircraft of the type the German Air Force had used in the war. Goering accepted — and soon a legend developed that he had rescued his own warplane from seizure by the French Army and flown it straight from Darmstadt to Denmark.

For the next few months Goering travelled from one Danish town to another, entertaining large crowds with his aerial acrobatics for fifty Kroner a time. He negotiated sales of aircraft and equipment and also served the Danish Airlines in an advisory capacity. Here he was in his own element, reasonably well off and independent. The Germany colony quickly took to the good-looking, well-mannered young hero with his exciting war stories and his amusing accounts of such eminent friends as the former German Crown Prince. Nights were spent at gay parties, most days in the air. It was almost like old times, and Goering lost little sleep over the grave news which reached Denmark from his own country. Let the Republic collapse in political and economic chaos — what did he care? Hermann Goering set course for a great future.

In 1920 he accepted an offer to go to Sweden as Flight Chief of the Svenska Lufttrafik in Stockholm. It was a well-paid job and there was a profitable sideline when wealthy businessmen engaged him to take them on hurried air journeys. Hermann Goering was a reliable pilot, a pleasant companion on these trips. One of his regular clients was Count Eric von Rosen, a Swedish explorer with whom he formed a personal frienship. The developments which this association set in train largely determined the course of Goering's life. It was always like that. Rarely did Goering pursue a chosen path. Outside influences, chance meetings, events which were stronger than his attractive but shiftless personality, guided his destiny. Often he put up a brave struggle to be just himself, but even his closest friends knew him in many guises behind which they could easily recognise the current dominating influence.

One winter's day Count Rosen asked Goering to fly him to his Rockelstad Castle, north of Stockholm. The weather was foul, but that could not deter the young airman. Against the advice of his colleagues, he took off from Stockholm Aerodrome with his passenger and, after a stormy flight, landed on the frozen Baven Lake close to the red walls of the Count's estate. When they arrived, much behind time, it was too late, too dark, to make the return flight and the pilot gratefully accepted Rosen's hospitality for the night. A huge fire was burning in the vast lounge of the castle which was decorated with paintings and trophies from a hundred hunting expeditions, with rare mediaeval armour, swords and spears. Tired and relaxing over a hot stiff grog, Hermann Goering abandoned himself to the impressive, captivating atmosphere. And, as in a dream, there appeared before him on the huge imposing staircase a young woman, a tall Nordic beauty, proud, aloof, yet very human and real.

None of the women whom Goering had met as a cadet, as a young officer in Muelhausen, or during the war had made a lasting impression on him. He was twenty-seven years old with many amourous adventures behind him, but he had never been in love. Now Fate granted him the rare privilege of falling in love at first sight. To Hermann Goering it came like a direct hit on his heart.

Count Rosen introduced, "My sister-in-law, Karin." Karin was Frau Nils von Kantzow, married to a Swedish officer for ten years and the mother of a boy of eight. She was five years older than Hermann Goering, young enough to be desirable, yet already of an age to impress younger men with the protective qualities of the heart in which they recognise their own mothers' sentiments. Goering sensed that here was a woman who could give him the love and protection of which the early separation from his mother had deprived him.

During the next few days weather conditions made it difficult for the pilot to take his machine back to Stockholm. He was not in a hurry. He stayed as Count Rosen's guest and came to know Karin better. There was no doubt that the wild spark of his love had warmed her, that a deep mutual affection had grown up overnight. When he eventually left Rockelstad he had made up his mind to marry Karin whatever the difficulties. In fact there seemed to be no obstacle once she had obtained a divorce. Goering did not worry unduly about the responsibilities which would fall on him as a married man. His passion was distracting rather than spurring him to greater efforts to build a permanent career for himself. From now on he lived only for his love. How he would live once he was married was a problem which did not burden his mind.

Karin's family was not enthusiastic about the prospect of a divorce, but Hermann charmed them and soon broke down their resistance. He became a regular guest at the home of Karin's parents to which she returned after a separation from her husband. The environment was congenial, familiar in many ways. It also subjected him to new influences from which he could never again free himself. Karin's father, Colonel C. A. von Fock, was a regular officer of the Swedish Army, and Karin was one of five daughters. "I wish I'd had five sons instead!" the old Colonel admitted quite frankly. Her mother was born Huldine Beamish, an English woman whose family had settled in Ireland and whose relatives still own property in Queenstown. A maternal ancestor was a captain in the Coldstream Guards, but the family's sympathies were with Germany where Karin's eldest sister lived until her husband, a German officer, was killed in the war.

This military background was obscured by incense — by real incense which permeated the whole house from a room which the daughters had converted into a chapel for their mother. The life of the family revolved around this chapel, a place of worship for members of all denominations which had been thrown open for a wide circle of friends and was operated like a religious society. Here, with strange Nordic rites, the Focks and their friends dedicated themselves to Christian principles, vowed to serve purity, truth, and love, and to foster complete integration of the individual and his Fatherland. As their symbol they adopted the Edelweiss flower, which grows only on the peaks of high mountains.

Baroness Huldine Beamish-Fock was the high priestess of this cult and Hermann Goering an eager disciple. A letter which he wrote to her reflects the grip which the Edelweiss Chapel gained on him: "I should like to thank you from my heart," he wrote, "for the beautiful moment which I was allowed to spend in the Edelweiss Chapel. You have no idea how I felt in this wonderful atmosphere. It was so quiet, so lovely that I forgot all earthly noise, all worries, and felt as if in another world. I closed my eyes and absorbed the clean celestial atmosphere which filled the whole room. I was like a swimmer resting on a lonely island to gather new strength before he throws himself once more into the raving stream of life. I thanked God and sent up warm prayers. . . . "

Hermann and Karin spent the next few months enjoying the high life of Stockholm, a popular, attractive couple, who were "made for each other." It seemed a happy, carefree life — too carefree to be useful. The Flight Chief was not now so anxious to take on special assignments, however profitable, if they involved even temporary separation from Karin. On the other hand, it was expensive to keep up with the "smart set." But Karin was not a woman to lose herself completely in the shallow existence of Stockholm society. The mysticism of the Edelweiss Chapel had been instilled into her from childhood. Her own ideas of patriotism, her strong sense of duty to one's country, communicated themselves to her impressionable partner. His country would soon be hers — and Germany was in trouble. As Hermann Goering was not doing so well in Sweden, they decided that he should return to Germany, take his part in the struggle for a German resurrection, and, incidentally, look for a job at home. Karin would follow him in good time.

In the summer of 1921 Goering was back in Munich, but the political atmosphere in Germany was not conducive to serious work for one whose fighting instincts had been roused again by the incessant exhortations of a restless and ambitious woman. The country was rent by violence. In the north an attempt by the Reichswehr to oust the Government had only just been foiled. Another move in the involved political game saw the Reichswehr helping the Government to fight the radicalised industrial workers of the Ruhr. In Bavaria the scheming generals financed, among others, a small new political group, the German Workers' Party, which, in turn, had undertaken to deliver the workers into the hands of the militarists. For a short spell after the war the Communists had been in control of the provincial government of Bavaria and the leader of the Social Democrats who had taken over from them, Bavarian Prime Minister Kurt Eisner, had been shot in the street by the young Count Arco-Valley. The Workers' Party in the meantime had received funds from the Reichswehr to acquire a small newspaper, the *Voelkischer Beobachter*, which fulminated against the Communists and the Jews. In July, only a few days after Goering had returned to Munich, Adolf Hitler was made "Fuehrer" of the Workers' Party — the N.S.D.A.P. (National-Sozialistische Deutsche Arbeiter Partei — National Socialist German Workers' Party).

With the help of a Reichswehr officer, Captain Ernst Roehm, a "Gymnastics and Sports Club" had been transformed into a militant praetorian guard, the S.A. (Sturm Abteilungen — Storm Detachments), to protect party meetings against Communists' interference. It was under the command of an ex-officer, the violent Lieutenant Klintzsch, who had only just escaped indictment for the murder of the Jewish Cabinet Minister Walter Rathenau. The moving spirit behind Adolf Hitler and the N.S.D.A.P., the Nazi Party, was Roehm, who devoted his special attention to the S.A., from which, one day, he hoped to raise a Reichswehr of his own. It was Roehm who organised the incorporation of the fiercest German putschists, the so-called Erhard Brigade, in the Nazi Storm Detachments.

Hermann Goering was as yet only on the fringe of these events. But instead of looking for a job, he studied the newspapers, devoured the political pamphlets which only added to the confusion of his mind. With anger he read of the Allied demand for reparations, and the astronomical figures startled him as they did most other Germans. Scanning the programmes of two dozen political parties, he could not decide which of them would be a suitable haven for him. It was an intricate situation. Two factions dominated the political life of Bavaria, both with negative aims. There was a strong separatist movement anxious to sever all connection with the Berlin Government and the contemptible Republic: "Los von Berlin!" (Away from Berlin!) was their slogan. The others hated the Republic just as much, but saw in Berlin the symbol of the unity of the Reich.

Life without Karin seemed intolerable for Goering. Each letter to her was another desperate appeal to come and join him in Munich. Towards the end of the year she followed his call. Colonel von Fock gave his daughter her share of the family fortune and sent her off with his blessing. For two months she stayed at the home of Hermann's mother, making plans for the wedding. She quickly changed the idle, wasteful life into which her fiancé had drifted. If there was no immediate prospect of a job, he should at least devote his time to studies. Although advanced in age, Hermann Goering enrolled as a student at Munich University, choosing history and political science as his subjects. His alert mind easily absorbed the vast amount of literature which unfolded before his eager eyes, the great panorama of his country's history. It was a fascinating subject. Goering was enthusiastic about his work and pursued it with all his energy.

On February 3, 1922, he was married to Karin von Fock-Kantzow. The wedding party at the Park Hotel in Munich was in the true Goering style. Goering's mother, his sisters, and brothers attended. Karin's eldest sister had come from Sweden; many airmen of the Richthofen Squadron, Goering's war comrades, were among the guests. Karin wore a white dress with a wreath of red roses in her hair; Goering's decorations were pinned to his civilian suit.

Major Bodenschatz, Goering's former adjutant, now a Reichswehr officer and Company Commander in Nuremberg, led the chorus in the singing of a mixed programme of old soldiers' ditties and new nationalist songs. The union of Hermann and Karin Goering was sealed to the strains of "Deutschland ueber Alles." The next day dawned as the young couple left the party to drive to their new home. Hermann carried his bride over the threshold of Hochkreuth, the little hunting lodge at Bayrischzell near Munich, which he had bought with part of Karin's dowry.

Goering studied, Karin painted and worked on her embroideries. The evenings were spent in earnest discussions in the spirit of the Edelweiss Chapel. Every day Karin raised her favourite subject and looked at it from a new angle — a man must work for his country. She sometimes accompanied her husband on his visits to Munich and on these occasions the couple rarely failed to attend at least one political meeting. These meetings grew even more stormy than before when speakers began to incite their audiences to resist a new Allied demand — this time for the extradition of the German war criminals. It was a matter of great personal concern to the man with the Pour le Mérite. The "war criminals" were the heroes of his youth, his leaders in the field, the men whom he regarded as the faithful defenders and true heroes of Germany. Protest meetings were called all over Germany. There was no question that Goering would support those who were determined to resist the demand. On a grey November Sunday a mass meeting was called on the Koenigsplatz in Munich. Hermann and Karin went as a matter of course: "I went to this protest demonstration as a spectator," Goering said later, "without having any connection with it. Various speakers from parties and organisations spoke. At the end Hitler, too, was called for. I had heard his name once before briefly and wanted to hear what he had to say."

Hitler was surrounded by a small group of his supporters and Hermann Goering found himself standing near to him. For the first time he saw the man with the short moustache, the flashing, unruly eyes. Hitler wore the dirty old raincoat without which he rarely went out. He refused to take the platform. Goering heard him telling his followers that there was no point in these feeble wordy protests. "I am not going to speak to these tame bourgeois pirates."

Goering nodded silent approval. He fully agreed with what Hitler said. He must take the first opportunity of hearing Hitler at one of his own meetings. The opportunity came two days later. Hitler, as usual, was speaking about the shameful Treaty of Versailles: "Only if Germany's protest is backed by strength will it carry any weight," he shouted. "Germany must be strong again!" These were words very much after Goering's own heart. This was exactly what he had been trying to explain to Karin in their long discussions at home. Excitedly, Karin nudged him to speak in support of Hitler, but Goering felt that he could add little to Hitler's arguments.

In the evening Karin and Hermann could not spare a thought for anything or anybody except Hitler. It was quite clear — Hitler was Goering's man. As instantaneously and impulsively as he had given himself up to Karin, he now offered his soul to the newfound cause. Next morning he went to see Hitler at the small headquarters of his Party. It was political love at first sight. Goering was full of admiration for the man who had found the words for which he had been groping and with which he himself would have wished to express his own undefined ideas. Hitler was flattered to receive a visit from the former Commander of the Richthofen Squadron, the highly decorated officer, a front-line soldier like himself. For years the relationship between these two men was determined by this first impression. Goering never ceased admiring Hitler for the way he formulated his own innermost thoughts and Hitler always looked up to Goering with a tinge of envy. Goering had enjoyed the higher education which he craved for himself. His social standing impressed Hitler in spite of his Socialist pretences. It was a case of two people seeking — and finding — in each other what they missed in themselves.

Hitler's intuition at once took a practical turn. For some time he had been looking for an outstanding soldier, preferably a highly decorated U-boat commander or airman, to take over the leadership of the S.A., a personality with a war record and personal authority to impress his brown-shirted legionaires. They needed real leadership. At this first encounter he told Goering what he expected of the S.A. They should not be organised along purely military lines, but should be trained for practical Party purposes. They should not be allowed to develop into a secret society or become the

Wedding of Hermann and Emmy Goering-Sonnemann at the Dom in Berlin in 1935 was a great State occasion. Hitler was best man. Here the couple are seen leaving to the sound of trumpets from the Wehrmacht's premier band.

Hermann Goering in Hamburg in 1937 at the "Joy of Work" Congress held in order to promote the German national drive for arms production.

instrument of conspirators. They should be seen in public in their uniforms, but these uniforms should be clearly distinguishable from those of the Army. The S.A. must be educated in his own Weltanschauung. Their purpose: the destruction of Marxism in all shapes and forms. There and then Hitler offered Goering the leadership of the S.A.

There and then Goering accepted and made only one reservation — that his appointment should not be announced for a few weeks; that he should first be allowed to join the Party like an ordinary member. He was anxious to avoid the impression that he had chosen Hitler's Party only to carve out a special niche for himself. Throughout his life Hermann Goering overdramatised his own genuine feelings. Now he was deeply moved. For a moment he searched for the right words, then he shook hands with Hitler and swore an oath of allegiance to his new Fuehrer: "I unite my faith with yours for better or for worse," he said. "I dedicate myself to you in good times and in bad, even unto death."

After five weeks Goering took over from Klintzsch as the new Commander of the S.A. In the hope that they would exert a moderating influence, he introduced a few of his refined friends into the formation. One of them was his war comrade Gehrt, who was destined for rapid promotion in the Party Army. But the S.A. was not easily tamed. The storm troopers were involved in street fights almost every day. Every political meeting ended in a battle with broken chair legs and with beer mugs flying. Hitler's plan to give the S.A. a character of its own ran counter to the ideas of Roehm and the Reichswehr generals who stood behind him. Goering's youthful idealism was no match for these hard, determined men in the background who knew what they wanted for the money they had invested in uniforms and equipment for the storm detachments. It was chiefly due to Roehm that the ranks of the S.A. began to swell soon after Goering had assumed command. Imperceptibly the new Commander was lured away from Hitler's original precept. Following Roehm's lead — and, incidentally, very much his own inclinations — he drilled the S.A. men in military style until it was able to parade almost as efficiently as a guard's division. On organised parades the formation was a model of discipline, but they were always liable to break out. Not even

Roehm could wholly suppress the rowdy instincts of this unruly crowd.

Behind the Frauenkirche in Munich is a small restaurant and beer house, the Bratwurstgloeckel, to which tourists in search of the typical Bavarian atmosphere invariably find their way to taste the incomparable sausages of a dozen varieties and the strong beer which is served in large tankards. In 1923, when I first visited the Bratwurstgloeckel, one big table was reserved every evening for a large party of regulars. As the evening went on they consumed an incredible quantity of beer. Their conversation was noisy and unrestrained. The members of the party were well known in Munich but I was, as yet, not familiar with their names. With the help of a waitress who is still around, I was able to reconstruct the composition of this Stammtisch (regular table).

The lady at the head of the table, one of the few women to attend regularly, was Karin Goering, who often accompanied her husband to these sessions. There was Hermann Goering himself, and the robust, red-faced officer was Ernst Roehm, about whose morals all Munich was whispering. With him was his friend Heines, who had the reputation of a killer, a member of one of the notorious secret Fehme (Revenge) organisations who waged a murderous war against pacifists and anti-militarists. Anton Drexler, one of the founders of the Nazi Party, missed few evenings and the "intellectuals" of the circle included Dietrich Eckart, a young poet who edited the Party paper, and Alfred Rosenberg, who was to succeed him after his death that very year. Best known among them was "Putzi" Hanfstaengl, a cultured, artistic member of a wealthy Munich family. Occasionally Bavarian "nationals" of other parties dropped in for a drink, among them Julius Streicher of Nuremberg who came for his first parleys with his future associates.

Chief topic of conversation in these days was the French occupation of the Ruhr. If the Government was taking this provocation lying down, Roehm argued, they had the S.A. to do something about it. Roehm demanded that the brown battalions should march against France. But Hitler had not raised his units to throw them into a hopeless battle. It was the first clash between Hitler and the man who had helped to put him on his feet. Goering sided with Hitler — if only to oppose Roehm, his powerful rival. Hitler's view carried the day: "The fight against the internal enemy is our chief concern," he dogmatised. "Only if we have secured victory at home can we deal with the alien enemies of Germany."

The fight against the internal enemy was to take the concrete form of a putsch with the vague aim to oust the Berlin Government; to take over Bavaria and carry the flag of the "national idea" in triumph to the north. It has been said that "atmosphere was everything" in Nazi Germany, that a simple enumeration of events often failed to provide an explanation of the general trend. That was certainly true of the Nazi Party in its early stages. To fight the internal enemy effectively, Hitler and the men around him performed astounding political contortions. One day saw them begging for the support of the Reichswehr. The next day they were prepared to make common cause with the police. In the same breath they laid their plans to supersede the army and to get the police under their control.

An essential precondition of success was a common policy of all the national groups and the well-armed fighting organisations (Kampfbuende) in Bavaria. A meeting of these organisations was called and Hitler and Goering attended. Though the Nazi Party was by no means the largest group, Hitler in a powerful speech pleaded for a free hand in the struggle against the Republic. Goering supported him and made a strong impression on the gathering which was largely composed of ex-officers. On Goering's suggestion Hitler was entrusted with the leadership of the entire national movement. Now was the time to strike, and the day chosen was May 1, 1923, on which date Communists and Socialists had arranged mass meetings and demonstrations in Munich. Under Goering's command the S.A. was mobilised for a march on the Bavarian capital. Hitler was there wearing a steel helmet and looking very martial. Everything was set for the great coup. The S.A. would take Munich by storm. At the last moment, however, Hitler lost his nerve. The S.A. marched — but kept a safe distance between themselves and the huge gatherings in the centre of the city.

The flop nearly broke Hitler and the Nazi Party. It was an almost fatal blow to the prestige of the Commander of the S.A. Hitler was anxious to disappear from the scene of his failure. With the help of his friends, he acquired a small house in Berchtesgaden, the

Plattenhof, to which he withdrew in silence and solitude. Goering had moved from Bayrischzell to a villa in Obermenzing, Nymphenburg, on the outskirts of Munich. Here Karin tried to keep up his spirits. She gathered his comrades around him and, though troubled by a lung ailment, remained the life and soul of the Party. She even persuaded Hitler to emerge from his seclusion to spend an evening at the house now and then, and Hitler, the shy, aloof man who secretly longed for the company of women, thawed out in her presence and became human, sane, and lighthearted. He adored Karin.

After two months both Hitler and Goering had sufficiently recovered to prepare another coup. But the situation had changed. In Berlin Dr. Stresemann had taken over the Government. To cope with the seething unrest in Bavaria, Herr von Kahr had been appointed Reich Commissar with dictatorial powers to carry on the provincial administration. Like everybody else in Germany, Kahr had ideas of his own, and so had General von Lossow, the Commander of the 7th Reichswehr Division which was stationed in Bavaria. The Police President of Munich, Herr Poehner, also pursued a personal policy, and, to add to the general confusion, there were the old wartime generals, Ludendorff and von Epp, and a strong element of monarchists who owed allegiance to ex-Crown Prince Rupprecht, the Wittelsbacher, of the former Royal House of Bavaria.

Like a snake in the grass, Hitler weaved through this mesh of conflicting purposes, allying himself in turn with Lossow who planned to wrest the control of the Reichswehr from Berlin, with Kahr who saw himself as the future dictator of Germany, with von Epp who was determined to restore the Wittelsbachers. Hitler's plan was to take them all in tow to assist his "National Revolution." As so often in later years, he hardly bothered to keep his own Party informed of his jumpy, often contradictory, schemes. The only man in whom he completely confided was Hermann Goering, whose S.A. was to be the armed instrument of the putsch. The coup was originally planned for November 10, and both Hitler and Goering felt sure that they could count on the support of the Bavarian Reichswehr. The Munich Police President knew of the plans and, waiting to see which way the wind would blow, did not interfere with them. Hitler regarded him as an accomplice. Von Kahr was to be won over with the promise of a high post in the Government which Hitler planned to form. Goering, the man of action, was little concerned with these complicated political manoeuvres. He simply relied on the armed formations of the S.A. to carry the day.

Describing the situation on the eve of the putsch, Goering later explained that he was ready to co-operate with anybody who was against the Berlin Republic, the "November Criminals," as they were known among the Nationalists. But doubts about the real intentions of Hitler's political associates had risen in him when he saw them in close association with Rupprecht. He feared that they would be content with a "March on Munich," and might try to use him and Hitler as tools to separate Bavaria from the rest of the Reich.

Goering's mother died suddenly. Her loss was a grave blow to him. Karin was convalescing after a bout of pneumonia, but still confined to her bed with a temperature. As often, when his mind was burdened by personal worries, Goering whistled up his own courage with an exaggerated show of determination. Discussing his doubts with Hitler, he suggested striking while the iron was hot and going ahead with the coup right away. On Thursday, November 8, he spent an hour at Karin's bedside. "This is a great day," he told her; "important meeting. I will be very late, but please do not worry!" Then he mobilised the S.A.

For that evening a meeting had been called in the cellar of the Buergerbraeu beer house. Von Kahr was to speak to an audience of three thousand about his plans for the administration of Bavaria. There was nothing unusual about this meeting. The Police President was present to hear his political chief; Ludendorff was there and so was Lossow — as could be expected on such an occasion. As the meeting was settling down to its business, Hitler drove to the beer cellar with his friend and Party comrade, Anton Drexler, who was unaware of Hitler's intentions. Goering posted a strong S.A. unit outside the Buergerbraeu.

Just as Kahr was about to begin his speech, Hitler entered, a revolver in his hand. In a dramatic gesture he fired a shot at the ceiling, swung himself onto the platform. The startled audience was spellbound, Kahr automatically stood aside. "Keep calm!" Hitler shouted, his whole body trembling with excitement. "I herewith proclaim the National Revolution. The hall is surrounded by heavily armed S.A. formations. The military barracks are occupied. Reichswehr and police are marching with us under the banner of the Swastika!"

There was not a word of truth in these assertions, but Kahr, Lossow, and Poehner were not sure. They decided to play for time. Hitler drew them into a separate room where they were joined by Ludendorff. While their parley went on, Goering took the platform to speak: "There is nothing to worry about," he said, when he noticed the hostile attitude of the meeting. "This is a revolution on behalf of the people . . . " But he was relieved when the crowd settled down and there was no need to call on his S.A. to maintain order.

The men whom Hitler had tricked into negotiations to form a "National Government" suspected that he was bluffing. In view of the threatening S.A. which surrounded the building, they pretended to fall in with his demands. Only Ludendorff took him at his face value. Kahr returned to the platform to announce that he was negotiating with Hitler. But the negotiations were adjourned until next day, and Hitler, overjoyed, joined Goering to prepare a "March on Munich" on the following morning. On November 9, S.A. units paraded in front of the Buergerbraeu. The senior members of the Party were to lead them across the river Isar to the Feldherrenhalle on the Odeonsplatz where the new Government was to be publicly proclaimed.

Intoxicated with the "success of his coup," Hitler never stopped to think that it would soon be apparent to Lossow that his Reichswehr had not made common cause with the S.A. It did not occur to him that Poehner might side with the Reichswehr against him. Triumphantly he set out on his march, ignorant of an official announcement which had hurriedly been posted all over Munich and in which Kahr declared that "the declarations which I have been forced to make at the point of a revolver are void. The National Socialist German Workers' Party . . . is herewith banned."

Hitler marched at the head of the column. With him were General Ludendorff and three Party leaders, Weber, Scheubner-Richter, and Kriebel. Behind them was Goering in a long, heavy, belted, black leather coat, high-necked but allowing the Pour le

Mérite to be clearly seen, with a Swastika armlet. He wore his steel helmet, also embellished with a large white Swastika. Rudolf Hess, one of Hitler's closest friends, walked with him. On the Isar bridge they were met by a police cordon armed with rifles. Hitler was perturbed when he saw them, but Goering did not bat an eyelid. Calmly he stepped forward: "One shot," he said, "and we shall kill all hostages in our hands!" It was a typical Goering threat. Hitler was overawed. He knew there were no hostages. But the bluff succeeded. The police gave way. The details of the following events emerged at the trial which Hitler faced after he was indicted for high treason. On the way to the Feldherrenhalle the marchers were joined by Julius Streicher who had hurried from Nuremberg to Munich. Ludendorff later said that he was not quite sure where they were going. The S.A. men thought the great general was leading them. In fact, he followed Hitler, who made for the narrow passage of the Residenzstrasse which leads to the Odeonsplatz. Here, too, a police cordon barred the way.

In 1950 the Feldherrenhalle and the Odeonsplatz still bore the signs of the heavy bombardment to which Munich was subjected during the war. The cream had been taken off the beauty of this wide square, the buildings were drab and grey and reconstruction of the tremendous bomb damage was only just beginning. Walking across the squares, amidst the ruins, I could, as in so many towns of post-war Germany, almost hear the echo of the bombs five years after the end of the war. Compared with the holocaust of these crashing bombs, the shooting of November 9, 1923, was a very small affair indeed. To this day it has not been determined how it all started. Hitler was carrying a revolver in his hand. Streicher was reported to have grappled with a policeman in an attempt to wrest a rifle from his hands.

Did Hitler, as on the previous night in the Buergerbraeu, fire the first shot? A police salvo carried confusion into the ranks of the marchers. Scheubner-Richter fell, mortally wounded, pulling Hitler with him to the ground, and dislocating his arm. Goering was struck by a bullet. Many were hit, others turned in flight. Only Ludendorff marched on, a lonely figure, the "Victor of Tannenberg," the hero of Germany, marching on, not knowing where . . . Sixteen Nazis were killed.

Two middle-aged sisters emerged from a house in the Residenzstrasse to aid the wounded who were shouting for help. One of them, Frau Ilse Ballin, wife of a Jewish merchant, found Hermann Goering prostrate, his head resting on the pavement. He was bleeding profusely from a wound high up in the leg. He had been dragged to his resting place by a few S.A. men before they had made off to escape a police charge and arrest. Frau Ballin called her sister, and together the two women carried the severely wounded S.A. Commander into the house. They washed his wound and applied an emergency bandage. They were going to call an ambulance, but Goering implored them to desist. He was in great pain, but glad to be out of reach of the authorities. Appealing to the sisters to save him a second time, he summoned his dwindling strength to devise his own strategy. Would they allow him to stay until darkness? If they would only help him to reach the clinic of a friend, Professor von Ach! He would not, he pleaded, survive the indignity of an arrest. . . .

Karin's sister Fanny, Countess Wilamowitz-Moellendorf, the widow of a German officer, had gone to the Feldherrenhalle to witness Goering's triumph and take the glad news to Karin's sick-bed. Karin did not show her bitter disappointment when Fanny arrived with the report of the débâcle. There was no news of Goering all day, until Professor von Ach advised Frau Goering that her husband would be brought to his clinic. Within a few minutes Karin was up and dressed. Her cheeks were burning, her hands trembling, but she hurried to her Hermann to find him delirious, fighting the battle of the Odeonsplatz all over again. The professor did not hide the seriousness of his condition from her. A bullet had pierced Goering's leg only an inch from the main artery. Gravel and mud had been pushed deep into the wound. It was inflamed and festering and there was danger of a hemorrhage.

Karin shook the hands of Frau Ballin and her sister: "We shall never forget what you have done for Hermann . . ." she promised. There was little time for words now. News came that Kahr and Lossow were not going to allow the instigators of the putsch to escape unpunished. They felt betrayed by Hitler and Goering, who had promised to make common cause with them but had jeopardised their position by premature action. Hitler's haphazard, violent intervention had compromised the National Movement throughout the country. Bigger things were at stake for Kahr and Lossow than the ambitions of a third-rate street-corner orator and his impulsive aide who was so eager to play at soldier. That was what even the "Nationals" thought of Hitler and Goering now.

A warrant was issued for the arrest of the putsch leaders. As soon as Goering recovered consciousness and was told the position, he asked Karin to get him away: "Rather dead than in prison!" was his resolution. Neither could Karin bear the thought of her hero husband behind bars. She knew she was risking his life, but what was life without honour as she understood it? In a letter to her mother she gave her own version of what happened next:

"We drove from Munich to Garmisch in the car of friends in whose villa we stayed for a few days until it became known where we were and people began to flock to the house, demonstrating and shouting 'Hurray.' So we thought it best to cross the frontier into Austria. We left by car, but were arrested at the border. Police with loaded revolvers drove us back to Garmisch, where the people gathered again, shouting 'Heil Goering,' and preparing to lynch the police.... The authorities took his passport and Hermann was taken to a hospital which was surrounded by guards and posts."

The escape had failed. Goering was under arrest, but received permission to stay at a hospital in Garmisch on parole. He gave his word of honour that he would not make another attempt to escape. That was not the way Karin wanted it. Within a few hours she had rallied a number of friends to help her and her husband get away. Only a few miles farther south was the Austrian frontier—and freedom. "Help came as if by a miracle," Karin wrote. "Hermann, in his nightshirt, over which he wore a fur coat, was carried into a car and crossed the frontier with a false passport." Goering's own version of this second and successful escape was more romantic. He described how his faithful Party comrades, in an arduous expedition, carried him across the mountains on a stretcher. Once in safety he tried to shield the Nazi supporters in the police and among the frontier guards who had allowed him to slip through. In Munich his elder brother wrote angry letters to the press in an attempt to refute accusations that Goering had broken his word. Whenever, in later life, Goering gave his "word of honour"—and failed to keep it—there were similar doubts, denials, and controversies.

4

ADRIFT

WHEN Hitler and Goering came to power in Germany in January, 1933, their political opponents — Socialists, Communists, pacifists, and Jews — fled in terror to escape persecution and the violence of the S.A. Hapless, dispossessed expatriates, they scattered over the Continent in search of refuge. Britain offered hospitality to many, the United States threw her doors open to them. "People without a Fatherland," wrote Martin H. Sommerfeldt at the time, "are the unhappiest of them all." But Sommerfeldt was not referring to the refugees from Nazism. He wrote these words in a biography of Goering which he proudly presented to his German readers. And he was writing of the years of exile through which his hero lived after his escape from the Bavarian police in November, 1923.

Karin took Hermann Goering to a Catholic hospital in Innsbruck, the capital of the Austrian Tyrol. His condition was grave; the trip had exhausted his strength, and he had lost much blood. An immediate operation was necessary; others followed, and his recovery was retarded by the depression which descended on him. Two daily injections of morphia hardly alleviated the pain; the danger of blood poisoning persisted and the wound had to be kept open until the infected channel, torn by the bullet, was cleared. In letters to her family and her friends Karin graphically described how Hermann suffered, how he bit the pillows to stifle his own cries. Anna Beran, a nursing sister, spent every night at his bed. Karin nursed him by day and tried to cheer him up with a running commentary about the political events which followed the putsch.

The German press, she told him, was not allowed to comment on the affair. Kahr, according to her, had broken faith with Hitler and was worried lest his treachery should become apparent. Austrian and Swedish newspapers filled in the blanks. A warrant for Goering's arrest with his picture was posted all over Munich, but Bavarians were writing "Heil Goering" across it. Kahr was behaving "worse than the French," said Karin, while pro-German Austrians were offering help and money, taking flowers to the hospital, and finding ever new ways to demonstrate their allegiance to Hitler's cause. Karin did not mention the hostile demonstration by patriotic Austrians who were far from enthusiastic about the visitor from Bavaria. During one of these demonstrations she was involved in a street fight in which one of her toes was broken. She moved to the hospital to avoid the dangerous streets.

Goering made only slow progress; morphia alone kept up his deflated spirits. Hitler's sister Paula, a small, tender woman, unlike her brother except for the flashing, glaring eyes, was a regular visitor at the hospital. Secret messengers and couriers maintained contact between the Goerings and their Nazi friends in Munich. Those who had escaped arrest organised an underground movement, distributed pamphlets, carried on the fight without their leaders. Hitler was in prison awaiting trial; so were Rudolf Hess, Weber, and Kriebel. Although he was as yet unable to walk, Goering sent heroic messages offering to return and face trial by Hitler's side, but he was advised to keep away. The thought of seeing Hermann in prison still disturbed Karin and she pressed him to accept the advice. Bravely she hid from her husband the financial worries which began to beset her when their house, their car, and their bank account were impounded by the Bavarian authorities.

Just before Christmas, Goering was able to leave the hospital, walking on crutches. The proprietor of the Tiroler Hof, a Nazi sympathizer, offered them a free room in which Karin and Herrman spent Christmas Eve alone. The tension was great, Goering in an almost continuous state of hysterics. After short spells of exhilaration and optimism, he would collapse and let his tears flow without restraint. It was more than Karin could bear at a season in which her memories went back to the happy celebrations in her Swedish home. To hide her own tears, she went out into the winter night and stood listening to the strains of "Stille Nacht, heilige Nacht," which came from every window. In her delicate state of health it was a rash thing to do. Just as Goering abandoned his crutches for the first time, Karin went down with a feverish cold. From Sweden came desperate letters; the Fock family feared that the sick and penniless couple would succumb to the strain. They sent food parcels, as much money as they could spare. The sympathy and the gifts hurt Goering's pride. But a letter which he wrote to Karin's mother did not reveal his feelings: "Kindest thanks for your thoughts," it ran. "We always think of you and know that you are with us in these hard times. I feel better now and should soon be fully recovered. Please have no worries about Karin. I hope to arrange everything as soon as I am well again. . . ."

A bunch of telegrams with New Year wishes from Bavarian and Austrian friends cheered Goering, but Karin commented: "I wish we had the money which was spent on all these messages. . . ." By February Goering's wound had healed, but the once-powerful, youthful man suffered mental anguish because the operations had affected his manhood. The doctor would give no date by which the patient could expect to recover his full strength and potency again. Every day he became more dependent on morphia to escape the torment of his mind. Physically, he was again fit enough to look out for something to do. Reports from Munich suggested that Hitler and his accomplices might get away with a nominal sentence or that an amnesty would soon follow the verdict of the courts. Goering took these reports as a signal to resume his political activities. Anna Beran was now nursing Karin whose condition was deteriorating.

The invitation of a small group of pro-German Nationalists to address them gave Goering an opportunity to make his first speech in Innsbruck. Karin was at home, the nursing sister praying at her bedside, as Goering rose to speak in the back room of a nearby inn. He had quickly grasped the problems of his Austrian friends who regarded the Catholics as their most dangerous opponents. In his best platform manner, he fulminated against "Rome" and the Vatican. Out of the blue he turned to the celibate, suddenly outraged by the thought that anybody should voluntarily forgo the normal relationship between the sexes of which his operations had made him incapable: "We demand," he screamed, "that the Catholic priest should lead a normal life and be allowed to marry!" The words slipped out before he had time to consider the implication, but the applause of his audience reassured him.

In an intensely Catholic country like Austria, such a speech was bound to create a stir. A notice about it appeared in the local press and was taken up by the Vienna newspapers. It came to the attention of Dr. Walter Riehl, a lawyer and leader of the extreme Right Wing of the nationalistic Pan-Germans, a fiery orator but withal an amiable man whom I have often heard expounding Nazi views in intelligent conversation and with better grace than Hitler. Riehl, while attacking the Jews from the platform, mixed with them freely in the cafés of Vienna. He was, of course, in complete sympathy with Hitler's aims, but would not allow the Munich Nazis to forget that he had founded a "German Workers' Party" in Vienna long before the N.S.D.A.P. was even thought of. Hitler never forgave Riehl for having anticipated him.

Many of the German "exiles" came to see Riehl in Vienna and the Austrian police had their hands full to control the weird collection of terrorists and putschists who transferred their activities to Austria. Goering too joined Riehl's group as Hitler's representative. The Austrian authorities had raised no objection to his stay in Innsbruck while he was ill and kept quiet, but their watchful eyes were on him as soon as he began to take part in the "work" of Riehl and his friends and to appear as a public speaker at their meetings. As I listened to Goering in Vienna, it was obvious to me that even his political friends were disturbed by his un-Austrian approach and the violence of his expressions. I did not realise at the time that he was overanxious to whip up the enthusiasm of his listeners because he was dependent on the small contributions which they were invited to drop into the collection boxes. It was not an easy way of making money, but he earned enough to buy Karin a portable typewriter, his first present since they had left Munich. It was a great joy to Karin who made much use of the machine, typing out long letters and writing thousands of words about her favourite subject — Hermann Goering. Without Karin and her typewriter, we should know less about the darkest years in Goering's life.

In April Hitler was sentenced to five years' detention in the Fortress of Landsberg, with the proviso that he would be released on parole after six months. Paula Hitler broke down when she heard the news, and Goering, unable to hide a sense of guilt at having left Hitler in the lurch, as always reacted with renewed fierce public outbursts. Fortified by his daily dose of morphia, he attacked the "Jewish Republic of Berlin," swore that he would only return to a truly "national Germany." The Austrian authorities were embarrassed by his attacks on a friendly government and were relieved when a German request for his extradition enabled them to act. Politely but firmly, Goering was asked to leave the country. Disappointed and bitter, he told Karin that from now on he would live only for the day when he could return to Austria in triumph.

Hitler was spending the time in comfortable confinement at Landsberg, dictating the first part of his book, the story of *Mein Kampf*, to his friend and fellow prisoner, Rudolf Hess. Ludendorff had been acquitted. "I regard this acquittal as an insult to the decorations which I am wearing," he commented, and turned his back on politics for the time being. The world had taken little notice of the trial. Even Germany began to forget Hitler and his movement. In Russia a new, vigorous, behind-the-scenes leader, Josef Stalin, was consolidating the power of the Communist régime. But in Italy the Fascist idea seemed to have taken root. Italy offered asylum to Hermann Goering. At the end of April, 1924, he took Karin to Venice. Though their funds were low, they moved into the expensive Britannia Hotel and, for a few days, lived, Karin said, "as if Hermann had inherited a million." Rome was their final destination, to meet Mussolini, Goering's greatest ambition.

With their last money the couple moved into a small hotel in a back street of Rome and waited until their friend Philip von Hessen, who was wooing the King of Italy's daughter, secured Hermann an audience with Mussolini. The Italian dictator, whose "march on Rome" (in a sleeper) had taken the Fascists to power, received Goering in the Palazzo Venezia. He carefully listened to his account of Hitler's struggle and to the "inside" story of the November putsch. "When Hitler is released from prison, he must come and see me," he said. "I shall be most interested to meet him." But that was a long way off. Goering returned from the interview, not elated because he had at last met the Fascist dictator, but even more depressed by the success of the man whose views he shared but had been unable to impose on Germany. In the meantime, without work or income the position of the Goerings was clearly untenable. Their hope of an amnesty did not materialise, and the emphasis, anyway, was not now on a return to politics. They were only anxious to obtain the release of their house so they could sell it, the return of their car, the loss of which had been a bitter blow to Goering, and to get money. Twice Karin travelled to Munich to organise help for her husband. She saw Ludendorff, who was polite and sympathetic but obviously no longer interested in Goering or the Hitler movement. She visited Hitler in Landsberg, but the Party had no funds to help the exiled comrade. Hitler gave Karin his picture inscribed "To the honoured wife of my S.A. Commander, Frau Karin Goering, in memory of her visit to the Fortress of Landsberg on 15 April, 1925. Adolf Hitler." This picture, linking, as it were, the two people who dominated his life, remained Goering's greatest sentimental treasure. In a silver frame it stood on his desk when he was already a Minister, Reichsmarschall, and the second man in the Reich. But when Karin brought it to Rome — and nothing else — Goering was at the end of his tether. There was nothing left for them but to go to Stockholm and to throw themselves on the mercy of Karin's family.

The trip was made by a devious route via Austria, Czechoslovakia, and Poland and the Free City of Danzig. Here he told his in-laws, touching German soil again after nearly two years, he went down on his knees to pray. His prayers remained unanswered. Goering's return to Stockholm, which he had left as an ambitious, optimistic, energetic man in the prime of his life, was a sad performance. Karin's relatives knew that drugs had taken a terrible hold on him and that there could be no thought of resuming his career as an airman. The family found a small flat for the couple, who were lucky at long last to obtain the release of their own furniture which was sent from Munich. The villa in Obermenzing was sold and the money sustained them for a few months. Goering was in a shocking condition. Day after day he paced his small room, restlessly, aimlessly, struggling against his craving for drugs, until, inevitably, his trembling hand reached for the syringe which brought him solace. His weary mind sought the delusions which ever bigger doses of morphine conjured up before his eyes. Slowly he was being driven to the verge of insanity. Karin, to add to their troubles, had developed a weak heart, and a slight epileptic tendency aggravated her condition. Unable to nurse Hermann, she consented that he should be taken to Konradsberg Hospital near Stockholm. When the money ran out before his condition improved, he had to be removed to an asylum at Langbro.

In 1933 I tried to obtain details of Goering's illness, but all documentary evidence of his detention in Langbro had disappeared. As soon as he had assumed control of the Prussian police, Goering, incensed by the revelations about his drug habit, had sent one of the most efficient German agents to Sweden to recover the relevant documents. But others had anticipated his move. His registration card as a patient at the Langbro Asylum had been photographed by representatives of an anti-Nazi group, who published it before the year was out.[1] According to the photostatic copy, Goering was admitted to the asylum on September 1, 1925. Karin was desolate. Without Hermann there was nobody on whom to shower her motherly love. Oh yes, there was! There was her son Thomas, now thirteen, and living with her first husband, Nils von Kantzow. She would devote herself to Thomas while Hermann Goering was away. When von Kantzow refused her request to let her son stay with her, the family could not dissuade Karin from launching a law suit for the custody of the boy. Von Kantzow quickly settled the argument by producing a doctor's certificate, according to which "Captain Goering" (Goering had been promoted to the rank of Captain on leaving the Air Force) "suffers from morphinism and his wife Karin Goering, née Baroness Fock, suffers from epilepsy. Their home must, therefore, be regarded as unfit for the son Thomas Kantzow." Signed, "Karl A. R. Lundberg."

Young Thomas, however, grew up to become very fond of Hermann Goering. After Goering's death in 1946, he visited Germany and his stepfather's second wife Emmy, to offer her a home in Sweden. The Fock family always regarded Goering's aberration simply as a result of his injury and the desolate conditions under which he lived in exile. After six months he was able to leave the Langbro Asylum, cured from his pernicious habit, but still unable to take up a regular occupation. As his fortunes reached

[1] *The Brown Book of the Hitler Terror.*

their lowest ebb, he found his pride and his energy again. He had reached rock-bottom, but, as in the old days on the battlefields of France, he avoided the fatal crash, glided out of danger, determined to fight his way to the top again. The world would see what Hermann Goering was capable of. There are people whom the blows of Fate, deserved or undeserved, leave prostrate and paralysed. Goering did not belong in this category. His house in Munich was gone — he would have to get another house! One day he would have a castle, many castles, estates! Now he had to live precariously by selling one piece of furniture after another. One day he would have all the furniture in the world!

After a long interval, Goering's interest turned to Germany again. He had no direct news from Hitler who had been released from prison just before Christmas, 1924, to find his hold on the movement slipping from his hands. The Nazi Party was banned; the shots of the Odeonsplatz had scattered his followers, subjected them to new influences. Ernst Roehm had tried to keep the S.A. in being, but soon withdrew from the political scene. Gregor Strasser, a young chemist, had gathered new followers around him and gained great influence among Nationalists in northern Germany. Alfred Rosenberg, his editor of the *Voelkischer Beobachter*, was printing articles from one Joseph Paul Goebbels, whose name was becoming increasingly popular. The Reichswehr was doling out money to less clumsy and more reliable agents, and had secured a hold on the Berlin Government. And Berlin had succeeded in stabilising not only the minds, but also the currency, of Germany.

For a few months Hitler lived in virtual retirement in Berchtesgaden, where his friends had enabled him to buy a new villa, Haus Wachenfeld, and devoted himself to work on the second volume of *Mein Kampf*. His closest friend and private secretary was Rudolf Hess; his circle included again the wealthy Ernst ("Putzi") Hanfstaengl, Alfred Rosenberg, Julius Streicher, Max Ammann, the business manager of the *Voelkischer Beobachter*, and Adolf Mueller, the printer who gave credit when business was slack. Hitler seemed to be content to settle down to the comfortable life of a writer and publisher and to leave politics alone. But *Mein Kampf*, when it was first published, did not bring in much money, and his newspaper became a playball of political factions inside the Nationalist Movement. If he wanted to keep control of his interests, Hitler had to reassert himself as a politician.

His first step was to secure the removal of the ban on the Nazi Party. He humbled himself before the political powers of the day, promising allegiance to the Catholic interests in Bavaria, approaching industrial interests in the Ruhr through Dr. Otto Dietrich, a new member of the Party, and seeking new contacts with the all-powerful Reichswehr. Manoeuvring cleverly, he rallied the majority of the Nationalists once more to his cause, among them now men like Wilhelm Frick, member of the Bavarian Diet, and the Reichstag, whose votes Hitler was able to throw into the scales of the political balance. Gregor Strasser grudgingly accepted his leadership, but the two never saw eye to eye. Strasser insisted on pursuing a strictly Socialist policy, while Hitler missed no opportunity of serving his industrialist paymasters. When the Socialist President, Friedrich Ebert, died, Hitler and his friends supported the candidature of the aged Field Marshal von Hindenburg. Hindenburg, soon after his election, showed his gratitude by proclaiming a political amnesty. At long last Hermann Goering could come home to Germany.

5

POLITICS AND PEA SOUP

IN LANDSBERG, west of Munich, where Hitler once served his sentence, there is today a modern prison, a big grey block with many wings spreading out in windmill fashion. It is run by the American occupation authorities and accommodates war criminals convicted in the secondary Nuremberg trials, such as the "Wilhelmstrasse Trial" (the Wilhelmstrasse was the Whitehall of Berlin). Among the prisoners are the intelligentsia of the Nazi movement, the hierarchy of the Nazi civil service and industrialists who helped Hitler — some of them wearing the wine-red jackets which indicate that they have been sentenced to death. A notice inside the prison appeals: "... to all who have not forgotten us ... for a small donation ... a number of our comrades are unable to write home as they cannot afford the stamps." Polish soldiers in black helmets guard the prison where over four hundred executions have taken place since 1946. Pathetic figures of black-dressed women search the prison graveyard for the "numbers" of the men they mourn. Others crowd the waiting rooms with bunches of flowers and food parcels.

In the past few years the list of prisoners has included famous names — Alfred Krupp; Baron Ernst Weizsaecker, Germany's perennial foreign affairs expert; Karl Krauch, of the I. G. Farben Chemical Trust; Walter Darre, the former Minister of Agriculture; Dr. Otto Dietrich, once Reichs Press Chief. Two of the long-term prisoners often talk of the late twenties when Fate brought them together with Captain Hermann Goering and started them on the road that led to Landsberg. Paul Koerner, one of them, is listed as a former Secretary of State in the Prussian Ministry of the Interior and Goering's right-hand man in the administration of the Four-Year Plan; the other was once the brains behind the organisation of the

German Air Force, a bluff, intelligent air expert — the former Field Marshal of the Luftwaffe, Erhard Milch. Ever since he returned to Germany from Sweden at the end of 1927, these two men had belonged to the circle of Hermann Goering's closest friends.

Leaving Karin behind, Goering went to Munich to see Hitler, but the two men had moved apart since November, 1923, and their reunion was cool and inconclusive. Goering met Bodenschatz and a few of his war comrades, but his mind was not on the past. He was determined to make money. Thus, the Pour le Mérite airman, who had reached the ripe age of thirty-four, set out on visits to the leading firms of the German aircraft industry, the B.M.W. (Bayrische Motoren Werke) and Heinkel. He was calmer and stouter now, anxious to take up serious and profitable work. He was made welcome. It would be a good idea, they thought, if he went to Berlin to establish contact with foreign military missions and to plug B.M.W. engines and parachutes, which were produced as sidelines. Goering liked the idea and agreed to go to Berlin at once.

Looking over a number of small furnished flats in Berlin, Goering chose one in the Berchtesgadenerstrasse — he was always a sentimentalist — and set out to make his contacts. Paul Koerner, whom his friends called "Pilli," an ex-officer he had met during the war, joined him and bought his sole asset into the partnership, a motor car which he drove as Goering's chauffeur-cum-secretary. The two friends had little money, but what they had was husbanded carefully to keep up with some of their wartime friends who had got on in the world. There was Erhard Milch in an influential position in Germany's leading civilian airline, the Lufthansa, who could do much to put fat commissions into the pockets of the ambitious agent. Bruno Loerzer was also in Berlin, now married to the daughter of a wealthy man, and Goering called on his partner of many gay nights at Stenay, Prince Philip von Hessen.

His most successful "line" was the Tornblad parachute in which he interested the Dutch, the Swiss, and the Swedish Military Attachés, organising demonstrations, but no longer taking to the air himself. Tirelessly he pulled every string he knew, brought businessmen and airmen together, induced experts to write testimonials, thinking engines and parachutes day and night. No person whom he met was able to remain outside the ever-widening circle of his activities; he was clever, efficient, and made money quickly, but much of it went to Sweden where Karin was seriously ill in hospital. The rest was spent on high living which he regarded as an indispensable investment in his career — on expensive dinner parties, on presents for his business associates and their wives, on luxury trips around the country. He and Koerner were inseparable. Although it looked as if they were on top of the world, the two often finished the day without a penny in their pockets.

In the spring of 1928, when Karin wrote that she was now fit enough to join him, he took a bigger flat in the Gaisbergstrasse and decorated a big corner room with flowers. At last he would be reunited with her! Without Karin his busy life had still been empty. Now that he was healthy again, he missed her sorely. Though there are few vices which have not been attributed to Goering, his sense of loyalty to Karin was never in doubt. It would not allow him to deceive his wife; and throughout his life he was a faithful husband, a strict moralist in the sphere of matrimony. With the return of Karin, politics inevitably began to take a new hold on him.

During one of Hitler's visits to Berlin, he asked Goering to come and see him at the small Sans-Souci Hotel where the Fuehrer stayed on his rare excursions to the capital. Goering had found his feet, was again confident, full of enthusiasm about his work, his contacts, his personal friends. Hitler took note — these were useful people, indeed; Goering could be useful again. It was almost the same situation as when they had met first in 1922. Hitler's intuition was at work. He told Goering about the latest developments in the Party. As always, there was trouble with the S.A., which was under the command of an independent fellow by the name of Pfeffer and not at all the kind of organisation which Hitler had envisaged. There was no question, however, of ousting Pfeffer, and Goering did not feel inclined to resume his old post of S.A. Commander. Hitler had created a new small formation, his very own bodyguard, absolutely loyal to his person, the so-called S.S. — short for Schutz Staffel (Protective Guard) — with a leader devoted to him, one Heinrich Himmler, a poultry farmer. He had appointed Joseph Goebbels Gauleiter of Berlin and the fiery young man had tightened up the party organisation. An election was impending and Hitler was preparing to invade the Reichstag with his own representatives — while the Constitution provided for that "talking shop" it was best to conquer it from within. Would Goering consent to stand as a candidate for the Reichstag? Hermann Goering, Member of Parliament, representative of the people — he did not hesitate for a moment. He shook hands with Hitler and accepted.

Karin was at home, resting and working on her embroidery when Goering stormed up the stairs with Koerner. "Get ready, we are going out to celebrate . . . " Her weak body was shaken by emotion. Hermann was a success at last! There was a hurried call to Erhard Milch for a dinner party at Horcher's, the fashionable restaurant in the Berlin West End. For once Goering paid little attention to his food or to the bottle of red wine of which he was usually so fond. There was too much to talk about; his campaign had to be organised, the line of his speeches determined. Milch could help to make his campaign a real hit; Koerner could rally the old officer friends: "You have to approach your task in a dignified way . . . " Milch insisted, thinking of Goering's Party comrades, the S.A., whose rowdyism in the streets shocked even some of Hitler's own followers. There was no need to warn Goering, who longed for respectability, and was going to show his elevated friends how to conduct oneself on the political platform. A "revolution without radicalism" was the slogan which he turned over in his mind, a "respectable revolution" which a prince or a duke could support.

No doubt Hitler had called him in to counteract the bad impression which wild men like Gregor Strasser and Ernst Roehm created. After all, rich industrialists were providing the money, the politics of the Party had aroused favourable comment in the drawing rooms of men with powerful positions in the German business world. The Reichswehr was counting on them, the whole of Europe was watching! It was up to Goering to reassure the world about the Nazi Party. The plans which he discussed with Karin, Koerner, and Milch at Horcher's that evening guided Hermann Goering's career for years to come. It has often been said that Hitler nominated Goering as a Reichstag candidate to furnish his old friend with a regular income. The emoluments of a German deputy would be a welcome addition to the uncertain budget of the Goerings, but they were no more than a drop in the ocean of his personal expenditure.

Long before he was elected, Karin went out to inspect new flats and to look over valuable furniture which could be a suitable foil for her husband, "the Magnificent," of whom she saw little now that he had thrown himself wholeheartedly into the battle. Between conferences and Party meetings he would arrive to take her out for a quick meal — but "We are rarely alone nowadays," she wrote to her mother; "even at meals there are at least three or four people with whom Hermann continues his consultations." Usually one of these men around Goering was Goebbels with whom he had formed a close friendship, although the Gauleiter's ideas of an election campaign had little in common with Goering's sedate approach. Goebbels, anxious to draw attention to the Party at any cost, mobilised the S.A. to roam the streets and to challenge their political opponents. He revelled in the daily clashes with the Communists, who sent out their own "Red Front"; with the Socialists and their Reichsbanner; even with the formations of the Right-Wing Stahlhelm. The clashes led to a ban of the Party in Berlin, but it was lifted again in April.

The elections took place on May 20. Hitler's National Socialist German Workers' Party received 800,000 votes. Twelve Nazis were elected as deputies to the Reichstag. Hermann Goering was one of them. Goebbels, cynical, only too conscious of the paradox of his anti-democratic Party striving for representation in a democratic parliament, recorded his own election in his diary with these words: "Now I am an 'IDI,' an 'IDF' " (Inhaber der Immunitaet, Inhaber der Freifahrkarte — Possessor of Immunity, Possessor of a Free Railway Ticket). But Goering took his election very seriously. To Karin it was the pay-off for years of soul-destroying endeavour in which she had reached the limit of her physical endurance. She rallied her strength to attend the opening of the Reichstag and to watch Hermann take his seat.

There he was right out in front sharing a table with General von Epp, who had resigned from the Army to take up politics in the Nazi Party. Goebbels was there, and Gregor Strasser, Wilhelm Frick, and Gottfried Feder, a woolly-minded economist and early friend of Hitler — a small group but men who meant to make themselves heard. Karin was shocked to see Hitler's handful of deputies opposed by an overwhelming number of Communist members in Red Front uniforms: "They are wearing the Jewish David Star, the Soviet Star — it's all the same!" she said. "Scores of deputies of all parties are Jews," she noted, "except, of course, in Hitler's Party!" From the Reichstag she accompanied Goering to a meeting where he spoke about the "great victory of the Nazi Party," and, returning home almost completely exhausted after the greatest day of her life, she could only just manage to scan the letters and telegrams with congratulations for her husband: "Hermann, look!" she shouted with excitement, picking out one of the letters. Goering read it, and pride swelled in his breast as he recognised the handwriting of the Crown Prince: "Your extraordinary talent, your power of expression," Friedrich Wilhelm wrote, "your great physical strength are excellent for your new job as a People's Representative. . . . " The Crown Prince was thinking of the fights on the floor of the House which were a regular feature of the Reichstag sessions, but Goering did not like that part of the letter. He was not going to fight the Communists with his fists. He would have to explain to the Crown Prince and to many others that a new era had dawned . . . The following week the Goerings moved into a new big flat in the fashionable Badenschestrasse.

Well could Karin's sister write that "in the autumn of 1928 the position had become more secure." As a member of the Reichstag, Goering received eight hundred marks per month and expenses which he was paid as a Reichsredner (Reich orator), one of the select band of Nazi leaders who were the star turns at the Party's mass meetings throughout the country. Karin, ailing and mostly confined to her flat, modelled the new home on that of her mother in Sweden. She bought a small organ on which she played for hours, and, though there was no Edelweiss Chapel, she turned a corner of her room into a place of worship, decorated with holy pictures and flowers. There she knelt in meditation while her husband, smoking a large cigar and enjoying a bottle of wine, occupied himself with political papers.

Goering's approach to politics had always been the rough-and-ready attack of a problem if and when it presented itself. He was content to leave ideological, programmatic details to his friend Goebbels, to the intellectuals and philosophers of the Party like Alfred Rosenberg. It was all really very simple. The position in Germany, as he saw it, was determined by the great split of the country into two camps: "The bourgeoisie," he wrote in these days, "represents nationalism, hated by the working class as a symbol of terror and suppression; the proletariat represents Socialism, hated and feared by the cowardly bourgeoisie as a symbol of destruction and enemy of private property." [1] He did not like either, but—"unite these two conflicting forces and you have National Socialism!" That was Hitler's task and his.

He went about this task in his own very direct way. To his new home he invited people whom he wanted to win over to the ideas of the Party. He had met the young Prince of Wied, member of an aristocratic and adventurous family, one of whose relatives went out to conquer Albania. Prince Wied and his wife became regular visitors at the Badensche Strasse and brought many of their aristocratic friends to the hospitable house. Goering was spending even more money than before. His sumptuous parties with famous guests were often followed by meagre meals at which Goering, Karin, and "Pilli" Koerner were satisfied with soup and bread. To maintain a façade of opulence was vital to the Goerings; how they lived outside the ken of their rich friends did not matter much. He had been in debt before.

The Goerings became friendly with one of the Crown Prince's brothers, August Wilhelm, known to the German people as "Auwi"; there were few parties at Goering's which Auwi did not attend. He joined the Nazi Party and became the only member of the Hohenzollern family to sport the brown shirt of the S. A. The circle of Goering's friends included young diplomats of the embassies with whom he still negotiated an occasional sale of aero engines. Slowly and deliberately he threw his nets to catch bankers and businessmen like Hjalmar Schacht, the President of the Reichsbank, and Kirdorf, the Ruhr industrialist. He soon realised that there were economic problems as yet beyond his horizon with which he had to familiarise himself. Above all, there were the financial problems of the Party which only ever-increasing contributions from the treasure houses of the Rhine and the Ruhr could solve.

Munich Nazis who came to Berlin were often put up at Goering's flat, and it was a feature of his parties, much discussed in Berlin, that princes and dukes could meet members of the humble working classes at dinner. "A few days ago," Karin wrote to her mother, "we had Baron Koskull for lunch, Herr von Bahr and Prince August

[1] Hermann Goering, *Aufbau einer Nation.*

Wilhelm and two National Socialist workers. Count Solms came later and the Duke of Koburg with his daughter. You can imagine that the mixture astonished them. . . ." Auwi also became a Reichsredner; he and Goering formed a team travelling from town to town and appearing on the platform together. Goering's speeches at the time were simple and direct: "Down with Marxism! Follow the Fuehrer who will save Germany!" Hjalmar Schacht and his friends explained to him the implications of the most pressing economic questions of the day, such as the Young Plan, a generous Allied attempt to settle the vexed Reparations tangle. But according to Goering, "reparations" was a word not to be included in the Nazi phraseology. Germany was not going to pay anything to her enemies!

Champagne was flowing in the Badenschestrasse while other streets reverberated with the noise of marching and singing storm troopers. The battle of the streets assumed threatening proportions. Hitler had appointed Goebbels Chief of Nazi Propaganda and his technique was to incense the masses, to excite them with constant demonstrations. The S.A. persistently chanted the same slogan, "Deutschland erwache!" (Germany awake!) Political clashes ended with wounded men littering the streets. Others paid for their ideals with their lives. When an ill-reputed S.A. leader, Horst Wessel, was killed in a brawl which had nothing to do with politics, Goebbels seized on the incident and turned him into a hero and martyr of the movement. Next evening the Princess Wied arrived at Goering's flat with her latest painting showing the marching columns of the S.A. and their dead comrades, ethereal figures, marching with them "in spirit." Not much later the "Horst Wessel" song, the Nazi anthem, could be heard all over Germany:

> Die Fahnen hoch, die Reihen dicht geschlossen,
> S.A. marchiert mit mutig, festem Schritt,
> Kameraden, die Rotfront und Reaktion erschossen,
> Marschiern im Geist in unsern Reihen mit.

> Lift up the flags, close firmly the ranks,
> The S.A. march with proud and daring steps,
> Comrades shot by Red Front and Reaction,
> In spirit march along in our ranks.

Goering himself was marching more warily. He convinced Schacht and his banker friends that the S.A. was just a regrettable by-product of a political movement which was really firmly in the hands of gentlemen like Hermann Goering. An intense patriot, Schacht expected the up and coming Nazi leaders to support a policy which would strengthen Germany, first internally and then internationally. A strong, united Germany, these men argued, could do away with the Treaty of Versailles. Germany would be able to rearm and become an equal partner in the concert of nations. But Schacht and his circle were still doubtful about "that man Hitler," the rabble-rouser, the ex-corporal, the putschist, the uncultured upstart. They had never met him. It was up to Goering to arrange such a meeting.

If there had been any hesitation on their part to meet Hitler, it was dispelled in the summer of 1930. The Reichstag had been dissolved again and there were to be new elections. Goebbels performed miracles of organisation. Six thousand mass meetings were held. Goering, like all other Nazi leaders, toured the country in a mad rush to speak at two, three meetings every day. His tour took him from East Prussia via Berlin to the Rhineland. His fans followed from meeting to meeting, and there were people like the crippled Count Henckell-Donnersmark who had himself wheeled to four of the meetings at which Goering spoke. Karin could not bear to miss Hermann's triumphal tour. Though hardly able to move, she insisted on being carried into a car to meet him at Magdeburg. She heard him speak and returned with him to Berlin, driving all night. As she returned to her sick-bed Goering went off, sleepless, to new meetings.

During the trip Karin was spared every unnnecessary move, Goering fussing about her as he watched her strength ebbing away. The excursion ended with a relapse. The household had virtually to be handed over to the new cook, Cilli Wachowiak, a pleasant young country girl. The election campaign was taking Goering ever further away. "I am so lonely," Karin wrote; "my health makes it impossible for me to keep social contact with friends and acquaintances as other women do. God gives me strength only when I believe that I must help, psychologically, in the Hitler movement." A few days later she had to be removed to a Bavarian clinic. While she was away, Goering celebrated his greatest triumph to date. At the Reichstag elections on September 14, 1930, Hitler's Party polled six and a half million votes, eighteen per cent of the electorate. Into the Reichstag in close formation, Hermann Goering at the head of the column, marched 107 Nazi deputies. They formed the second strongest Party in the Reich. Hitler, the Fuehrer, had earned the right to be heard.

Berlin was strange territory to the Fuehrer, who always regarded Munich as his spiritual headquarters. Only Goering, well versed in the social graces, the jovial, happy, corpulent fellow with unbounded energy and a sense of fun, with easy manners and much charm, could make him feel at ease in the company of strangers. "Mein Fuehrer," Goering promised, "let me make a little party and you will see that you will be a tremendous success." Goering knew how to arrange these parties. Karin was back, a little better now, and was able to prepare the house for the great occasion. It was a small party, a simple party, the way Hitler liked it, designed at the same time to appeal in its simplicity to the other guests whom Goering could not, in any case, impress with a show of lavishness. Karin chose the menu: Pea soup, pork, and a Swedish apple-cake with vanilla cream. She borrowed the cook of her friend, Princess Wied, to help in the kitchen. Cilli served at table.

One of the guests was von Stauss, a banker, who had introduced Schacht to Goering; Schacht brought his wife and Fritz Thyssen, the immensely wealthy, powerful leader of the Ruhr industrialists. If Hitler could win over Thyssen — the magnates of German heavy industry and high finance would follow suit automatically. Hitler arrived after dinner.

Hjalmar Schacht, who stood trial with Goering at Nuremberg but was acquitted, has long since changed his views about Hitler and Goering. When I met him at the Luneburg estate of a friend, where he lived after his release, Schacht, youthful in spite of his years, quick-thinking, speaking English as fluently as German, was scathing and contemptuous of the Nazi leaders with whom he joined forces on that evening in Goering's flat. On that evening he thought that Goering's attitude was simple and restrained. After all these years he still recalled the pea soup. Karin, he told me, made an excellent impression. The party settled down comfortably to listen to Hitler who spoke for two full hours: "He said nothing," Schacht explained to me, "which could in any way surprise us. Equality of Germany in the international field, work for Germany's unemployed, were his chief topics. Rearmament was Hitler's means of achieving the first, State credits for public works were to create employment."

Goering said little until the bankers raised the question of the S.A., that public nuisance, the rowdies whose violent and disorderly conduct disturbed the business. Goering tried to placate them. "We shall restrain these people," he assured them. "Once we have your support, we shall be able to achieve our aims in a perfectly legal manner." Thyssen went away convinced that the Nazi Party deserved support. Schacht was impressed: "I noticed in Hitler," he said, "an élan, an infectious will which would become real action once he was in power!"

When the bankers had gone and Hitler remained alone with Goering and Karin, they knew that their Nazi movement had gained a great victory. They could count on Thyssen's co-operation. And this co-operation meant — finance, money. Hitler kissed Karin's hand: "You are the mascot of my movement," he said. "When you are here all goes well!" He did not long persist in this mood. Both men realised that this first step towards a solid alliance with the Schachts and Thyssens necessitated radical action inside the Party. Their thoughts turned to Ernst Roehm, who, a few months previously had returned to Germany from South America where he had spent a year reorganising the Bolivian Army. Hitler had once more entrusted him with the leadership of the S.A. and once more Roehm had pursued his own path. Roehm would have to be curbed! Matters were also coming to a head in the simmering conflict between the Hitler-Goering faction of the Party and Gregor Strasser's clique.

Strasser soon learned of the portentous meeting in the privacy of Goering's flat. He, too, was a man of quick action and he challenged Goering: "You are selling out the Party to the moneyed interests!" Hitler had made off to Munich. For Hermann Goering a first big crisis, such as often accompanies success, had arrived. These were no simple problems with which to deal in the "soldierly manner" to which he was accustomed. There was no hope of winning Strasser over to his views. He would have to be a little more subtle than he had been hitherto. How could he explain to a man who always put the emphasis on the Socialist points in the Party programme that Hitler saw no hope of success without Thyssen's financial support? A split in the highest ranks of the Nazi Party was inevitable.

Goering has often been described as the "diplomat of the Nazi Party." Time after time his amiable personality was pushed into the foreground to gain new friends for the Party, to allay suspicions against which Hitler fought in vain. Hitler had a habit of withdrawing into the solitude of Berchtesgaden and leaving Goering to deal with awkward situations. As Hitler's faithful paladin — his own description of himself — Goering always knew what was in the Fuehrer's mind when he left it to him to find a solution. Though the official appointment came a little later, he was now Hitler's political representative in Berlin with full power to act. This power implied the need for action. And out of this need, Goering the diplomat was born.

At this stage of his career, Goering had not yet learned to look far ahead. But now it was necessary to take stock to see where he stood and where the others stood. Inside the Party Strasser and Roehm were the enemies. Strasser, particularly, could almost be identified with Marxism, and Marxism, in Goering's view, was "revolution, unrest, street fighting, plunder, murder, arson, disorder." Did it occur to him that this cap fitted the S.A.? The Jews were obviously up in arms against the Nazi Party. Now Goering saw the Jews threatening him behind the shield of every political party. Karin had said so herself; she had noticed that the Jews were "dominating the Reichstag." Then there were the Catholic Parties. Damn it! If the Catholics claim that the Pope is infallible, National Socialists could claim that Hitler was infallible too. General von Schleicher, a power behind the scene of Reichswehr politics, was friendly with Roehm — therefore Goering's enemy. And the Government . . . the instability of the Reichstag, where it was almost impossible to get a clear majority for the most important measures, the evil mood of the people and the political parties forced Chancellor Heinrich Bruening to run the country by emergency laws. Goering felt that they were operated to the disadvantage of his Party, that Bruening was determined to keep him out. As the second Party in the country, surely the Nazis had a right to power in the State.

Perhaps the old gentleman at the head of the country, perhaps Hindenburg would help. Goering set out to get the ear of the President. The Field Marshal would not deny an audience to the famous airman and holder of the Order Pour le Mérite, however obstinately he refused to see the ex-corporal, Hitler. Goering was invited to Neudeck, to the President's residence; he went for a second time, and again, and was making good progress. "It will not be long now," he told Karin, who was only just hanging on to life. "We shall soon be in power. Once Hitler and Hindenburg meet . . . there will be no further obstacle, Hitler will be Chancellor of the Reich!" Karin knew that her days were numbered; all she wanted was to live long enough to see that day. To bring it nearer, Goering ranged far and wide over the political scene. It was as yet impossible for him to oust Roehm, but a breach was made in Strasser's front when Hitler quarrelled with his brother Otto, who left the party.

Hitler put his faith in Goering. "Through Hindenburg to power!" was his slogan — the Nazi always thought in terms of getting "an die Macht" (into power); and "Through Goering to Hindenburg" was Hitler's device. From money which the rising circulation of the *Voelkische Beobachter* and increased sales of *Mein Kampf* brought in, he bought Goering a present, a big, supercharged Mercedes motor car, "to replace the car which Goering sacrificed to the movement in 1923." For the last time Karin rallied and, together, in the new car they went on a tour through Germany. On their return to Berlin, Karin expressed the wish to travel to Stockholm — at once! Hermann Goering felt that she wanted to go home to die. In the spirit of the old Edelweiss Chapel, she was determined to be reunited with her own country, even if only in death.

Although the long negotiations with Hindenburg and his entourage were about to produce results, Goering accompanied his dying wife to Sweden. Her own mother died and the shock was a final blow to her. Karin took to her bed and the family gathered around her. Goering prayed and waited. On October 14, 1931, a telegram arrived from Berlin. Hindenburg had at last consented to see Hitler. Would Goering introduce his Fuehrer to the Field Marshal? There is no record of the conversation between Karin and

Hermann which followed the arrival of this telegram. Goering had reached another turning point. There could be little doubt that the "old man" had decided to appoint Hitler Chancellor of Germany. None but the Nazis, with their hold on the mass of the radical unemployed workers, could bring order into the political chaos. Hitler and Goering were nearing the peak of achievement. Next day Goering travelled to Berlin. In the late afternoon of October 16, he and Hitler were shown into Hindenburg's study. Without offering the leader of the Nazi Party a seat, Hindenburg curtly asked him to speak. Hitler, ignoring the insult, launched out into a oration. For a while the President listened until, abruptly, he said: "Thank you very much for coming here." The interview was at an end, a complete failure.

In Stockholm at this hour Karin Goering lapsed into a coma. At 4 A.M. on October 17, 1931, she died. Goering could not face the trip back to Sweden alone. His eldest brother, Major Karl Goering, and Pilli Koerner accompanied him.

There are people who bury their sorrow deep in their own hearts. Goering found relief from his oppressing thoughts only by giving vent to his feelings. Among his personal friends he would talk about Karin incessantly, about her life and her death. He knew that she had given her life to him and to the Nazi movement. Without her he could not have survived his trials in Austria, Italy, and Sweden. Without her he would not have found strength to take up the struggle again. That she had died while he was pursuing his politics, that, in her last hour, he had chosen to be with Hitler rather than with her, remained forever on his conscience. That eventual success, his own rise to power, would not now be mirrored in her soul seemed to make the endeavor almost worthless.

6

INTO POWER

HERMANN GOERING never again set foot in the flat in the Badenschestrasse. For a few weeks after Karin's death he lived at the Kaiserhof Hotel which had become Hitler's Berlin headquarters. Returning from conferences, Hitler gathered his entourage around him in the big lounge where the élite of the Nazi movement was always on show. Berliners made a point of dropping in at the Kaiserhof at teatime to see the Fuehrer and the big men of his party; even tourists rarely missed the opportunity of watching the spectacle. Goering had changed. His voice was louder now as if to drown his own thoughts, his manners rougher and his movements jerkier. When I discussed him with the men who were closest to him, they admitted that there was a possibility — yes, thinking back it was likely — perhaps it was true that he had taken refuge again in the syringe . . .

Whether or not he was taking morphia again, his energy was not flagging. He delved into the political game like an experienced gambler, very sure of himself and confident that he could match the highest stakes. The economic crisis which started with the collapse of the Credit-Anstalt, Austria's biggest bank, and had swept across Europe, had gravely affected Germany. Six million people were unemployed, and in the tense atmosphere orderly government was threatening to break down. The German people were constantly called to the polls. Since Goering had been unable to obtain the support of Hindenburg, Hitler listened to other counsels, and when the President's term of office came to an end in March, 1932, he decided to stand as a candidate for the Presidency in opposition to the Field Marshal. Though Hindenburg was re-elected with nineteen million votes, over thirteen million Germans voted for Hitler.

It was not a move to endear him to Goering's industrial friends, who still regarded Hindenburg as a safe rock in a stormy sea. But the money they had invested in Nazi propaganda had paid dividends for the movement and bought the masses. Goering moved into a bachelor flat in the Kaiserdamm, taking Cilli with him, his last personal link with Karin. Goebbels had, in the meantime, married the former wife of a rich businessman, Frau Magda Quandt, and their house became the meeting place of the "very important people" who had previously been entertained at the Badenschestrasse. Magda also replaced Karin in Hitler's affections. Goering's evenings were spent in the company of friends — Pilli Koerner, Erhard Milch, Bruno Loerzer, and Ernst Udet, with whom he tried to recapture the happy days of his youth, to fight over again the glorious air battles of France. Major Karl Bodenschatz came up from Nuremberg for an occasional visit. It was as if the old Richthofen Squadron had come to life again. Talk turned to the not-so-distant future when the Treaty of Versailles would be torn up and Germany would have an air force again. They founded an "Air-Sports Association" which later revealed itself as a "National Socialist Flying Corps," encouraged the Hitler Youth, the junior S.A., to play with toy aeroplanes and to take up gliding. In their minds the new air force was already taking shape.

Goebbels organised a succession of political meetings and, accompanied by Pilli Koerner, Goering travelled around the country to speak, seeking distraction from his work by occasional visits to the theatre which he loved. In the hustle and bustle of his widespread activities, he felt again lonely. After a Saturday rally in Weimar, he decided to see a play at the local theatre, *Minna von Barnhelm*, by G. E. Lessing, which revolves around a beautiful, typical German lady of high station. It is a play which every schoolboy reads in his teens, and Goering knew it almost by heart. Lounging in his box, he enjoyed the language, hardly looking at the stage, reciting long passages to himself in silent chorus with the actors.

When he looked up, Minna von Barnhelm held the centre of the stage: "A very attractive woman," he whispered to Koerner. "I'd love to meet her!" Koerner took Goering's every wish as a command; quietly he slipped away to backstage. Would the leading lady allow him to introduce Captain Goering, the Reichstag Member? The leading lady was Emmy Sonnemann, a tall, stately blonde, a dignified woman who had made a name for herself in the provinces as an actress in straight plays. Emmy Sonnemann resisted the approach on that occasion, but Hermann Goering was introduced to his future wife soon afterward at a party in Bad Kochberg: "It is very funny," Emmy Sonnemann said when she told me how she met Goering, "but at that moment I just did not realise about whom Pilli Koerner was talking. I knew about the Nazis, of course, but when I eventually met him, I was not sure whether his name was Goebbels or Goering."

With the longing of a lonely heart, Goering attached himself to Frau Emmy. He still mourned Karin deeply, but for many months before her death she had been more of a friend than a wife to him. However much he had loved her, the weak, sylphlike figure, too tender to touch, he had, perhaps without knowing it himself, longed for a woman whose body could offer him as much as her soul. Subconsciously, he had felt this desire a long time before. Among the paintings which he had bought here and there to decorate the flat were his two show pieces, canvases by Lukas Cranach, depicting just the kind of woman who was in Goering's mind. From now on Weimar saw a lot of Hermann Goering.

Emmy was different from Karin not only in appearance. The theatre was her life, politics a strange, remote world. She had been married before, but her marriage had failed. Men were playing as small a part in her life as politics. When Hermann arrived with tales of world-shaking negotiations from which he might easily emerge as a Cabinet Minister, if he talked about the Fuehrer and the complexities of the political situation, Emmy listened good-humouredly and politely, but without great interest. She was more concerned with the plans for a forthcoming performance of Goethe's *Faust* at the Weimar State Theatre. For her to get the coveted part of Gretchen seemed infinitely more important than that Hitler should become Chancellor. Goering soon gave up talking politics to her. To his own surprise, these evenings with Emmy and his escape from the crazy world of Nazism and Communism, of Parliament and Reichswehr, became a necessity for him.

Refreshed and rested, he returned to Berlin time after time to throw himself into the parliamentary struggle. To the Reichstag he brought some of the strong expressions which came so easily to his tongue. Excitable, impatient, he crossed swords with Communists, Socialists, loving every minute of these verbal duels. To him the Reichstag was a "talking shop," never mind what the people thought about these cheap quarrels. If they held the Reichstag in contempt, so much the better for the Nazi Party. Ruthlessly he fought the Government. He was even prepared to join the Communists in their attacks if he felt it would help to bring the Government down. In July, 1932, the Government resigned.

Again Goering and the National Socialist Party were involved in an election campaign. Goebbels spent millions to cover the country with posters. Hitler's face was on every hoarding. Conditions in Germany had further deteriorated and the masses wanted a change; matters could only change for the better. The Nazi newspapers, including Goebbels' own *Angriff*, battered the German people with a constant barrage of propaganda, aimed to hit them at the core and to set off a political explosion. Almost dazed and overwhelmed, they went to the polls again on July 31, 1932. From this election the Nazis emerged as the strongest party in the Reich. They almost doubled their strength, secured 230 seats, leaving the Socialists, with 133 and the Communists with 89, far behind. "We are in the saddle now!" Goering exclaimed in undisguised triumph.

He had not counted with the old gentleman of Neudeck. The Nazis the strongest party? That would mean Herr Hitler as Chancellor! "No, no!" said the President. Goering rushed to Neudeck. Hindenburg told him coldly: "Let the Nazis join a coalition. Hitler can be Vice-Chancellor under von Papen!" "The Fuehrer a Vice . . . Never!" Goering replied. His disappointment turned to rage when Gregor Strasser, in a conference of the Party leaders, suggested that a share of the Government was better than to remain in opposition. "The Fuehrer a Vice — " Goering thundered again. "Never!"

But he did not fall a victim to the political frustration which gripped Hitler and his friends. As parliamentary leader of the strongest party in the Reichstag, a new honour and a position of great influence had fallen to him. On August 30 Hermann Goering was elected President (Speaker) of the Reichstag. A proud and happy man, he was led into his new office by the permanent officials. He did not speak, but I know what he thought. He walked to his new desk. The stationery for the exclusive use of the Reichstag President was neatly stacked on one side. Goering picked up one of the cards and a red pencil. Quickly he wrote a few words, put the card into an envelope, and beckoned an attendant to deliver the note to Frau Emmy Sonnemann in Weimar at once. I talked about his message with Emmy Sonnemann-Goering when I spent a few days with her at Sylt in North Germany in the summer of 1950. She fumbled in her bag and from a bundle of old papers she brought out the card and gave it to me. On it was written in Goering's strong, characteristic hand: "Ich liebe Dich. H."

Then he went to work. His official duties obliged the Reichstag President to negotiate with members of all parties. He met Torgler, the Communist leader, and talked to him in a civilised manner even if, on the same day, he hurled insults at him on the floor of Parliament. He invited the Social Democrats to discussions in his office while his Party carried on a vicious campaign against them. But most of all, he tried to win over extreme right-wing groups to support his machinations against his chief enemy, Franz von Papen, the Chancellor, who held the Government fort against all Nazi assaults. But it was of no avail. Hindenburg's rebuff had clearly damaged the Party's prestige. Goering felt Hitler's eyes often resting on him, questioning, accusing. His much-vaunted friendship with the eighty-five-year-old President had not helped the Party.

Goering could not bear to lose Hitler's confidence. If Hindenburg would not have his Fuehrer, the battle would be fought in the streets where the S.A. could make its weight felt. Goering had so far been a restraining influence, but now, when it was a matter of life and death, he would not interfere with either Goebbels or Roehm. When, in the amazing contortions of the political underworld, the Nazi found themselves fighting the Government hand in hand with their deadliest enemies, the Communists, Goering still did not interfere. The Government resisted the assault of this strange, united front, but worried lest either the Communists or the Nazis were planning a bloody revolution and convinced that many a plot was hatched under the cover of the parliamentary immunity, von Papen ordered the Prussian police to search the offices of the Communist Party in the Reichstag.

Rudolf Diels, a young official of the Prussian Ministry of the

Interior, was sent to obtain permission from the President of the Reichstag to conduct the search. He was an expert on Communist affairs and Goering received him with open arms. He could learn much from Diels. Diels, in turn, was flattered by this friendly reception. It was useful to be on good terms with Goering; one day, Diels thought, who knows? Goering may be a minister. But Goering would not sanction the search. Once he opened the doors of the Reichstag to the police, they might not stop at the offices of the Communists!

There was murder in the streets and distress in the Nazi hierarchy. Hitler was in Berlin to take a hand in the negotiations, to help Goering extract more money from Thyssen, Kirdorf, and their friends. But the shrewd businessmen were hesitant. Already nearly a hundred million marks had been spent on the Nazi Party — for what? The public was losing interest, the Nazis making common cause with the Communists. It was wiser to wait and see. When yet another election came, Hitler, Goering, and Goebbels were already scraping the bottom of the barrel. For the first time since 1926 they lost votes. But even with only 196 seats in the new Reichstag, they were still the strongest party. Goering was re-elected President of the Reichstag.

Von Papen had been brought down, but Hitler waited in vain for Hindenburg's call. The Field Marshal, supported by his son, Colonel Oscar von Hindenburg, and his military clique, was still determined to keep Hitler from the Wilhelmstrasse Chancellery. Only a soldier could handle the situation. The President called on the Reichswehr General Kurt von Schleicher to form a government. For some time Schleicher had nursed a plan to break up the Nazi Party. To this end he invited Gregor Strasser to become Vice-Chancellor in his Government. Strasser was willing, but Goering got to know about this scheme. Together with Hitler he squashed Schleicher's ingenious plan. From that day, Strasser was a marked man.

Baulked on the threshold of success, torn by internal conflicts, the Nazi Party's fortunes began to decline. "If the Party breaks up," Hitler said, "I shall kill myself!" Alone, he walked through the streets of Berlin where Emmy Sonnemann met him. She would never forget the meeting, she told me. She was on one of her rare visits to Berlin and for the first time noticed the hundreds of unemployed young men idling in the parks. It was a depressing sight. "Good morning, Frau Sonnemann," Hitler greeted her. Emmy thought he looked miserable. "I told him," she recalled, "that I felt terribly about all these strong, healthy people out of work." Hitler flared up: "Leave it to me, Frau Sonnemann! Leave it to me! Once I have assumed power not one healthy man will be unemployed in Germany!"

Right then he seemed farther away from that day than ever. But nothing was impossible in the Germany of 1932 and 1933. In Nuremberg in his defense speech, Hermann Goering gave a seemingly reasoned account of the events which preceded Hitler's appointment as Chancellor. It was an account of Goering, undismayed, skilful, optimistic, carrying on his negotiations, taking every opportunity of visiting Neudeck in the hope of bringing Hindenburg and Hitler together after all. But it was not Hermann Goering who paved Hitler's way to the Wilhelmstrasse. The Fuehrer had made contact with von Papen, whom Goering still regarded as an enemy. He was delighted to learn that Papen had "declared war" on Schleicher who had ousted him. So they both hated Schleicher; it was a good basis for co-operation. But a Papen-Hitler alliance would still not have changed the mind of Hindenburg. Neither Hitler's dynamic personality nor Goering's skill as a negotiator performed this miracle. It was an extraordinary palace intrigue which put the Nazis in control of Germany just when their star had begun to wane.

On Sunday, January 22, 1933, Goering, according to his own account, was in Dresden when he received an urgent summons from Hitler. In Berlin the Fuehrer told him that a great new opportunity had presented itself. Colonel Oscar von Hindenburg wanted to see Goering. Hitler was elated and distressed in one breath. It was the first time that the initiative for conversations had come from the Field Marshal's circle. But his pride was hurt because Colonel von Hindenburg wanted to see Goering instead of him, the Fuehrer. The meeting took place on the same evening in the flat of an intermediary, Herr Joachim von Ribbentrop, the son-in-law of a rich champagne merchant. Papen was present and Otto Meissner, a high official of the President's Bureau. Colonel von Hindenburg was the spokesman for the group.

They were very frank with Goering. General von Schleicher,

Oscar von Hindenburg said, had betrayed his friends and his class. It appeared that a scandal had been brewing in connection with State funds for "needy" East Prussian landowners, the Junkers, who were Hindenburg's closest friends. Accusations had been made that most of the money had gone to the richest among them, who had bought new estates, expensive motor cars, and spent the rest on excursions to the Riviera and other luxuries. The Socialists had demanded a probe and Chancellor Schleicher — incredible! — had granted their request. Such a probe might even involve the family of the Field Marshal. Schleicher must be removed from office before this can happen. If the Nazis were prepared to enter the Government, Colonel von Hindenburg would persuade his father to appoint Adolf Hitler as Chancellor of Germany.

It is doubtful whether the doting President knew the details of the game which was played in his name. There is no evidence that at this stage even Hitler was aware of what had happened. Goering only told him that he had, at long last, succeeded in his endeavours to change old Hindenburg's mind. There would be conditions, of course, but before the week was over Hitler would be master in the land. The conditions turned out to be severe. Hindenburg, or rather his advisers, worked them out in great detail. Hitler would be Chancellor, but Franz von Papen would be Vice-Chancellor to keep an eye on him. Goering would be a Minister without Portfolio, but Foreign Affairs would be conducted by a gentleman of Hindenburg's own class, Baron Constantine von Neurath. Papen, since the Laender (provinces) had their own governments, would also hold the key-post of a Prussian Prime Minister; Goering would have to be content with the Prussian Ministry of the Interior as his second job. A National Socialist, Wilhelm Frick, as Reichs Minister of the Interior — all right! But the Reichswehr was to remain under the control of a general — Werner von Blomberg. Goebbels would be put in charge of propaganda, but the rest of the Cabinet would be made up of Conservative Nationalists like Count Schwerin von Krosigk, Baron von Eltz, and the Stahlhelm leader, Franz Seldte. It was to be just another Party Cabinet in which Hitler and Goering would be virtual prisoners of the "more reliable elements." Hindenburg had a two hours' conversation with Hitler. For the first time Field Marshal and corporal shook hands. At 10.15 A.M. on January 30, 1933, the appointment of Hitler's Government was announced.

At 2.30 P.M. I was among a group of journalists who filed into the reception room of the small Palace of the Reichstag President, Hermann Goering's official residence. Goering spoke a few words. It was a humble, sweetly reasonable Goering, obviously overwhelmed by the stroke of luck to which he owed his success. In this mood Goering was charming, captivating, far removed from the turmoil of the streets which were already filled with Nazi supporters. Berlin reverberated with their droning voices in which I could detect a hidden menace as they burst out singing: "Deutschland, Deutschland ueber Alles! Ueber Alles in der Welt!" The "Horst Wessel" song soon became part of the noisy symphony.

As dusk fell, the S.A. were out parading through the Wilhelmstrasse with flaming torches. On the balcony was Hitler greeting them with his outstretched hand. Inside, Goering, in the uniform of an S.A. leader, hugged a microphone. The whole of Germany heard his voice which trembled with emotion: "My German comrades! As I stand here at the microphone, hundreds of thousands are crowding outside the Reich Chancellery. They are in a mood which can be compared only with the enthusiasm of August, 1914, when the nation stood up to defend Fatherland, Honour, and Freedom. January 30, 1933, will enter Germany's history as the day on which the nation, after fourteen years of torture, need, defamation, and shame, has found its way back to itself . . . gratefully, we look up to the leader of our great movement . . . we also thank the aged General Field Marshal von Hindenburg, who has united himself today with the young generation. By the side of the venerable Field Marshal . . . now stands Adolf Hitler, the young leader of Germany . . . now all hands will be busy, confidence will return . . . and the future will bring everything for which the Fuehrer and his movement . . . have fought tirelessly and hopefully in spite of all reverses and disappointments: Bread and Work for the German people, Freedom and Honour for the nation."

Hitler's enemies were undismayed. It would not be long before this reckless orator, who had lured the masses with his promises, would be exposed as a charlatan.

7

"... AND HERE WE STAY!"

NOT very long ago I walked along Berlin's Wilhelmstrasse, past the ruins which are all that remains of rows of impressive buildings. An old "rubble-woman," one of the miserable creatures whom the Russians have put to work clearing away the remnants of the bomb-shattered blocks, had made her home in the cellar of No. 63, which used to be the proud Prussian Ministry of the Interior. It was still an imposing structure when, from his first, short press conference as a Cabinet Minister, Hermann Goering, accompanied by Pilli Koerner, drove to his new Ministry.

For years the fight against the Nazi and Communist enemies of the Republic had been directed from these offices. To Goering the Ministry was the fortress of the enemy. Now he was able to take it over as the undisputed master. Quickly and without a word he passed the ranks of the officials who had assembled to greet their Minister. There was only one man in his house with whom Goering would have any dealings, a man on whom he could rely to join him in the final battle against the Communists. "Call Diels," he told Koerner. The meeting was short but of tremendous consequence for Goering. I have already said that Goering, in the course of his life, appeared in many guises. In the first few months after he assumed office, he appeared in the guise of Rudolf Diels. It was an ugly mask.

Through the Prussian Ministry of the Interior Goering obtained control of the police, the weapon with which to defeat the Communists. Diels was the expert on Communist affairs and Goering chose him over the heads of a hundred deserving officials for the most important position in the organisation—as Chief of the Political Police. Just the man to escape intact from the holocaust of Nazi politics and the war, Diels has written a book[1] about his activities as Chief of the Gestapo — a book which I should normally have shunned as much as the Gestapo itself. But rather than talk to him, I have read his book. From its pages emerges a Goering so cunning, so versatile, so evil, as to beat Lucifer at his own game. From its pages also emerges a Rudolf Diels, so pure, so good, so helpful to Nazis and Communists (yes, Communists), to Jews and pacifists as to put Archangel Gabriel in the shade. With an artistry which must be the envy of all writers, he describes his part in the tragic events of those days. He was always there, always involved in the most gruesome affairs — but always, of course, on the side of the angels. There were horrible beatings — Diels saved the victims. The long murderous arms of the Nazis reached out for their enemies — Diels helped them to escape. Everybody was thirsting for blood — Diels pulled the cup from the lips of the vampires.

In Nuremberg in 1946 I heard Hans Gisevius, another Prussian civil servant, saying from the witness stand: "The political police was under one Rudolf Diels. . . . He was a professional civil servant and one might have expected him still to retain the ideas of law and decency. But in a brutal and cynical way he set his mind on making the new rulers forget his political past as a democrat. . . . It was Diels who created the Gestapo office; he suggested to Goering the issue of the first decree for making that office independent. It was Diels who let the S.A. and the S.S. enter that office; he legalised the actions of these civil Kommandos."

That evening I re-read what the daughter of William E. Dodd, the American Ambassador in Berlin, had to say about Rudolf Diels:[2] "He belonged to the S.A., but claimed that they hated him and that he received his real support from the S.S. men. . . . He liked and trusted no one (though he gave, seemingly, his loyalty to Goering), and no one liked or trusted him. No matter how fine and innocent a character might originally be — and Diels' certainly was not ever — a job of the nature of his would invariably and inevitably corrode the character. Towards the end of his career in this post he became more neurotic than anyone I knew in Germany — even those whom he persecuted. . . . I am sure Goering himself was dis-

[1] *Lucifer ante Portas.*
[2] Martha Dodd, *Through Embassy Eyes.*

trustful, but I felt, either from watching the two together or hearing Diels talk, that Goering was afraid of him. I was intrigued and fascinated by this human monster of sensitive face and cruel, broken beauty. . . ."

Now Goering looked into this unusual face. "You are going to take over!" he said to Diels. Elated but embarrassed, the young official had to tell his leading colleagues that the Chief refused to meet them. He himself had already passed the greatest test, had been able to answer Goering's first question: "Yes, the dossier of the Communist Party is quite up to date . . ." and had added off his own bat: " . . . and the same applies to the Social Democrats, of course!" During the previous week Goering had spent a sleepless night trying to formulate vague plans for the "elimination of the opposition" which had always been at the back of his mind. He would give Diels his instructions within a few hours, he said.

At the first Cabinet meeting that afternoon, the battle against the "internal enemy" was the only item on the agenda. Goering expounded his ideas: "First we must make a clean sweep of the old heads of police departments!" Hitler nodded assent. Next morning twenty-two of the thirty-two police chiefs in the country found themselves without jobs: "Secondly, the S.A. is to become an auxiliary police force!" Agreed. This measure took to the Ministry of the Interior and to Police Headquarters the leaders of the Storm Troopers who for years had trained their guns on every policeman in their way. Hitler was not in the mood to listen to any of the non-Nazi ministers, some of whom, including General von Blomberg, he now met for the first time. He gave Goering "full powers" — nobody dissented. Then he sent a request to Hindenburg — would the President approve the Swastika banner as Germany's official flag? Cabinet meeting concluded.

Next morning Goering reappeared at the Ministry. He had asked Diels to call a meeting of all officials concerned with the police: "Just tell them that I do not expect any advice or suggestions," he said: "I shall be telling them . . . !" For a man who approached such problems in a soldierly manner, primitive things took precedence over complicated principles. Goering's directions were to the point: "I do not like the idea of the police running around with batons to beat up the population. Away with the batons!" he insisted. If the police felt threatened, they should shoot! The old officials shook their heads as he said: "*I* shall be responsible for what the police do. Every bullet fired from the barrel of a police pistol — is *my* bullet! And I shall say so in public!" He did say it in a speech in Dortmund a few days later, and added: "If you call that murder — *I* am the murderer." The rank and file of the police liked that. For years they had been the targets of Nazi and Communist shootings. Now was the time to hit back!

Out of curiosity rather than for a political purpose, Goering asked for some of the "top secret" files. On his desk Diel piled up a mountain of documents which made the new Minister forget the duties of State which had so suddenly fallen on his shoulders. There was a bundle of love letters which his friend Alfred Rosenberg, the apostle of the pure Aryan race, had written to a Jewish girl. She had tried to blackmail her lover and had been arrested by the police, who had kept the letters. There were documents dealing with a case against Adolf Hitler who had been suspected of perjury when he applied for German citizenship. Gottfried Feder, Hitler's friend and expert on economic affairs, it appeared, had been involved in an embarrassing correspondence with Jewish moneylenders whom he had threatened with violence. It was all there in black and white. The details of a law suit against Joachim von Ribbentrop made fascinating reading. He had refused to pay the aristocratic lady who had adopted him, enabling him to add the "von," the symbol of a German knighthood, to his name. Instead of reading the dossier of the Communist criminals, Hermann Goering, slapping his thighs with laughter, immersed himself in the study of these entertaining revelations.

Back home at the Kaiserdamm there were personal matters awaiting attention. Goering had decided to move to the Palace of the Reichstag President at once. Cilli would go with him, but in his new position he would need a valet. At his request a friend, Baroness Holdorf, had inserted an advertisement in the *Kreuz-Zeitung*, a small paper favoured by ex-soldiers. From the candidates who had applied for the job of "first-class valet for gentleman in good position," she had chosen an ex-naval N.C.O. with a good "national record," Robert Kropp. Kropp had taken part in one of the postwar putsches against the Republic. He had since been employed by several wealthy businessmen. Baroness Holdorf instructed him to report at Flat 5, Kaiserdamm. Having waited from 10 A.M. until 3 P.M., Robert Kropp, to his surprise, was taken into Goering's presence. "I have read your testimonials and your record," Goering told him. "You will do. What wages do you expect?" "I had a hundred and forty marks in my previous job." "You'll start here with eighty marks. If you are satisfactory, you will get a rise. If not — out you go where the builder has left a hole in the wall!"

I found Robert Kropp fifteen years later as a hall porter in the Berchtesgadener Hof, the smart hotel in Berchtesgaden which the American Army run as a holiday centre for senior officers. His station was the servants' entrance: "Have to do all sorts of jobs here," he said. The staff treated the small, wiry man with respect, and listened attentively to the unending tales of his experiences in Goering's employ. He refuses to talk to strangers, and would not have talked to me had not Frau Emmy Goering introduced me with a personal note. Though few people know his full name, Robert, after 1933, became a much-discussed, mysterious figure whose influence on his chief was said to have grown with the years. No other man has spent as much time in Goering's company as Robert. No man knew more about Goering's private life which had such an important bearing on his public activities. Robert was frank with me, obviously honest, although careful not to cast any reflection on his master's character. As one of the American interrogation officers said to Robert in June, 1945: "There is no point in questioning you chaps. You won't say anything against your chief!" Robert's association with Goering only ended after the Reichsmarschall's capture and detention. Robert accompanied him into captivity.

As Hitler and his advisers sat in daily conference to thrash out details of high policy, Goering concentrated on the Communists. He had no time for Emmy Sonnemann now, and she was not anxious to join the gatherings of politicians and militarists around him, among whom she felt a little lost. He was still the perfect, considerate cavalier, but he had no private life and work was his only love. Later his laziness was a standing joke wherever two Nazi leaders put their heads together. He was not lazy now. His day began at 7 A.M. with a hurried bath and a shave, after which he dabbed his neck and cheeks with powder to dry the skin. It is a habit not infrequent among men of the German upper class, but soon aroused much comment: "Goering powders himself," foreign diplomats whispered; "... and uses rouge!" a rumour added.

He took an even more hurried German breakfast — coffee and rolls — and then studied the newspapers: "Make a note," he would say to his secretary, "that these democratic rags shall be taken off the streets!" He need not have bothered. Goebbels saw to that, although his appointment as Minister of Propaganda was only made official four weeks later. The car was waiting as Goering was helped into one of the heavy, ankle-length overcoats which were specially made for him and which he wore over a stylish S.A. uniform of his own design. And off he went to his office at the Prussian Ministry of the Interior. He chose his personal staff, acting on the advice of Diels. Though none of them were members of the Nazi Party, Diels could vouch for their national, anti-Marxist outlook. A Prussian official, Dr. Erich Gritzbach, was added to his secretariat. Frau von Kornatzki was chosen to deal with his correspondence; an old friend, Martin H. Sommerfeldt, to act as his Press Chief — his first task to rewrite and bring up to date a short Goering biography [3] which he had published a year earlier. As an S.A. functionary, his chauffeur and friend, Paul ("Pilli") Koerner, was qualified to be installed in the Prussian Ministry with the title of Secretary of State.

Hitler had lost little time moving into the Chancellery and the men who had previously gathered around him in the lounge of the Kaiserhof received invitations to "lunch with the Fuehrer" at his office. It was a daily Tafelrunde (friends meeting regularly around a table) — Hermann Goering, Rudolf Hess, Joseph Goebbels, Alfred Rosenberg, Wilhelm Frick, Ernst Hanfstaengl (whom Hitler had called from Munich to establish contact with the foreign press), Wilhelm Brueckner and Julius Schaub, his personal aides. Hardly ever were any of the other Cabinet Ministers admitted to the meetings of this intimate circle where the fate of Germany was under discussion and the real decisions were made.

In the afternoons Goering worked at home. While officials of his Ministry waited, he sat in conference with leaders of the S.A., whom he had often opposed while their activities disturbed his negotiations with the industrialist supporters of the Party. The Com-

[3] Martin H. Sommerfeldt, *Hermann Goering, Ein Lebensbild.*

mander of the Berlin S.A. formations, Obergruppenfuehrer (Upper Group Leader) Count Wolf Helldorf, owner of a small estate but a soldier of fortune by choice, was a daily visitor; so was his friend, the ex-waiter Karl Ernst, another high S.A. leader. They were both "police officers" now, entrusted with the special task of combating the Communist menace.

For the first time in his life Hermann Goering tasted the nectar of personal, of absolute, power. These men listened with reverence to his every word. His astute mind could detect in their suggestions a humble plea that he should turn them into his own orders. Only now did the "Fuehrer" principle of the Nazi Party, the complete authority of each leader over all below his rank, become a delectable reality.

What the Minister said was final — there was no question of contradiction. Often, in the long years while he had waited for this, Goering had wondered what it was really like to govern. The Richthofen Squadron was an experience in leadership; he had run it like a little empire of his own. But there were always superior orders and the force of circumstances was already overpowering when he took over. He had been Commander of the S.A., but it had been a small assignment indeed. Now he was one of the rulers of over sixty million people — under Hitler, to be sure, but with responsibilty for the most important sector of government, as he saw it. There were some compelling and awkward circumstances again, but nothing, nothing would be allowed to stand in his way.

Goering often talked quite frankly about January, 1933, when his life and outlook were changed with one stroke. And laughingly he explained that to him it all came very naturally. At his Ministry Rudolf Diels reported about the purge. Of course, he had got rid of men like Dr. Robert Kempner, the organiser of the police measures against the S.A. and illegal Nazi activities. But it was impossible to throw out every non-Nazi. What, then, was the best way to assure complete Gleichschaltung — a technical electrical term which the Nazis borrowed to describe the elimination of all non-Nazi elements from public, industrial, even family, life. The answer was obviously to remove the nerve centre of the organisation, the Political Police, from the democratically polluted atmosphere of the old force. There would have to be a new secret department.

"Good," said Goering, "we shall have such a department, call it the Geheime Staats-Polizei (Secret State Police) and move it to new offices!" The Gestapo was born. Diels and his friends did the rest.

Experts were at hand to deal with constitutional questions. There was obviously no room for a Prussian Landtag (Diet). Let the constitutional lawyers devise a substitute for this outmoded democratic institution — something like Mussolini's Fasci, a totalitarian organisation in which authority would rest with the élite, not with the majority. Prussia, the biggest province, would set an example to the other Laender. Goering had only to issue the instruction — Ministerial Councillor Kramsch and his officials would have to rack their brains about the details. How easy it was to govern! He made his decisions, mentioned them casually to the Fuehrer at lunch; Hitler, to whom a hundred similar measures were submitted every day, gave his lieutenants a free hand. He approved their measures without giving them much thought. Goering beamed with satisfaction and his officials did the work. He had to read documents, listen to reports, deal with hundreds of requests which poured into his office from old fighters and new supporters. His days were full, but only the question of the elimination of the Communists held his interest. Sooner or later they would have to be put behind bars! Diels had worked out a scheme for "instantaneous action." At a given sign it would be possible for every Communist leader in every part of the country to be arrested in one big sweep. That was the kind of staff work which Goering appreciated: total action. Proudly he showed the plans to his friends Helldorf, Ernst, Prince August Wilhelm. All S.A. leaders would have to assist in a police task of such magnitude. The whole S. A. would be mobilised — not a single Communist functionary or member of the Reichstag would be allowed to escape; not one of their Party haunts should be spared. They were to be kept under constant surveillance. First they would be put behind lock and key; decisions about their fate could be made later: "Perhaps," Goering suggested, "we might reform a few of them . . . !" "Erschiessen!" (To shoot them!) was Karl Ernst's suggestion.

A home for the Geheime Staats-Polizei — Gestapo for short — was found in the Prinz Albrechtstrasse, and Rudolf Diels lorded it over a carefully selected staff of cold disciplinarians and radical

Nazis drawn from the S.A. In the provinces S.A. leaders were appointed as police chiefs. A few new officials came in from the ranks of the S.S., Hitler's Schutz Staffel, but neither Goering nor the S.A. leaders cherished collaboration with the privileged supermen under Heinrich Himmler's command, who quickly began to form a state within the State. These men were liable to take matters into their own hands and to disregard even Hermann Goering's orders.

Hindenburg had made it a condition of Hitler's appointment that his Government should seek the country's approval at once. The Reichstag had been dissolved and elections were scheduled to take place on Sunday, March 5, 1933. To Goering this seemed a tedious, unnecessary procedure. Hitler had agreed with him a long time ago that there would be no Reichstag, no Parliament; that the State would have a completely new structure. The Communist Party would be banned; it was inconceivable that Social Democrats should be allowed to voice their pacifist views. There was certainly no need for other national parties in a country under the control of National Socialists: "The Reichstag is a nuisance!" Goering said. "Away with it!"

A hundred different versions about the Reichstag fire have been published. Documents have been produced to give minute details about every phase of the portentous incident. Whole books have been devoted to the subject, and an independent trial, conducted by reputable international lawyers, took place in London long after the Nazi Government had closed their own files. My own research on the spot started on the day after the fire, but I can add little to the mass of often conflicting evidence. Rudolf Diels took over the investigation — he is, incidentally, the only person connected with the events who insists that the Nazis had nothing to do with the fire. According to him the young Dutch Communist, Marinus van der Lubbe, started it single-handed. Marinus van der Lubbe certainly did set fire to the Reichstag.

Robert Kropp told me that Helldorf and Ernst, the two S.A. leaders, were regular visitors at Goering's palace during the weeks preceding the fire. My informants at the time, notorious and predatory members of the Nazi underworld, said that the S.A. leadership had received information towards the end of February that a young Dutchman, aged about twenty-four, had been heard muttering in a

Wirtshaus (public house) in Hennigsdorf, near Berlin, that "the Nazis will never let the Communists take their seats in the Reichstag. What's the use of a Reichstag without Communists?" In his slow, drawling voice he mumbled something about "burning the Reichstag down" when one of the bystanders revealed himself as a member of Storm 17 of the S.A., beckoned him to come along to his barracks: "Says he is going to put fire to the Reichstag!" the storm trooper reported. The Reichstag had never been held in great esteem by these men, but the arrest of this little foreign agitator had to be reported to higher authority.

The news reached Karl Ernst, Ernst told Helldorf, and both mentioned it at Goering's dinner table: "Let him burn the Reichstag if he wants to!" Goering said, turning to other, more important topics. He had given Ernst an idea. For a day, while he asked Storm 17 to release van der Lubbe but to keep an eye on him, Ernst toyed with this idea. He mentioned it to Goebbels, who thought it was not bad at all. If Goering says, "Let him burn the Reichstag!" — if Goebbels thinks it is not a bad idea — of course, let van der Lubbe burn the old Communist stronghold! Let us help him to do it! Ernst's men were apprised of the plan of their commander. They were to make friends with van der Lubbe, encourage him to go ahead with his plan, help him in every way.

Ernst was responsible for the S.A. Guard of Honour at the Palace of the Reichstag President; he knew that an underground passage, part of the heating system, connected it with the Reichstag. If van der Lubbe and a few S.A. men were to set the Reichstag on fire, they could easily make their getaway through this passage to Goering's palace and slip out by the back door, leaving Lubbe to be caught as the Communist who had burned down the Parliament building of Germany. And that would be the end of Parliament.

This is how the plan originated, how it developed, and how it was carried out on the evening of February 27, 1933. Goering was quick to grasp the possibilities arising out of the fire. As he was dashing to the burning building, he made up his mind. Meeting Hitler on the scene of the fire, he realised that the Fuehrer had come to the same conclusion. "A sign from Heaven!" the Fuehrer said. To Diels, who had arrived a few minutes earlier, Goering issued his order: "Arrest all Communists!" The plans were ready, the police and S. A. Kommandos went into action. When Goering, later, heard that the world regarded him as the real instigator of the fire, he said: "I knew people would probably say that, dressed in a red toga and holding a lyre in my hand, I looked on at the fire and played while the Reichstag was burning. . . ."

He was no Nero, but he certainly did not play either. During the night and on the following days over four thousand Communist functionaries and members of the Reichstag were arrested. Many Socialist leaders, hundreds of harmless people who had incurred the wrath of the S.A., were abducted and disappeared in police stations, state prisons, or in the barracks of the S.A. Social Democrats, pacifists, even Right-Wing Nationalists out of step with the Nazis, fell victims to this wave of indiscriminate arrests. They spread all over the country. S.A. leaders like Heines, when prisons were too crowded to accommodate their victims, herded them together in improvised barbed-wire enclosures. They called them concentration camps. The S.A. and police used their pistols freely. Over five hundred anti-Nazis were shot in the following months.

For days after the fire armed S.A. bands, authorised as "auxiliary police," roamed the streets. I was lucky to be out when one such group came to arrest me at the Hessler Hotel in Berlin where I was staying. Leaving my luggage behind, I made for the station and took the next train to Vienna. Six weeks later Paul Markus, "Pem," the well-known German journalist, now a British subject, introduced me to an unfortunate namesake of mine whom I had never met before. The S.A. had arrested him instead of me, taken him to Licherfelde Barracks and tortured him for three days until they realised their mistake. My "crime," it appeared, had been to connect Eric Jan Hanussen (real name Steinschneider), a professional telepathist, with Helldorf, Ernst, and the Reichstag fire. Helldorf, Ernst, and their storm troopers were regular guests at Hanussen's lavish private parties. He knew about their project, and predicted "full success" for their future. Two months later he was found murdered. It was not safe to know too much about the fire. A second victim of the ruthless elimination of those "in the know" was Dr. Bell, a former friend of Roehm, who was kidnapped in Kufstein by the Munich S.A. and killed. The third was Dr. Oberfohren, leader of the German Nationals, a staunch anti-Communist, yet not a man to approve of incendiarism. In a long memorandum he had put down what he knew about the fire. Not much later he was found dead — "suicide," said the official announcement.

But the murders, the arrests, the concentration camps, even the ban on the Communist Party, were only accompaniments to the real result of the Reichstag fire. The fire was still smouldering when Hermann Goering, as President of the Reichstag, signed and published an "Emergency Decree for the Protection of the Nation and the State." His officials had not been idle. The decree was the perfect pattern of a dictatorship such as the modern world had not known before. All articles of the German Constitution guaranteeing civil liberties were suspended. "Consequently," Paragraph 1 of the Emergency Decree stated, "restrictions on personal freedom and on the right of free expression of opinion, including the freedom of the press, and of the right of association and assembly, are permissible. . . . In addition the privacy of correspondence, of the post, telegraph, and telephone, is suspended and house-searchings and the confiscation or restriction on the rights of property are permissible. . . ." The death penalty was introduced for many minor offences.

German democracy had come to an end. The elections took place as scheduled, but with the elimination of the Communists and with many Socialist leaders in flight or in hiding, the Nazi Party easily carried the day. The "emergency" remained in force as long as the Nazi Government lasted. The provisions of the ominous first paragraph of the decree were employed against people of every political shade. Non-Nazis lived in constant fear of the "knock at the door" which might spell arrest. It began with Communists, Socialists, pacifists, intellectuals, Jews, but such measures never remain restricted to those against whom they are devised. I was amused to hear fifteen years later how a member of Goering's own staff had complained that "he never knew when the S.S. might come to take him away."

On September 15, 1933, the new Prussian Constitution was ready and Goering launched his venture with an elaborate public ceremony and a great speech. His constitutional advisers had created a State Council to supplant the Prussian Diet. The Prime Minister of Prussia (an office which Goering had assumed in the meantime) was responsible for the appointment of the State Councillors. According to the new law, he chose most of them from among the S.A. and S.S. leaders. His friends, Koerner and Ernst, were obvious choices, so was August Wilhelm, Prince of Prussia. Roehm and his protégé, Edmund Heines the terrorist, staked their claim for seats on the Council and were duly appointed. The S.S. delegated Heinrich Himmler and Brigade Leader Daluege, the Nazi Party among others Dr. Robert Ley. The famous conductor, Wilhelm Furtwaengler, consented to represent the arts, Field Marshal von Mackensen the Army. Prince Philip von Hessen was one of the aristocrats who graced the new assembly and Industry sent the banker, E. G. von Stauss, and Fritz Thyssen into the Council.

Drums were beating and flags flying when the State Council was ceremoniously inaugurated in the great hall of Berlin University on September 15, 1933. "We have reached a turning point in the life of the State," Goering orated. "With the Prussian State Council we have laid the foundation of a truly National Socialist Constitution . . . which will spread beyond Prussia. Only the Fuehrer principle can save the people!" With hands outstretched in the Nazi salute the assembly greeted Goering, who ended his speech: "The Prussian State Council is opened with the call: A 'Sieg-Heil' [victory hail] to the Reichs Chancellor, the Fuehrer of our people!"

Goering's eyes gleamed for an instant. There was nothing in his demeanour to betray the grave doubts about the wisdom of his State act which had risen in him. The Fuehrer, to whom he had paid homage, was not present at the ceremony. Goering knew that, while he had worked on the Prussian Constitution, Hitler had come to the conclusion that there would be no separate provinces and no Prussian State in his Third Reich. As Goering spoke, Hitler's own constitutional advisers were already putting the finishing touches on a plan for complete centralisation and unification of Germany. Never was a still-birth more elaborately celebrated. In his hour of triumph, Goering already felt his Prussian pedestal shaking under him.

A week later he was the central figure in another sensational act. The Reichstag fire trial started before Senate IV of the Reich Court in Leipzig. It lasted fifty-four days. Diels and his Gestapo had prepared the indictment of Marinus van der Lubbe. No effort had, of course, been made to trace his accomplices, even though it was clear that more than one man was responsible for the fire which had started simultaneously in a dozen, widely separated places of the big assembly hall. To demonstrate that the Nazi Government had faced an international Communist conspiracy, four men, alleged to have been associated with van der Lubbe during the days before the fire, had been arrested and indicted together with the Dutch boy — Ernst Torgler, Chairman of the Communist Parliamentary Party; the Bulgarian Communist, Giorgi Dimitrov, and his two compatriots, Tanev and Popov. On Diels' instigation, Prime Minister Goering consented to appear as a witness to add strength to a shaky indictment. For hours Diels briefed his chief about the questions likely to be raised. Goering felt uneasy. The memory of the Hitler trial of 1924 oppressed him — Goering did not like trials.

Eighty foreign journalists crowded into the gallery. The German press was restricted to twelve reliable Nazi representatives. The whole world was waiting to hear Goering whom it regarded as the real culprit. In S.A. uniform, breeches and shining boots, Goering stepped forward to give his testimony. Rudolf Diels, in the well of the Court, could not keep his eyes off him. Outwardly calm and very sure of his subject, Goering explained that he had only been waiting for the signal which, he knew, would herald the Communist coup to take over the State. His immediate reaction, he said, was to hang van der Lubbe on the spot. But he had waited until his police had been able to uncover the ramifications of the vast Communist conspiracy.

All went well with Goering's testimony until Dimitrov requested permission to question the principal witness. I hate to strip this historical event of some of its glamour. Few people, as they watched and listened, realised the background of the drama which developed. Goering was deeply hurt about the world-wide accusations which had been hurled at him. Of the crime of incendiarism he felt genuinely innocent. But he also knew that Dimitrov was innocent. The man who faced him across the floor of the courtroom was not an ordinary foreign Communist, but one of the leading agents of the Comintern, the Kremlin's international underground organisation. Though Hitler had not told him, he guessed that the Fuehrer might agree, "in the interests of the State," to release Dimitrov once the trial had served its propaganda purpose. The Soviet Government had offered to exchange him for two top-ranking German agents who were held in Russia. It was a shadow duel, the tips of the swords were blunted, but it looked as if blood would flow at any minute. Dimitrov teased his powerful opponent with cunning stabs. Not for a second did his position in the dock embarrass him in his exchanges with the almighty Nazi Minister. His questions soon involved Goering in contradictions and involuntary admissions of many flaws in the indictment.

"What has the Minister donc," Dimitrov asked, "to get the police to check van der Lubbe's movements, his stay at Hennigsdorf, his acquaintance with two people there and thus to find the true accomplices? What has your police done?" Van der Lubbe, shifting absent-mindedly in his seat, was forgotten, as the whole Court looked at Goering, who answered: "Obviously as a Minister, I have not followed every trail myself. For that I have my police."

DIMITROV: As you, in your position, have accused the Communist Party of Germany and foreign Communists, has that not directed investigation into certain channels and prevented the search for the real incendiaries?

GOERING: For me this was a political crime and I was convinced that the criminals are to be found in your Party. (*Shaking his fist at Dimitrov and shouting*): Your Party is a party of criminals which must be destroyed.

DIMITROV: Is the Prime Minister aware that this Party rules a sixth of the earth, the Soviet Union, with which Germany maintains diplomatic, political, and economic relations, from which hundreds of thousands of German workers benefit . . .

CHAIRMAN: I forbid you to make Communist propaganda here.

DIMITROV: Herr Goering makes National Socialist propaganda. . . . Is it not known that Communism has millions of supporters in Germany . . .

GOERING (*screaming*): It is known that you are behaving insolently, that you have come here to burn the Reichstag . . . In my opinion you are a criminal who should be sent to the gallows!

CHAIRMAN: Dimitrov, I have told you not to make Communist propaganda. You must not be surprised if the witness gets excited.

DIMITROV: I am very satisfied with the reply of the Prime Minister.

GOERING (*screaming*): Out with you, you scoundrel!

CHAIRMAN (*to the police officer*): Take him away.

DIMITROV (*already being led away by the police*): Are you afraid of my questions, Herr Ministerpresident?

GOERING: You wait until we get you outside this Court, you scoundrel . . . !

By losing his temper and allowing Dimitrov to score important points, Goering had spoiled the propagandist effect of the trial. Whenever he was stung, Goering was likely to let his tongue run away with him. "I am not concerned with meting out justice," he shouted; "my task is to destroy, to exterminate." No wonder Sir Austen Chamberlain, the British Foreign Minister, commented in the House of Commons, "What is this new spirit of German Nationalism? The worst of the All-Prussian Imperialism, with an added savagery . . ." A subservient judiciary had done its best to conduct the trial along prescribed lines and to bring it to the prearranged conclusion. Van der Lubbe was sentenced to death and executed. Giorgi Dimitrov (who later became Prime Minister of Bulgaria and one of Stalin's closest collaborators) was acquitted. He and his Bulgarian friends were allowed to fly to Russia. Ernst Torgler was also acquitted, but taken into "protective custody," never to leave the Nazi prison and concentration camp alive. The Reichstag fire had destroyed German democracy. With the trial, Goering and Diels had dealt German justice a mortal blow.

8

MAN OF IRON

IN THE hectic days which followed his appointment as Cabinet Minister, Prussian Minister of the Interior, and Commissioner for Air, Hermann Goering for the first time in many years was almost too busy to worry about his private affairs. His office as President of the Reichstag had already eased his financial position which had become increasingly pressing in 1932. As Reichstag President, he received a salary of seventy-two hundred marks per year and a substantial personal allowance; he paid no rent for the palace which was his official residence. As Cabinet Minister, he was entitled to a further twelve thousand marks, plus two thousand marks for his work as Air Commissioner. By mid-1933 he was given another twelve thousand marks tax-free to cover his expenses as President of the Prussian State Council. Yet it was irksome to hear Hitler announce publicly that he would not accept the legal salary due to him as Reichs Chancellor. The *Voelkische Beobachter* and *Mein Kampf* were earning the Fuehrer a fortune. Goebbels made big profits from his own newspaper, *Der Angriff*, even Julius Streicher's *Der Stuermer* was making much money. Goering started negotiations, soon successfully concluded, for a share in the leading Ruhr daily, the *Essener National Zeitung*; it became his official organ and a new source of income.

Hitler took the view that the special circumstances of the Party's sudden rise to office warranted unusual measures. He regarded Goering as the "show-piece of the movement," whose duties brought him in constant contact with some of the wealthiest people in the land; so that he should have the means to represent the Party and the country adequately, he created a fund to provide for Goering's extra expenses. As a Minister, he should have a house of his own—

at the expense of the State. The State would pay if he entertained Germany's leading personalities, diplomats, and foreign statesmen. Financial consideration should not restrict the activities of the Fuehrer's most intimate collaborator.

Goering had never been unduly worried by his debts; he accepted these lavish emoluments with equal equanimity. It was very nice of the gentlemen of the aircraft industry to suggest that he also take up a few shares of the Benz-Motor Company and the Bayrische Motoren Werke, the firms with whom he had done much business in the past. Yes, he would certainly take a financial interest in the Junkers Flugzeuge Company. No deposit was needed; his benefactors had no doubt that, with an airman of his outlook in charge of the Air Ministry, the industry would soon boom and their own shares would treble their value. Goering faithfully listed all these emoluments in his income-tax return. Among other presents, Mussolini kindly sent a token of his friendship, a Madonna statue which Goering had admired during a short stay in Rome the previous year. From other countries came gifts — it was well known that the Minister was a great lover of the arts. The city of Dresden sent three Lukas Cranach paintings, his favourites — he would have to start collecting them! But he particularly liked the gift of a large canvas by Claus Bergen showing his own Jasta 27 in combat with British fighters.

He was admiring the picture when Robert announced a visitor. Bustling into the room, a happy smile playing around his lips as usual, came Karl Bodenschatz, now a full colonel in the Reichswehr. "Congratulations! Congratulations!" boomed the tall, good-looking officer who had come from Nuremberg to offer his best wishes to his former commander. Bodenschatz was one of the few permitted to address Goering with "Du," the German "thou" which is only used among close friends. "Look what I have got here!" Goering showed his old adjutant the Bergen painting. Bodenschatz told me of the childish joy which paintings, old statues, and antiques evoked in Hermann Goering: "I used to accompany him on his leave to Brussels during the First World War," Bodenschatz recalled," and he spent most of his time sniffing through antique shops and trying to find a bargain."

From their enjoyable conversation about Bergen's painting to a related but weightier subject was but one step: "Bodenschatz," Goering said, "what we have discussed so often in the past is now becoming a reality. I am Commissioner for Aviation, in reality the first German Air Minister since the end of the war. What I have promised when we parted at Aschaffenburg in 1918 I shall keep — we shall have a German Air Force again. Not a military affair as yet — you understand! The Treaty of Versailles is still in force. But as soon as the Fuehrer has completed the political preparations to do away with the Treaty, I want to be ready. . . . There is much work to be done. I need a reliable friend to work with me — will you be my adjutant again?"

It was a great opportunity for the company commander from Nuremberg. Next day Colonel Bodenschatz joined Goering's staff as his personal assistant and chief adjutant at the Air Ministry. "Familiarise yourself with the whole sordid story of our decline," Goering told him. "It will only encourage you in your determination to help in rebuilding our strength!" Goering explained that he had twice tried in vain to interest the Reichstag in German aviation — for the first time in 1929, but few people had taken notice. Again in 1931 he had pointed out that Britain was spending three times as much as Germany on development of civil aviation. But he told Bodenschatz that he had already made a most important initial move for the creation of a new German Air Force.

The occasion was the anniversary meeting of the German Aero Club. That meeting was the birthday of the Luftwaffe. The vast gathering of aircraft and engine manufactures, of shareholders and former airmen, gave Goering a tremendous reception. He beamed as he heard them referring to him good-humouredly as "Der Dicke" (Fatty) or "Der Eiserne" (Man of Iron). Hundreds of these people had vested interests in aviation. Hermann Goering, they had no doubt, would make their interests prosper. Bruno Loerzer was with him. He would be put in charge of the "Air-Sports Association" and could be relied upon to train the members in the spirit of the Richthofen Squadron. Ernst Udet, with sixty-two victories in the air, the highest scoring surviving airman of the First World War, had tried his hand as an aircraft designer and, like Goering himself, had earned a living as a stunt flier. He would have an important post in the Air Ministry. One by one the pioneers of German aviation were taken into a corner by the new Air Minister and received their briefs. There were Otto Mader and Heinrich Koppenberg of the Junkers Works, Kurt Tank of Focke-Wulf, Ernst Heinkel, Claudius Dornier, and Fritz Nallinger of Benz Motoren.

"The position is shocking," Goering told them, "but do not let that worry you!" There was not much to build on as yet, they all agreed, but now they could go ahead in great style. Hitler had authorised him to say that the Government would make large credits available to the industry. They were to intensify experimental work and to develop the few available types like Junkers' three-engined "Ju 52"—an ideal prototype"; Heinkel's "He 70," Focke-Wulf's "F.W. 200." Dornier was to concentrate on flying boats. "You can take your pick, gentlemen," Goering said, "from six milion unemployed. We shall put them to work building new aerodromes, factories, aircraft, and engines. We shall pay men to take up flying and get experienced N.C.O.'s from the Reichswehr to disipline them. Even if they are not allowed to wear the uniform of airmen, they must be trained like real soldiers!"

Now was also the time to reward an old friend for many kind services. Erhard Milch would join him at the Air Ministry as his Secretary of State. There was a little problem here—Goering knew that Milch had Jewish blood in his veins, and though he, personally, was not particularly concerned with such details, it might create difficulties for his principal official. A solution was soon found. Milch was the son of a Jewish apothecary from Breslau, but his mother was a pure Aryan. What if Frau Milch were to admit that she had deceived her husband, that Erhard was really born out of wedlock? The harassed old lady did not want to hamper her son's career. She would do anything to help him to achieve the highest honours in the new State! Frau Milch made a solemn declaration that she had committed adultery with a minor German aristocrat. Erhard Milch's original birth certificate was withdrawn, a new one was issued. Baron Hermann von Bier figured on it as his father. The road to the top was clear for Erhard Milch.

The Aero Club meeting had been a great success, but Goering thought that the premises of the club would soon be too small for their purpose. He told Bodenschatz of one of his pet projects. "We

German airmen have never had a real home of our own in Berlin," he said. "We shall not need the Prussian Landtag any more. Let's rebuild it and turn it into a Haus der Flieger (Airmen's Club). I cannot imagine any better use of the old Quasselbude (talking shop). There would also have to be a new Air Ministry. Goering called on the State architects to submit plans for a big new building with at least five thousand rooms, and, most important, with a roof on which aircraft could land and take off. The Air Minister decided to take up flying again. One of his favourite airmen, Captain Hucke, introduced him to such novel techniques as night flying. What a joy it was to have the stick of an aircraft in your hand again!

At his trial in Nuremberg, Goering said that it took a long time before he was able to give the German Air Force the character which he visualised. There were not enough raw materials, not enough aluminum, to build the type of aircraft which he wanted. He regarded Russia as the main potential opponent; England and France, even Italy, had to be considered. The Atlantic lured—there would have to be aircraft capable of carrying the war to North America; "I regarded it as my duty," Goering said, "to take all possibilities into account!"

Goering was most reluctant to leave Germany when Hitler asked him to go on his first official diplomatic mission abroad. But the Cabinet had decided to send von Papen to Rome to reassure the Vatican about the Nazi Government's treatment of the Catholics. Hitler did not trust Papen and decided that Goering should accompany his Vice-Chancellor. Goering had often attacked the Church of Rome. Now he could tell the Pope that what he said was not Government policy. It was an unusual situation for the two political enemies of yesterday to join forces on this trip to Rome. Their uneasy partnership soon received a severe jolt—there was a heated conversation between the two men when a telegram from Hitler arrived in Rome removing Papen from his post as Prussian Prime Minister—and appointing Hermann Goering in his place. Goering was content to leave negotiations with the Vatican to his Catholic colleague. Together with Erhard Milch, he sat in conference with Marshal Balbo, head of the Italian Air Force, like him an airman of distinction. At long last he met men who appreciated his ideas of government; in the members of Mussolini's Government Goering found congenial companions.

By the time he returned to Berlin, documents had piled up on his desk. Diels reported that new-type machines had arrived from Switzerland, with which it was possible to record private telephone conversations automatically. What a brilliant invention! But control of these machines would not be left to the police. Goering decided to create a "Research Department" of the Air Ministry — "research" meaning supervision of the "internal enemy," including the highest ranking personalities in the State. Everybody was a potential enemy. A special staff prepared a daily dossier of "interesting" telephone conversations; extracts in the form of "Brown Sheets" were submitted to the Air Ministry personally every morning. It was Goering's jolliest hour of the day. Robert brought his coffee, turned on the gramophone to play some soft music, and Goering studied the Brown Sheets, roaring with laughter at one minute, raving with fury in the next, as he read what people said about him, Hitler, and the Nazi régime. The Brown Sheets helped him to become the best-informed man in Germany, an ever-present witness of his friends' and enemies' most intimate conversations.

From Italy he had returned with a bright new Italian decoration to add to the Pour le Mérite, the Iron Cross I and II Class, the Order of the Zaehring Lion, the Karl Friedrich Medal, and the Hohenzollern Order, which had been conferred on him in the First World War. He wore them all at a reception, and soon the Brown Sheets told him that his order-bedecked breast had created quite a stir. A general in a telephone conversation had told a friend the latest joke — the rate of street accidents at night had gone up in Berlin because Goering would never dip the lights on his tunic. "Not bad," commended Goering. He knew that the Gestapo had arrested several people who had ridiculed the Nazi régime, but when he heard that a popular Berlin soubrette, Claire Waldow, was being held because she had made fun of his silver epaulettes and his medals, he ordered her immediate release. "Idiots!" he fulminated. "If they make jokes about me, it only proves how popular I am!" One comedian, in particular, made a reputation for himself with a witty and biting Goering parody. "Let's go and hear him," Goering told Bodenschatz, "but make sure that he does his act even though I am there!" The comedian trembled as the Lord of the Gestapo, the man with power over life and death of all Germans, listened to his song. He was not at his best that night. "I bet he suffered more," Goering commented, highly amused, "than if I locked him up!" He protected Werner Fink who made fun of him at the Katakombe, a Berlin night-club, but Fink made a mistake to think that other Nazi leaders would be equally tolerant. When — encouraged by the success of his Goering stories — he told a harmless joke about Hitler, he was sent to a concentration camp.

In August Field Marshal von Hindenburg, as Supreme Chief of the Reichswehr, fulfilled one of Goering's dearest wishes. He promoted him to the rank of General of the Infantry. Heinrich Himmler conferred on him the honorary appointment of an Upper Group Leader of the S.S., and he had also resumed his old rank in the S.A. Now he called in Herr Stechbart, the well-known uniform tailor in the Tauenzienstrasse in Berlin's West End. He needed a general's uniform and an S.S. uniform; he was getting stouter, and his old S.A. brown shirt did not fit any longer; he had neglected his civilian wardrobe. "Fit me out completely." he told Stechbart, who did not as yet realise what working for the new customer would imply.

Robert told me that clothes were a constant worry to Hermann Goering. As he grew fatter, Stechbart had to come to his house almost every morning to alter his suits and uniforms. Then Goering would spend a weekend in the country and, wrapped in thick pullovers, take his valet on a "quick-march," lasting sometimes over two hours. "So he lost weight again and on Monday none of his suits fitted him. I had to call Stechbart again . . ." It was probably the after-effect of his early and neglected rheumatism that caused Goering to be troubled with pains in his limbs. His clothes seemed to weight him down. Stechbart had to perform feats of supreme artistry to build his suits and uniforms so that they sat loosely on his body without giving the appearance of being too big. As soon as his chief came home in the afternoon, Robert said, he would take off everything and slip into a dressing gown specially designed to allow free play to his bulk. He wanted very full sleeves and much room around the chest. Goering loved these long coats, had them made in all colours and of different materials. In the end he had over forty — a complete set in each of his residences.

Goering's growing size also brought food problems. He was accustomed to a typical Bavarian diet — dumplings, noodles,

Nockerln (small dumplings), mountains of meat. His tremendous expenditures of energy created a craving for sugar — he took it in the form of sweets, chocolates, sweetened whipped cream. But these dishes, in turn, increased his size and the discomfort that went with it. While the world thought of Hermann Goering enjoying all the sweet things in life, he actually suffered daily tortures — eating his favourite meals with a bad conscience, and spending hours trying to get rid of his extra avoirdupois. He changed his suits or uniforms three or four times a day. "People thought it was only vanity," Robert told me. "Of course, he liked his clothes, but he had to change once or twice not only to keep comfortable, but to be able to carry on with his work at all."

Goering with his uniforms and decorations, the fat Goering, subject of a hundred jokes (they said he wore a set of rubber decorations in his bath, that he put on a miner's helmet when the coalman called), emerged as the most popular figure of the Nazi Government — a laughing, clowning, jovial, happy-go-lucky fellow. Abroad, the cruelty of the S.A., the outrages of the Gestapo, were laid at his door. His speeches lost nothing of their violence even when the passions they roused among his supporters became a serious embarrassment to him. Anxious to pacify international public opinion, which was solidly against the Nazi Government, Goering, as he had done in 1932, was forced once more to try and curb the S.A. The permanent officials of the Prussian Ministries joined him whole-heartedly in his campaign against the brown-shirted intruders: "The revolution is over!" Goering shouted, but it was impossible to get rid of the spirits which he had conjured up.

In spite of their protests, he closed down the wild S.A. concentration camps which Ernst, Heines, and other radicals had built all over the country. "But we shall keep one or two of these camps and run them properly," he declared: "I don't know why the English should object. My father told me that they introduced concentration camps in Africa thirty years ago and put the Boers behind barbed wires — women, children, and all!" As the S.A. and their leaders were getting out of control, he asked Himmler with his S.S. to take over guard duties at the camps. He heard that Ernst Torgler complained about his treatment in such a camp. There was no question of releasing the arch-Communist until he had reformed. "I want to see Torgler," he told his officials, who could hardly believe their ears.

There has rarely been an interview quite like it. Under armed guard, Torgler was taken to the Prime Minister's office. Two deadly enemies faced each other: "I hear you have a lot of complaints," Goering said. Torgler told him that he had been beaten, humiliated, tortured, that he did not get enough to eat: "Mind you, Torgler," Goering answered, "I am not sorry for you; I cannot help wondering what you would have done to me if our positions had been reversed. But I shall give orders that you be treated properly." The guards did not pay much attention to Goering's orders. Every day now brought news of S.A. excesses: "I have no sympathy with the people you are badgering," Goering told Karl Ernst, "but, for God's sake, behave decently. You are ruining our prestige!" "But you have said yourself that we should shoot . . ." "I have said a lot of things, my friend."

Every day Goering spent at least an hour in private conversation with Hitler. He told him of his difficulties with the storm troopers and their leaders. We know only from Goering's own account how Hitler reacted, and this account is highly coloured. But it was no secret in Goering's entourage that Hitler also was not happy about the S.A. It had always eluded his control. Ernst Roehm was not the man to follow Hitler slavishly, as did all the others. Hitler also suspected that he had allowed the Communists to infiltrate the S.A. He heard they were saying in Berlin that the S.A. was like a beefsteak — outside brown, inside red. Once or twice Goering met Roehm to discuss the S.A., but Roehm only reiterated his longstanding ideas: the S.A. should be the army of the Nazi Party and the country. Goering gained the impression that Roehm wanted to supersede the Reichswehr, make himself commander of all the armed forces in Germany and thus become the most powerful man in the State.

Defence Minister General von Blomberg was under a similar impression and protested to Hitler against S.A. intrusion into the sphere of the army. Accusations against Roehm came from all sides; hints about his morals and those of his friends were made openly. Parents complained about the homosexual approaches to which their young sons in the S.A. were subjected. Goering assiduously collected all available information until he was able to give his Fuehrer a dramatic account of the position. Hitler had always known about the evil practices in the S.A., but now he was glad to use them as a pretext for action. According to Goering's report, Roehm, the despicable pervert, was conspiring with General Schleicher and Gregor Strasser to bring about the fall of the Hitler Government, to eliminate the Reichswehr and Hindenburg. He had designated S.A. Leader Prince August Wilhelm of Hohenzollern as President of the "Fourth Reich," of which Schleicher would be Chancellor, Strasser Vice-Chancellor, and Roehm himself Minister of Defence in charge of the Army. His S.A. henchmen were to be the generals of Germany.

Hitler hurriedly consulted with the Reichswehr. He received the assurance of full army support if he crushed this conspiracy. Hitler and Goering, relying on the help of Heinrich Himmler and his loyal S.S. Black Guards, laid their plans. To crush such dangerous enemies could only have one form — complete elimination, Goering said, using one of the régime's favourite expressions. Just as in the case of the Communists on February 27, 1933, so with the S.A. on June 30, 1934. Whether a coup was imminent or not, Hitler was determined to strike. Goering made one attempt to avoid a crisis. In a speech he frankly addressed himself to those in high places who criticised the Fuehrer and showed signs of disaffection: "We shall be utterly ruthless," he warned them. Roehm sent him a message — "not to be silly!" Goering was not being silly by any means. If they did not want to listen — very well. Now he mobilised the police to be at Hitler's disposal. Himmler called on the S.S. to be prepared. Hitler went to Bavaria where Roehm was known to have gathered his S.A. friends around him. Goering, personally, was entrusted with the conduct of operations in Berlin. In the early hours of June 30, Hitler, at the head of an armed S.S. unit accompanied by Goebbels and Dietrich, raided Ernst Roehm's house in Wiessee, by the Tegernsee (Tegern Lake). Later in his apologia, he said that he found Roehm in bed with a boy friend. They were taken to Stadelheim Prison and shot.

In Berlin mass arrests took place under Goering's supervision. The police and the S.S. took up one of his public announcements. "Perhaps I may shoot too short or too wide, the main thing for me is to shoot!" General Kurt von Schleicher was shot as he opened the door to an S.S. Kommando; his wife, who tried to protect him, was shot dead. Gregor Strasser was shot. Karl Ernst was shot. With a list of names before him, Goering checked the reports of killings and arrests until he spotted the name of an S.A. leader, Gehrt, like him holder of the Pour le Mérite. Gehrt had served with Goering in the Richthofen Squadron. "I want to see this fellow!" he demanded. Gehrt, with hundreds of others, had been taken to the Lichterfelde Barracks; one after another of the arrested men had been called out — to be shot. Gehrt was staggered when his name was called and he was told that Goering wanted to see him. "I have asked you to come here," Goering told him, "because you are a soldier and once were my comrade. That makes your treasonable activities only worse! I wanted to deal with you myself!" He ripped off Gehrt's Pour le Mérite and flung it into a corner: "Now take him away!" Gehrt was shot an hour later.

Prince August Wilhelm, also under arrest, was brought into Goering's presence. But it appeared that he had known nothing of the whole plan or the part he was supposed to play in it. Konrad Heiden [1] describes the encounter between the two old friends. "Where," Goering asked, "have you last spoken to Karl Ernst?" "On the telephone." "What did you discuss with him?" Ernst, the Prince said, only wanted to take his leave before going abroad. "You are lucky to have told the truth," Goering said as he switched on a gramophone which played a record of the conversation. "I am glad that you have decided to go to Switzerland for a few days!" Goering told the Prince, who looked at him with a blank expression. "Have I not told you that you have the dumbest face in the world?" Goering continued. "Of course, you want to go to Switzerland!"

No complete list of the victims of the June Bloodbath is in existence. Goering had asked Franz von Papen to stay at home on June 30: "It will be a hectic day!" he told him. Papen followed his advice, but three members of his personal staff, Klausner, Jung, and Bose, were killed; Dr. Fritz Gehrlich, who once accused Goering of corruption, was killed; Herr Gustav von Kahr, seventy-three years of age, the man who foiled Hitler's putsch in 1923, was killed;

[1] Konrad Heiden, *Hitler, Das Leben eines Diktators.*

so was Dr. Villain, a sadistic S.A. leader who had caused Goering much trouble in the Prussian police. Among the S.S. officers who conducted the manhunt was Josef ("Sepp") Dietrich, the Commander of the Leibstandarte, the S.S. unit which was Hitler's personal guard. "You have gone too far!" Hitler shouted at Dietrich, when arriving by air in Berlin he heard of the vast proportions which the murder campaign had assumed. "Mein Fuehrer," Dietrich said, "ours is the responsibility for your security; for once we must have the right to let ourselves go!"

Hitler was in hysterics. He had had killed most of his best friends, men who had fought with him since his beginnings, men without whom he would never have succeeded. Heavily he leaned on his faithful Goering who had met him at the aerodrome. Together they went to the headquarters of the gruesome operation. An aide handed Goering a message. As he read it, he knew that he had served the Reichswehr well. Here is a copy of the telegram:

MINISTER PRESIDENT GENERAL GOERING BERLIN
088/Teleg. 4012

ACCEPT MY APROVAL AND GRATITUDE FOR YOUR SUCCESSFUL ACTION IN SUPPRESSING THE HIGH TREASON STOP WITH COMRADELY THANKS AND GREETINGS

(signed) VON HINDENBURG

The S.A. was reduced almost to the status of the Sports Club from which it had been developed in 1922 and 1923. The vacuum was soon filled by the S.S. Himmler's praetorian guard took over Goering's police. Before long Heinrich Himmler became Germany's Police Minister, and his young aide, Reinhard Heydrich the "Killer," Chief of the Gestapo. The organisation which Goering had created dominated the life of Nazi Germany. But not even in his wildest dreams could he have forseen that one day he, too, Hermann Goering, would be a prisoner of the S.S.

9

EMMY

On a cold morning of January, 1934, a shivering crowd of Berliners gathered at the corner of Unter den Linden and the Wilhelmstrasse. "Good old Hermann!" they called out as they pushed nearer to the smiling Nazi Minister. Goering in a heavy fur-collared coat, a big scarf only just revealing his rosy cheeks under a service cap, shook a big collecting box noisily under their noses. In his best huckster's style he shouted: "Ein paar Pfennige, bitte [A few pennies, please]. It is more blessed to give than to receive!" Like all Cabinet Ministers, he was taking part in the public collection for "Winterhelp" to aid millions of hungry Germans and to lighten the heavy burden of unemployment benefit. A few hundred yards away Joseph Goebbels had posted himself, silent, aloof, anxious to avoid contact with the masses, hating his part in this propaganda stunt which was his own idea. Goering loved every minute of it.

The country was hungry; there was not even enough fuel because much of the Ruhr coal output had been earmarked for export to earn foreign exchange; a sharp wind was whistling into thousands of uncomfortable homes. There was a big open fire in Goering's office as he settled down to put the final touches on arrangements for the two new homes which he had acquired. Hitler had agreed that he should take over an old, empty palace in the Leipzigerplatz in the centre of the city, yet separated from the bustle of the streets by a wall and rows of big trees. The State would bear the cost of rebuilding and redecorating. For weeks Goering conferred with architects about the design; Hitler, the amateur architect, took a great personal interest in all details. He was himself working on plans for a new Chancellery and the two men spent hours comparing and elaborating their conceptions of a novel National Socialist style.

When Goering's palace was completed, visitors were overwhelmed by the view of a white alabaster staircase leading up to the reception rooms. His study was built to resemble Mussolini's office in the Palazzo Venetia, which had ingrained itself in the mind of the impoverished Hermann Goering of 1925. Deep carpets swallowed every sound, guests were received in an all-red-and-gold drawing room, left waiting to admire paintings and tapestries which Germany's museums had put at the disposal of the Minister to decorate his residence. Heavy silver almost weighted down half a dozen tables, a big vitrine revealed a collection of old Roman cups which Marshal Balbo had sent from Libya. Emmy Goering told me that the palace was not big enough for its purpose; there were too few rooms — since her husband put apart much space for offices. Accommodation was needed for his aides and his secretarial staff. The palace was not very big, but the new Nazi style in architecture, as in many other things, conveyed an impression of grandeur, exaggerating real size and concealing mediocrity and insignificance.

Goering visited the Schorfheide, a thick forest and vast heath twenty-five miles north of Berlin, to inspect an old small former Imperial hunting lodge of which Prince August Wilhelm had often spoken. "His work," Emmy Goering told me, "had kept him from his beloved mountains, from nature, from hunting — one of his hobbies. The little lodge was just the type of country house which he had missed ever since he came to stay in Berlin." A personal credit, advanced by the banking house of Thyssen, enabled Goering to buy the lodge. Wild animals roamed the woods around it, and often, when the pressure of work had worn him down, Goering disappeared for a day or two to stalk deer or shoot bears. He was a fine marksman who took his hunting seriously. With an old battered hat such as Winston Churchill wears on his holidays, with a leather jacket and big, bulky trousers, it was almost impossible to recognise the usually immaculate man with the reputation of a clothes-horse.

Losing himself in the wilderness, alone with nature, he was painfully aware that this was just the life which Karin would have loved; the hunting lodge just the remote hide-out to which they had planned to retire one day. The lodge became a passion, a symbol of the opportunities which Karin had missed by her untimely death. He called it Karinhall — it was really Karin's by right, he thought. Indeed, it shall be Karin's, he decided. He drew up plans for an extension, for a few roms to be built around the original lodge which he wanted to preserve as he found it. More than once his pencil strayed with his mind and, whatever he meant to draw, there appeared in black and white before his eyes the design of a mausoleum for Karin to rest in and remain with him forever. Only a small pretence was needed for him to move from doodles to a decision. The Swedish press carried many hostile comments about the Nazi Government, a source of indignation to Goering who regarded Sweden as his second home. A report appeared that Karin Goering's grave had been desecrated by Swedish Communists, who regarded Goering as their vilest enemy. Karin would find real peace in the Schorfheide. Goering decided that her body should be brought home.

Early in June Karinhall was completed and Goering asked friends and members of the diplomatic corps to be his guests at a housewarming party. He told them of his plan to develop Schorfheide into a reservation for rare wild animals, to import bison, elks, and bears, to rescue the aurochs from extinction, and to cultivate every type of creature which would flourish in this district. Karinhall would grow to become a monument of Nazi culture, a unique integration of architectural beauty and scientifically developed nature. Goering conducted his guests in cars over the estate, joyfully accepting their compliments. At least one of them, William E. Dodd, the American Ambassador, could not help making a mental comparison between economic conditions in Germany and Goering's ambitious and costly project. But Madame Cerutti, the wife of the Italian Ambassador, voiced the views of others who encouraged Goering in his daydreams: "In his conception of a princely existence, he reminds me of the Borgias," she commented with unconcealed enthusiasm and little awareness of the double meaning.

Finally, Goering led his guests to the marble-covered entrance of a vault which had been hewn in the ground. Part of the forest had been cleared; he would be able to sit in meditation on a wooden bench under a big lime tree in the centre of the clearing. From the tree a short path led to the vault. Ambassador Dodd said that he felt embarrassed by this ostentatious display of a mausoleum, but

Goering was too absorbed in his thoughts of Karin to notice that some of his guests edged away quickly and took their leave long before the appointed time. In his mind he was working out the details of Karin's last journey. It would be a public holiday. Hitler had consented to attend the ceremony of the burial at Karinhall. The Fuehrer would pay homage to the "Mascot of the Movement" and thus express his appreciation for her part in his struggle to power.

To Sweden Goering sent Pilli Koerner and an S.A. Kommando unit under Group Leader Wecke, who had earned rapid promotion in the police raids on anti-Nazis in 1933. Prince and Princess Wied, as Karin's closest friends, went to Drotthingholm Cemetery. The crews of a German torpedo boat flotilla were on parade as the white coffin was lifted from the grave; they accompanied it as it was carried to the station. In Trelleborg it was placed on a ferry, covered with flowers, and taken to the small German port of Sassnitz, where Goering boarded the boat to welcome his dead wife. To Eberswalde, the station which serves the Schorfheide, the Reichswehr had sent a band and a convoy of mounted artillery guards officers who accompanied the procession to Karinhall. Here Hitler and the members of his Government were waiting to honour Karin Goering. To the sound of a hundred hunting horns and trumpets, the coffin was deposited in the vault.

The officers of his entourage noticed that Goering, in the second half of 1934, was a relaxed, composed, balanced personality. He showed no more signs of instability; his exaggerated exuberance and almost superhuman zeal to accomplish the impossible had subsided. In retrospect, they are not sure whether the radical elimination of the S.A. opposition or the sentimental reunion with Karin had brought peace to his mind. But he had changed again; Rudolf Diels had been promoted into obscurity and gone to Cologne as head of the local government. The Prussian police had lost its fascination for Goering. Though not a man of letters, he avidly responded to a suggestion that he should explain the Nazi Government to Britain. In forty-eight hours he completed dictation of a book,[1] which was published in London. He accepted an offer from the Association of German Hunters to become its official patron. Hitler, to whom he

[1] *Germany Reborn.*

explained that the timber industry afforestation and related problems needed special attention, appointed him Reich Chief Forester, and granted funds for the development of the Schorfheide. Builders were put to work on further extensions and a group of scientists engaged to devote themselves to zoological research, of which the Schorfheide became a super-laboratory.

As Karinhall was turned into a show place, Goering bought another hunting estate in Rominten, East Prussia, and in a big Junkers 52 aeroplane flew there every fortnight to spend the weekend hunting and shooting. He also began to see more of Emmy Sonnemann, whom he had persuaded to refuse an attractive offer from the Burgtheater, the famous Vienna State Theatre: "I cannot let you go that far away," he insisted. Emmy Sonnemann-Goering was brought before a de-Nazification Court after the war to defend herself against the accusation of having "profited from Nazism," a punishable crime. The prosecution contended that her association with Goering helped her to obtain a profitable engagement in Berlin. Emmy told me that she simply had fallen in love with Hermann and only too gladly acceded to his request to remain in Germany. "You belong to the Prussian State Theatre," he said — and as Premier of Prussia, he was also the supreme chief of this theatre. By that time it was well known in Berlin that Goering was extremely fond of Emmy Sonnemann. The Prime Minister did not need to exert himself unduly to find a niche for her at the State Theatre. Gustaf Grundgens, a great German actor, an unusual man in many ways, was the Director. "I engaged Emmy Sonnemann on her merits," he said in 1948. Obviously Hermann Goering's lady friend was also a strong box-office attraction.

Now that Karin was home and his political work gliding gently into more regular grooves, Goering proposed to Emmy and they announced their engagement. "She is marrying him because he is a mighty man and a Minister," said Berlin: "She wants to feather her nest — typical of an actress!" was the general comment. It is difficult to analyse the feelings of a woman who marries above her station. Emmy Sonnemann was doing well on the stage. Her salary was ten thousand marks per year. Her position brought her into contact with many prominent men in Germany. Hermann Goering, it is true, was the most eligible of them. "I loved him," Emmy said to me in 1950, speaking very quietly and very simply; "I thought he was the most wonderful man in the world — and I still think so!"

The engagement was celebrated with a trip to Athens. Prince Philip of Hessen took them in his car: "The beauty of the Acropolis, the glorious light of an evening in Greece, the inspiring atmosphere . . . !" Emmy recalled. Goering revelled in this atmosphere which brought to life the ancient history of the Greeks, a subject which he had neglected in school, but which had fascinated him ever since. His ideal was a combination of the soldierly virtues of Sparta and the aesthetic qualities of Athens. It never occurred to him that the two philosophies may not mix. But politics were really ten thousand miles away. Hermann Goering was more himself on this trip than he had been for many years; once he left his desk, his documents, the telephone, and his ever-growing staff of adjutants and secretaries, once he put Hitler and his Tafelrunde behind him, there was no more charming man under the sun.

Hitler realised that more than anybody else. Distrusting and disliking his Foreign Minister, Baron von Neurath, he mapped out a heavy programme for his first lieutenant. It was a job much after Hermann Goering's heart. In complete harmony with the leaders of German industry, Hitler came to the conclusion that it was necessary to conquer the Southeast European markets. Austria would have to be absorbed in the Reich — and Germany was to inherit the economic and strategic position of the old Austro-Hungarian monarchy. Hitler sent Goering on a mission to the Balkans, which were partly under Italian influence; known as the "Little Entente," they were also under the wing of France.

If these links could be broken, Germany would have a clear field. In Austria a strong National Socialist Party harassed the Government with street disturbances and political intrigues reminiscent of the German Nazi campaign in 1932. They were determined to bring down the dictatorship of the Catholic Chancellor, Engelbert Dollfuss. Once Austria could be isolated, Goering was convinced, it would fall like a ripe apple into the hands of the Austrian Nazis — and of Germany. He visited Poland — Foreign Minister Joseph Beck took him on an extensive hunting trip in the forest of Bialowice; he went to Jugoslavia and was treated royally. In Hungary, Regent Admiral Nicholas Horthy found that he had much in common with the German, an officer and gentleman like himself. The British press noted that Hermann Goering seemed to be succeeding in his attempt to achieve a rapprochement between Germany and Eastern Europe.

Goering's own newspaper, the *Essener National Zeitung*, strongly reflected his views and accompanied his Balkan trip and his attempt to isolate Austria with a violent campaign against the Dollfuss Government. The Austrian Nazis, whose Party had been declared illegal after an unprecedented terror campaign, took these comments as a signal to rise in a putsch. Goering had frequently received Austrian Nazi leaders and discussed the situation with them, but he was too optimistic about the success of his diplomatic exchanges to encourage their putsch plans. Encouragement from other German quarters, however, was not lacking. The Austrian Nazis murdered Dollfuss in July, 1934. Goering raved. He was not sorry for Dollfuss — "this pocket edition of Papen," as he called him — but the consequences of the abortive putsch were embarrassing for Germany. Mussolini thought that the Reichswehr was planning a march into Austria and sent three Italian divisions to the Brenner. It was a serious setback to Goering's afforts to woo Italy. The Balkan States were roused in fear and suspicion of Germany. The Western world was perturbed. Goering suggested to Hitler that von Papen should go to Austria as Ambassador to pacify their minds and restore confidence. He was killing two birds with one stone. "At least we get rid of him that way," he said. Papen, whose closest friends had been murdered only a month previously, was glad to escape the dangers which lurked in Berlin.

Events moved so fast that Goering had little time to linger over the temporary collapse of his East-European plans. His entourage and well-wishers missed few opportunities to show their admiration for him. Goering Streets sprung up all over Germany; a plaque was fixed on the house where he was born. A new balloon was named Hermann Goering — not without causing some lively badinage among his friends. A new Rhine bridge was given his name. The Bavarian Government offered him a piece of land in Berchtesgaden, near Hitler's house, to replace the property he had lost in 1923. Here he would build another retreat for himself — the resolution that he had made in his darkest days in Stockholm was rapidly turning into reality.

Then Field Marshal Paul von Hindenburg died. In a long conference with Hitler, Goering dissected the political situation which arose from his death. The Reichswehr had lost its nominal head; the conservative elements of the antiquated national parties their last protector. "*You* will be the new President of Germany, mein Fuehrer," Goering said to Hitler. "And *you* will be my Prime Minister!" Hitler answered. Goering has described the scene to his friends — it was a replica of the occasion, he said, when Hitler offered him the command of the S.A. In the Nuremberg trial Goering testified that he advised Hitler to follow the American example and unite the offices of President and Premier in his own person. It is, however, a fact that he was deeply disappointed when Hitler adopted this course, although nobody would have guessed his real feelings when he took the platform to support Hitler's candidature. He was always Hitler's faithful paladin.

Germany's diplomatic affairs soon claimed his attention again; prominent British airmen came on an official visit and he charmed them as he did most people when he set his mind to it. In Ward Price, the famous British correspondent, he found a representative of the British Press with whom he could get on. The West was beginning to penetrate the thick veil which he had thrown over the secret German air rearmament. "Let's end all this secrecy!" he advised Hitler. And, after consulting Blomberg about the feelings of the Reichswehr, Hitler gave him permission to reveal the existence of a new air force. In an interview with Ward Price, Goering proudly proclaimed that Germany was demanding "equality in the air," that a new German Air Force was taking its place in the international arena. Goering assumed the rank of a "General der Flieger" (General of Airmen). The German Air Force was born in the Aero Club of Berlin in February, 1933; in March, 1935, Goering christened the growing baby. He called it the Luftwaffe. Goering was its parent and godfather; the nurse was Erhard Milch, who proved himself an organising genius.

Having reached his first military target, having established his political and private position, Hermann Goering was ready to get married again. He fixed the date — April 10, 1935. On the eve of his wedding he appeared at Emmy Sonnemann's home. "Here you are!" he said with an acted show of brusqueness. Onto her table he flung a chain, closely studded with diamonds, and a glittering tiara, the like of which she had never seen before. It was worth fifty thousand marks. "Thanks for the chain!" Emmy said, ". . . but this thing — I dare not wear it!" What woman would not like a tiara? With a heavy heart Emmy tried to give it back to him. "What are people going to say? There is so much misery in Germany — so much poverty!" "You are a stupid woman," Hermann told her. "However poor people are — they love a show! You are doing them a favour, you are giving them something to talk, to dream about. And besides that," he added smilingly, "I should not take you on without it!"

At noon on Wednesday, April 10, the voice of a breathless radio announcer came over the air from Berlin: "I am now taking you to the wedding of the Prime Minister, General Hermann Goering, and State actress, Emmy Sonnemann — the wedding procession is now on the way from the Chancellery to the Town Hall where the civilian ceremony will be conducted. The streets are lined with thousands of people — the famous Richthofen Squadron is flying overhead. The formations of the N.S.D.A.P. are on guard along the whole route — the people are cheering — it is drizzling but nobody moves — here is the car of the bride — in a beautiful dress; Hermann Goering, our Hermann, is in the uniform of a General der Flieger — and now the Fuehrer's car approaches — there are cheers, enthusiasm, shouts — can you hear them shouting: Hoch Hermann! — Heil Hitler!"

Adolf Hitler was a witness at the wedding. "My dear Frau Goering — it is a very happy day!" he said. "If you have any wish — I shall be honoured to grant it to you — tell me!"

"I only wish, mein Fuehrer," Emmy said, smiling, "that politics would give Hermann a rest; I'd prefer him to be an actor!"

"Don't joke, Frau Emmy" — Hitler did not understand jokes. "I repeat — if you have a wish, now or ever, I shall grant it!"

Emmy insisted on a church ceremony to follow the civil wedding. It was an awkward request because the Nazi Government was involved in a grim struggle with the ecclesiastical authorities, but Goering consented. Reich Bishop Mueller, a Nazi nominee, performed the ceremony in the Dom. Hitler toasted the couple at a wedding breakfast at the Hotel Kaiserhof, which three hundred guests attended. On his way home, driving slowly in a new

Mercedes car, Goering, Emmy by his side, reviewed a formation of the police which was on parade at the Leipzigerplatz. In the evening they attended a gala performance of Richard Strauss's *Egyptian Helena* in the State Opera.

Gifts arrived from all over the country. Museums sent valuable paintings, carpets, tapestries, silver, goldware, jewels. From the Munich Pinakothek came two Lukas Cranachs. "Emmy Sonnemann must feel like a dream come true," said a foreign diplomat. "It was overwhelming," Emmy Goering agreed, holding back her tears as she spoke of "the greatest day in my life." She was rudely awakened from her dream in 1948 when she faced her trial in Garmisch-Partenkirchen. "Do you know," the public prosecutor asked, "that the 'Group of German Industry' had been requested to give you one of three wedding presents — a painting, a famous porcelain service, or a Landhaus (country house) — and that, according to the minutes of the meeting, the gentlemen, a little stunned by the blunt request, chose the Landhaus because at thirty thousand marks, it was the cheapest?"

Emmy Goering did not know. She did not know, either, that overzealous officials of her husband's entourage "simplified a collection" for the purchase of a wedding present by ordering the deduction of small sums from the pay-packets of the employees in Goering's Ministries without bothering to get their consent. "I wish to God we had never received a single present. We had enough already!" Emmy Goering cried, and I am convinced she meant what she said. By nature a modest woman in spite of her regal appearance, she did not cherish the thought that, with Hitler a bachelor, she had suddenly become the "First Lady of the Reich"; that people addressed her as "Hohe Frau," and Berliners, borrowing a term from Imperial Germany, referred to her as "Landesmutter" (Mother of the Land). She was sad because her stage career had come to an end. Once more as "Queen Louise" she appeared at a performance in honour of Hitler's birthday. Then she stepped off the "boards which mean the world" and became a figure on the stage of international politics.

Today, like ghosts in an eerie prehistoric landscape, two dirty lion figures, their marble ears and manes chipped and broken, rise from the dim light of an evening in the Schorfheide — behind them a waste of masonry and rubble. Now and then a shot rings out as soldiers of the Soviet Occupation Army hunt the stray deer which have survived the destruction of Karinhall. The lions and a slab of stone with the Goering family crest are all that remain of the elaborate portal through which Hermann Goering took his bride in 1935. Karinhall was not yet the vast building into which it grew as Goering ordered one extension after another to be made —adding a new wing even after the outbreak of war. But already a room had been put aside to house the lorry-loads of gifts from many parts of the globe. He chose a place for every single object; put up big showcases for the invaluable treasures. "This is my museum!" he said. That was how he wanted it to be. Only a small part of the house was really habitable. His favourite room was a big lounge, built in a hunting style, with hunting trophies on the walls and bearskins scattered on the floor. Here he would sit and relax with a bottle of wine or a big tankard of beer, puffing at his Churchillian cigar.

In 1945 a unit of the advancing Soviet armies found Karinhall in ruins, blasted by the engineers of the "Hermann-Goering Division" before their retreat. They dug into the mausoleum, broke open Karin's coffin in search of valuables. The body disappeared. In 1935, when Emmy arrived, it was much in evidence. Like many widowers when they marry a second time, Goering forced the memory of his first wife on his new bride. From now on Emmy Goering virtually lived with the late Karin. Karin was Hermann's fetish. A small yacht, one of the wedding presents, he named *Karin.* "Karin would have liked that," he said, looking over a landscape painting which he had bought. "This would have been just the place for Karin!" he sighed. "It would have been better for him had Karin lived," Emmy told me sadly. "Perhaps he would not have suffered this terrible fate!" I doubt it. Emmy had none of Karin's ambitions. Quietly she tried to fit herself for the new rôle in which she was cast. Hermann Goering was an easy man to live with, she told me. But she saw little of him. It took over an hour to drive from Berlin to the Schorfheide and Goering rarely arrived before midnight. Emmy, her friends and guests, patiently waited with empty stomachs for him to join them at dinner. "We cannot keep the servants up so late!" Emmy gently protested at last.

Goering thought it was a great joke. He rang the bell, called the servants together. "Listen, my friends!" he said, "I may be a mighty man in Germany, but at home my wife is in command. There will be dinner at 10 P.M. from now on — and if I am not here, you get on with it, even if there is nothing left for me!" He was so powerful now that he loved to show himself amenable to Emmy's discipline. Of course, he continued to arrive around midnight. His family and his guests continued to wait for him. But he had learned to shed the cares of his office when he was with Emmy. "People will not believe how little I knew of his politics," Emmy said. Goering realised that his wife's interests lay elsewhere. He tried his best to take up these interests. They talked of plays and of the stage. "He adored George Bernard Shaw," Emmy recalled; "he knew long passages of Shakespeare by heart. He loved the language of the German classics."

He also loved detective stories of which Robert always provided a large selection. And he could toy for hours with mechanical instruments — experiment, devote himself to problems which baffled his aeronautical experts. When an engineering firm sent him a large toy railway, he was delighted, ordered extensions, learnt the intricacies of shunting and organising a time schedule for the large network of rails. Many of his eminent visitors had to listen to his elaborate explanations about the mechanics of his railway. Some of them got bored with it, but others, like the Duke of Windsor when he visited Karinhall two years later, took up the game and were soon as fascinated as Goering himself. The Duke of Windsor, incidentally, during his visit to Schorfheide, was asked an awkward question: "When you were King, how many uniforms did you have?" The Duke confessed that he did not know exactly. He had uniforms of the various regiments in which he held honorary appointments; he had a boy scout uniform — this amused Goering intensely — and he was a member of many organisations whose uniforms he wore on ceremonial occasions: "Why do you want to know?" the Duke wondered. "Because I cannot understand that the British press should make a fuss about my uniforms!" was

Goering's answer. "Why, I saw Sir Nevile Henderson, the British Ambassador, the other day at an official function — he had three times as much gold braid on his coat as I have on any of my uniforms!" The Duke laughed: "I should not worry about that if I were you!"

Goering's personal staff grew with Karinhall. He engaged a cook with whom he discussed menus in great detail — how to eat well without putting on any more weight was the problem. Emmy needed a personal maid. Cilli was promoted to head-housekeeper. There were always house guests. Emmy's sister Else spent much time at Karinhall; Goering's own sisters, Olga Riegele and Paula Hueber, became extremely fond of Emmy and loved the Schorfheide. A room was set aside for Colonel Bodenschatz. Pilli Koerner used to accompany his chief home and to stay the night. Erhard Milch, now a general in the Luftwaffe, brought members of his technical staff along — Goering could get away from politics, from aeroplanes never. Even after his midnight meal, he retired to his room to read documents which he had brought with him from Berlin. In the morning he usually handed Bodenschatz a bundle of papers which always included a sheet marked "Fuehrer," listing subjects he wanted to discuss with Hitler.

Goering's honeymoon, six weeks after the ceremony, was a diplomatic expedition. It was made in his special train and the newlyweds were accompanied by a staff of twenty. The destination was Southeast Europe. Goering wanted to take up his Balkan conversations where they were broken off after the murder of Dollfuss. The Minister for Church Affairs, Hans Kerrl, was in the party; he took his wife, who was a pleasant companion for Emmy. Prince Philip von Hessen went — the King of Italy's son-in-law symbolised German-Italian friendship. Milch, Koerner, and Bodenschatz went as a matter of course. Dr. Gritzbach had become an indispensable member of Goering's staff, an adviser on whom he could rely to suggest solutions of the trickiest political situations, always on hand with facts and figures and details of historic precendents on which most statesmen base their diplomatic moves. He taught Goering that, for those who knew their history; there was little new in diplomacy.

Belgrade was the most important city on the itinerary. Prince

Paul, the Regent of Jugoslavia — King Alexander had been assassinated with Barthou in 1934, the bloodiest of the inter-war years — received Goering in private audience. From their interview they emerged as firm friends. Prince Paul gave him a ring, set with an inch-square emerald, which Goering always wore until his jewels were taken from him. He was overjoyed with the present, but embarrassed because he could not return the compliment on the spot. "We must take a selection of presents with us next time," he told Robert. On his return to Berlin, he asked Markgraf's, the well-known Berlin jewellers, to fit out a small travelling case with golden cigarette cases, rings, brooches. From then on, Robert carried this case with him wherever they went, and Goering was able to produce suitable presents for everybody, as if from a hat. A banquet at the Garde Casino in Belgrade concluded the visit to Jugoslavia. Gritzbach and Milch had spent the time in long conversations with Premier Jeftich. Goering had no doubt that he could count on Jugoslavia. He took time off to enjoy the sun and the beaches of Dubrovnic.

The trip took the party also to Poland, where Goering met Laval for the first time; to Hungary, where he renewed his contact with Admiral Horthy and Premier Goemboes; and to Bulgaria. In Sofia Goering was received by King Boris, and Prince Cyrill arranged a hunt in the Bistrice district for the visitor from Germany. No other Nazi leader had as yet been paid such compliments; none had developed the faculty of talking politics casually and on equal terms with Europe' kings and statesmen. On the surface, Goering's bonhomie, his good-tempered, open-hearted, friendly approach, surprised all who met him. Julius Caesar said that he preferred fat people because they are rarely dangerous. Goering certainly seemed to bear him out. In the Balkans he was a great success.

10

GUNS OR BUTTER

On Goering's return to Germany, Hitler outlined to him his plans for 1936 which would be the year of Germany's destiny. He had decided to take a further step towards his chief political objective, the renunciation of the Versailles Treaty. He was going to end the demilitarisation of the Rhineland. Germany would have to be strong — if only to avoid any "incidents." Goering told him that, in the light of all available information, he regarded the plan as premature. Conversations with Blomberg showed that the Reichswehr was also in favour of extreme caution and delay. But Hitler's word was a command to Goering. He saw Dr. Hjalmar Schacht, to whom the Nazi Government had entrusted the conduct of financial affairs, and Schacht gave Goering an inkling of the economic difficulties of the Reich.

Germany was not poor by any means, Schacht explained, but the country's resources had been swallowed up by the armament industry. He was in favour of making Germany powerful enough to face the Western States on equal terms. That was the purpose of the régime of austerity he had devised; that the aim which he had had in mind when he introduced a strict exchange control at a time when money was freely exchangeable in every country in the world; that was the only national justification for such arbitary acts as the repudiation of foreign loans. But there was a limit to the people's endurance, Schacht thought, and Hitler's demand on German economy went beyond the endurable limits; they obviously aimed at something more than equality with the West. Now there was an acute shortage of fats — there were shortages of most consumer goods — and the ugly companions of rearmament and austerity, hoarding, black marketing, and profiteering, raised their heads.

The shortages were grim but unavoidable under the circumstances, Goering replied. But Schacht need not worry; he would explain to the German people, they would listen to him. Goering was overworked and tired, suffering from the effects of a radical slimming cure. "No fats," his doctors ordered, and he told them, "That is all right with me; that's patriotic now!" Wearily he worked on a speech dealing with questions with which he was not really familiar. If he could find a popular approach, that would get him over all technical difficulties. When he thought that he had discovered a suitable formula, it was arranged that he should make a ceremonial State visit to Hamburg. "I want to address a mass meeting," he demanded. "I want to get the biggest audience ever!"

In the glare of arc lights he mounted the platform. "Party comrades, friends . . ." he began, and patiently allowed the cheers to subside: "I have come to talk to you about Germany, about our Germany. *Germany* —" emphasising every word — "*must have a place in the sun!*" Strength, rearmament, was the way to achieve this aim. "But rearmament," he said, "is only the first step to make the German people happy! Rearming for me is not an aim in itself. I do not want to rearm for militaristic ends or to oppress other people, but solely for the freedom of Germany! Meine Volksgenossen, I am for international understanding. That is why we are rearming. Weak — we are at the mercy of the world. What is the use of being in the concert of nations if Germany is only allowed to play on a comb!" The cheers encouraged him: that was a fine, useful phrase, he thought. Raising his voice, he shouted: "I must speak clearly. Some people in international life are very hard of hearing. They can only be made to listen if they hear the guns go off . . ." Under a hail of "Hurrahs," he adroitly turned to the subject of fats: "We have no butter, meine Volksgenossen, but I ask you — would you rather have butter or guns? Shall we import lard or metal ores? Let me tell you — preparedness makes us powerful. Butter merely makes us fat!" The crowd roared. The wires buzzed. "Goering has done it," a report told Hitler; "he handled the crowd beautifully. He slapped his fat belly and they cheered him when he asked them to go without butter. He is amazing!"

One of the great dilemmas of European policy became manifest: Goering could do nothing wrong in German eyes. He could do nothing right in the eyes of the Western world. No other example demonstrates more clearly the gulf which separates German mentality from that of the West European people. No sooner had the agencies transmitted Goering's speech to Paris, London, and Washington than a storm broke over Germany: "Guns before Butter!" the headlines screamed. It was as if, out of the blue, Germany had declared war. And the press was not far wrong. Goebbel's Propaganda Ministry took up the cue and German economists, reassured about public reaction in Germany, increased the quota of essential raw materials which were diverted from general use to the armaments industry.

Although reports about output of aircraft and tanks were still not encouraging, Hitler persisted in his determination to reoccupy the Rhineland. There would be no opposition from foreign countries, he was sure. Goebbels advised that national unity should be demonstrated by an election. There were now no other parties except the N.S.D.A.P. and elections were a hollow demonstration, but the world, he thought, might be impressed by this democratic procedure. On March 7, 1936, Goering dissolved the Reichstag, "to give the German people an opportunity to approve the first three years of National Socialist policy." As they had no choice, the German people approved. A week later Germany occupied the Rhineland. France and Britain took no action. The Rhineland was, after all, German territory. If the Reichswehr generals, if Goering had been hesitant, Hitler had given them an example of his political prescience.

Goering's admiration for Hitler was unbounded. Enthusiasm ringing in his voice, he challenged the Western Powers in another speech: "If Germany faced a phalanx of enemies, they would not deter us. Perhaps other people have been asleep. Germany has certainly not been asleep. As long as Adolf Hitler lives, Germany cannot be brought to her knees!" With a large entourage, he went to inspect the token forces which had been moved into the Rhineland. A show of strength by France would have sent these few battalions scurrying back across the Rhine. But it was too late — or too early. From London I reported that Britain may be content with protests now, but one day Germany might find that Britain, too, had a few guns up her sleeve.

Encouraged by the success of his first military operation, Goering was resolved to become Germany's leading soldier (after Hitler), as he had been Germany's leading National Socialist and diplomat. At his receptions the representatives of the Luftwaffe were given places of prominence. Even if his air force was as yet not a perfect instrument of war, it could be used as a powerful argument in negotiations with foreign countries. King Boris of Bulgaria, when he returned Goering's visit in August, 1936, was given an inkling of things to come. At a breakfast which Goering gave him at Karinhall, the party looked like a Luftwaffe staff conference. General Stumpff, the Chief of Staff, was there; so were General Albert Kesselring, Colonel Ernst Udet, and many other high ranking officers. Goering wore the new insignia of a Colonel-General's rank, to which Hitler had promoted him. The list of guests included State Councillors, Prince Philip von Hessen, and Gustaf Grundgens, the theatre director, but civilians were overshadowed by the glittering uniforms. The Luftwaffe entered the field of foreign affairs.

To build up Germany's strength while intensifying efforts to gain friends and allies appeared to Goering the ideal way of serving his country's interests. The Olympic Games gave him an opportunity to pursue the second course. Goering provided the most sumptuous entertainments Germany could offer her guests from abroad. His party at Karinhall had the visitors gaping. Foreign reporters have tried to estimate the cost of this party; Goering never considered it — the State paid, anyway. But he personally supervised every detail of the arrrangements. Every day he had a new idea. "I have a plan," he said to Emmy, "which will please many of our 'old fighters' " — as the earliest members of the Nazi Party were called in Germany. It was a costly and complicated plan, but he carried it out. In the grounds of Karinhall he built a replica of the Bratwurstgloeckel, the Munich beer house where he and his friends used to congregate in the old days "Karin often went with me . . . !" he mused. The effort was lost on most of the foreign visitors, who preferred the performance of a monster ballet of beautiful girls, the fireworks and illuminations which turned the Schorfheide into fairyland. But they also commented on the tremendous expenditure which had been made in these festivities.

It was difficult to reconcile this expenditure with the intensified austerity and rumors of impending major decisions on Germany's economic policy. The rumours proved to be correct. From the expensive glitter of his party, Goering went into conference with Hitler and Dr. Hjalmar Schacht. Hitler wanted still more money for armaments. It was for Dr. Schacht to provide it. He wanted industry to stop producing luxury and household goods: "These gentlemen will have to forgo some of their profits!" he declared. "The national interest demands it." Schacht said it was impossible to extract further sacrifices from the German people. "Very well!" Hitler said; "if you cannot do it, Goering will make them toe the line. Goering shall take over!" There would be a plan to make Germany self-supporting, independent of foreign countries, and strong enough to deter the world from interference. It would have to be done within four years. Goering would be in charge of it. But Goering was of two minds. He had neither the knowledge nor the experience to counter expert economic arguments. Schacht he held in great respect and was inclined to believe him. But his own Luftwaffe needed funds and Schacht had been ever slower to provide them. If the Fuehrer gave him a free hand he could make the Luftwaffe the mighiest weapon in the world.

He ordered the experts to design an economic Four-Year Plan — to cover every aspect of the German economy, to allocate a part of the common effort to every individual. In October he accompanied Hitler to Nuremberg to the Parteitag (Party Day), the yearly mass meeting of leaders which had developed into a big public demonstration. For the first time the Luftwaffe flew over the Nuremberg Stadium and the assembled Nazi cohorts in a massed formation of four hundred war planes. Foreign visitors looked up, but they were brought to earth by Hitler's speech. He had decided, he said, to concentrate the country's economic resources. There would be an all-embracing Four-Year Plan: "All must pull together in a common effort to carry out this plan!" The official announcement to give effect to Hitler's decision provided: "Colonel-General Prime Minister Goering takes measures to fulfil the task. He has power to make decrees and the general administrative authority necessary for his task. He is empowered to listen to all, including the highest Reich authorities, all offices of the Party, its branches and organisations, and to issue orders to them." The decree made Goering economic dictator of Germany.

That evening Goering confessed to Emmy that he was a little bewildered by his new job. To be honest — he understood very little about economics. He decided to create a special office for the Four-Year Plan, as the new organisation was named, and to appoint Koerner as its leading permanent official: "Pilli has little to do in the Prussian Ministry, anyway," he laughed; "he can keep an eye on the experts and industrialists." Next day he called a big conference of leading economic experts. It was attended by financiers, industrialists, coal owners, leaders of the business community. Goering asked for suggestions and listened to many impromptu speeches. "It's like a butter dough, this economic business," he told Emmy after the conference; "you have to keep on beating it until it turns to something good!"

It was a tough dough, as Goering soon found out. His rough-and-ready methods had been successful in the Prussian police; they had found response in the Air Ministry and among the Luftwaffe generals; they had pleasantly surprised foreign diplomats. But economics were not so tractable. The simple solutions which he suggested, the drastic measures which he introduced, brought him into sharp conflict with Dr. Schacht, to whom he owed much of his early success. One of Goering's moves was to ask for State funds to acquire an industrial organisation of his own. He bought the Salzgitter Iron Works for the Four-Year Plan and renamed them "Reichswerke Aktiengesellschaft fuer Erzbergbau und Eisenhuette Hermann Goering," to give a visible expression to his personal interest. He accepted a block of shares in the firm, "to encourage other capitalists to make investments," he explained later. To give German industrialists an example of what an industry under his control could achieve, he appointed a friend, Dr. Wilhelm Voss, as manager and ordered him to modernise and expand the firm, regardless of cost. He proceeded to buy up other firms and to incorporate them in the Hermann-Goering Works. His orders to Koerner were to get results: "This is a military operation!"

Dr. Schacht, when I talked to him at Lueneburg, told me about the developments which followed: "It was inevitable," Schacht said, reviewing the situation which arose, "that a conflict should develop between Goering and myself. He used his powerful position in the State to sanction a policy which was draining the resources of Germany beyond repair. To save foreign currency he insisted, for instance, on the exploitation of German low-grade iron mines at stupendous cost. The Hermann-Goering Works operated at a tremendous loss and he called on the State for ever-increasing credits which could never be repaid. To cover up losses, he ordered that other flourishing firms be bought up. Party protégés were put into leading positions to control the reluctant and bewildered experts. The whole thing developed into a gigantic watermelon on which Stupidity, Corruption, and Swindle were inscribed in capital letters. . . ."

Dr. Schacht had been anxious to help his country, but he was disturbed about the dilettante approach to problems as to which he was one of the world's greatest experts. He also recognised Hitler's and Goering's ulterior motives. He offered his resignation. Hitler felt himself betrayed by the expert — one of the few men to contradict him, but he would not accept the resignation. Dr. Schacht told me that from then on the men around Hitler began to regard him as an enemy. The radicals, he was convinced, were after his life. The break came when he refused to accept Goering's authority in economic matters. There was a scene — Goering went to see Schacht at his office. "How can you think big in such a small room?" he asked. Dealing with a topical problem, Goering began by saying, "I order you to . . ." Schacht interrupted, "You can issue your orders only to my successor . . ." Goering's face was red. He let himself into Schacht's chair. "I am sitting in your chair now! I am your successor!"

Goering, however was not in every respect as reckless as Dr. Schacht assumed. Sometimes there was method in his madness — as when he encouraged leading German industrialists to acquire industrial interests in Austria. He provided the funds with which Germany obtained virtual control of the Alpine Montan Gesellschaft, Austria's most important iron and steel works. He suggested that Austria should be supplied with German-produced arms — "even if our Italian friends dislike our competition," he said. With all available means he carried out the economic penetration of Austria, which undermined the independence of the Government of Dr. Kurt Schuschnigg, who had succeeded Dollfuss. His policy later greatly eased the strategic move of the Anschluss.

Goering's quarrel with Dr. Schacht deprived Germany of its outstanding economic expert, one of the few German leaders who retained the confidence of the Western world, an advocate of a moderate German nationalism to which few people objected. Schacht was a close personal friend of Sir Montagu (later Lord) Norman, the Governor of the Bank of England, whom he often visited at his home in Kensington. He also had many friends in the United States, where his mother was born. But Germany's loss was Dr. Schacht's gain. For those who survived the experience, it was an advantage to have been one of Goering's enemies. Like Franz von Papen, Dr. Schacht was acquitted at Nuremberg, where he had joined Hermann Goering again — in the dock. Afterward he told me that he was finished with politics.

Goering devoted all his energies to the Four-Year Plan which outwardly seemed to prosper and to grow. Eventually the Hermann-Goering combine absorbed a large proportion of Germany's industry. It branched out into Austria and Czechoslovakia and gained economic control of the Balkans where Goering had sought markets for Germany. By that time the position was reversed and Balkan industries had to work for Germany. In 1936 and 1937 Goering stumped the country to get support for his economic policy. He explained the more complicated problems in simple words and the people did his bidding. Although he had long handed over police and concentration camps to Himmler, recalcitrant industrialists never forgot that they were dealing with the man who had created the Gestapo and had shown in June, 1934, how he could deal with opposition. His warnings to the "Economic Fifth Column" could not be misunderstood. Goering worked day and night. And though German economy suffered, the Luftwaffe grew.

Milch and Koerner were old friends and co-operation between the office of the Four-Year Plan and the Luftwaffe was smooth. Professor Junkers, Dr. Heinkel, and Claudius Dornier had gone ahead with the development of their aircraft factories. New models were turned out — civilian types at first, but all of them designed for quick conversion into war planes. At a conference with Goering, Milch reported progress: Heinkel's factory in Rostock was working to capacity; a new factory had been built in Marienehe. Their star model was the He (Heinkel) 111. In Bavaria a brilliant young designer, Willi Messerschmitt, of the Bavarian Aircraft Works, was forming his own company — the Messerschmitt Works. His latest model, the Bf 109, would be renamed Me 109. The Do (Dornier) 17 was highly satisfactory. Ernst Udet reported about the excellent development of the Hs (Henschel) 123, an all-metal aircraft with two machine guns. The Ju (Junkers) 86 was also already available.

The Air-Sports Association had become the National Socialist Flying Corps, an S.A. of the air under the command of General Christiansen. At Schleissheim, as in a dozen other centres where thousands of airmen had previously been trained for the Lufthansa, war pilots were now being turned out at great speed. Goering was never satisfied with the numbers of men available as pilots, for the Luftwaffe ground organization, and his air regiments, the future parachutists, to which one of his friends, General Student, devoted special attention. Every means was permissible to increase their number. When the reorganised S.A. under a new Commander, Viktor Lutze, celebrated Goering's birthday by appointing him Honorary Commander of an élite formation, the S.A. Standarte (Regiment) Feldherrenhalle, he accepted gratefully. Next day he ordered that the unit be incorporated in the Luftwaffe to be trained as parachutists. Lutze and the S.A. were not pleased, but the Luftwaffe generals appreciated the gesture.

A big air display and air races were held in Zurich in the last week of July, 1937. German aircraft took part in strength. They proved themselves superior to most types. The German press jubilantly recorded one German air record after another. The Lufthansa was spanning the globe, and its pilots were gaining invaluable navigational experience as well as a knowledge of territories over which they might one day be called to fight. It did not matter now that the world knew about the Luftwaffe. On the contrary. An American airman whom Ernst Udet "kindly" permitted to try his hand at a new Me 109 wrote glowing notices in the American press and declared that he had seen Spitfires in England, but that he preferred the Messerschmitt type any time. Goering rubbed his hands

— that was just what was needed to impress Western statesmen. Most of the leading First War airmen had returned to the German colours. The Richthofen Squadron was again the outstanding formation. Doerning, one of Goering's Jasta commanders, was in command. And the Luftwaffe had already proved its worth in a trial gallop under actual war conditions.

The Spanish Civil War was raging, and Goering had seized on it for his purpose in many respects. In the diplomatic field he was in constant contact with Mussolini, encouraging him to resist British demands for "Non-Intervention." He was determined to go much farther. In a conference with Hitler and Defence Minister Blomberg, it was decided to send a Luftwaffe unit to Spain to fight the Republicans. Heinz Bongarz, the chronicler of the Luftwaffe, describes how already on July 26, 1936, State Secretary for Air General Erhard Milch called a conference at his Ministry. Present were Generals Kesselring, Wilberg, and Stumpff and "a few striking-looking southern types." Milch said: "You all know that the Spaniards, under the leadership of General Franco, have risen to liberate Spain. The greater part of Spain is in the hands of the enemy. The enemy's fleet dominates the sea and makes it impossible for Franco to take his Moorish divisions from Africa to the Spanish mainland. Franco asked the Fuehrer to put at his disposal a transport fleet of Ju 52's and crews to take his forces from Tetuan to Sevilla. . . . General Goering has decided to entrust General Wilberg with this task. . . . Wilberg, you have full powers. . . . For reasons of foreign policy, strictest secrecy is essential!"

Only eighty-five men formed the first contingent of "Special Staff W." Goering gave them twenty Ju 52's and six He 51 single-seater fighters. Disguised as a "Travel Group Union," the party set out in civilian clothes while the planes were flown to Africa. From this small beginning, with secrecy finally abandoned, grew the "Legion Konder," the German Air Force in Spain. By November it comprised sixty-five hundred men; its commander was General Sperrle, whom we shall later meet again. His chief of staff was Colonel Richthofen, a relative of the late "Red Knight." As soon as General Sperrle had gathered sufficient information about modern combat conditions, he was recalled to pass on his experiences to other Luftwaffe officers in Berlin. He was succeeded first by General Volkmann, who was to meet his death in France in the war; later Richthofen took over. Constant changes of personnel on all levels gave a maximum number of Luftwaffe staff their baptism of fire. The Luftwaffe left its mark at Guernica, a foretaste of things to come. When it returned to Germany, its task accomplished, Goering publicly congratulated and decorated his heroes. He was convinced that he had created a fighting force with no equal in the world.

11

CONQUEST BY TELEPHONE

LONDON held the attention of the world in May, 1937. The politicians, if they did not exactly take back seats, were only part of the vast audience which gathered to watch a fascinating spectacle — the Coronation of King George VI. Every country delegated an outstanding personality — its king, premier, or most venerated statesman — to go to London and pay homage to the new King-Emperor. Hermann Goering thought it would be an opportunity for him to present himself to the West as he had introduced himself to the Balkans. He was positive that he would go down as well in London as he had done in Belgrade and Budapest. Joachim von Ribbentrop, the intermediary at whose flat Goering had negotiated Hitler's appointment in 1933, had been rewarded for his services with the post of German Ambassador in London. He was instructed to advise the British Government and Buckingham Palace that Hermann Goering would represent Germany at the Coronation.

The news leaked out, and the late Miss Ellen Wilkinson, the charming red-haired fury of the Labour Party, raised the subject in Parliament, of the German representation at the ceremony: "Can we have a guarantee," she asked of the Foreign Office spokesman, Viscount Cranbourne, "that this country will not be insulted by the presence of General Goering?" There was a scene in the House of Commons; cries of "Why?" "Why?" and "Shame!" and the Speaker called for order. The British press was hostile to the idea and Goebbels' Propaganda Ministry in Berlin announced that "The statement . . . that General Goering was to represent Herr Hitler at the Coronation . . . was premature. . . ." At the Chancellery there was an angry scene. Goering implored Hitler not to allow the "red press of Great Britain" to dictate to him. He would go to London in any event. It was one of the few quarrels between the two old friends. Hitler hurriedly nominated General von Blomberg, the War Minister, as his special envoy. But Goering would not let the matter rest.

On May 11, the eve of the Coronation, Joachim von Ribbentrop nervously paced a small room at Croydon Airport. Half an hour later a Junkers 52 landed with an embarrassing visitor. Hermann Goering had decided to make a personal appearance in London. Unobtrusively he was driven to the German Embassy at Carlton House Terrace, the secret of his visit guarded by arrangements which were a credit to the tact of the British authorities. Ribbentrop, who was already entertaining Blomberg, spent a harassing hour explaining to his chief that public demonstrations were inevitable if he showed his face in public. Goering might do irreparable damage to the German cause at an occasion when Hitler's official representative could obtain much good will. He was shown the newspaper attacks and leaflets calling on all democrats to come out into the streets in protest against Gestapo Goering.

Discreetly the Foreign Office intimated that Goering was not persona grata. A well-known British peer with whom Goering had formed a friendship hurried to the Embassy to dissuade him from any rash move. After a restless night at Carlton House Terrace, Goering gave in. Early in the morning, as the streets were already filling with crowds, Goering drove to the airport, boarded his plane, and, an angry and disappointed man, flew back to Germany. His one and only visit to London had lasted just twelve hours, but it had escaped the notice of the press, and, though Goering's face was red, it was saved. Although I covered the Coronation as a reporter, I was as unaware of his escapade as my colleagues in Fleet Street. The secret had been kept so well that I could not believe the story when I heard it from a member of Goering's entourage thirteeen years later. I sent an inquiry to New Scotland Yard. In reply the Metropolitan Police Office wrote to me: ". . . The Commissioner asks me to say that it is known that Hermann Goering visited this country . . . in 1937 for the Coronation." It was only known to Scotland Yard.

Goering's failure was a favourite topic at Hitler's Tafelrunde at the Chancellery and the cause of much ribbing. Goering was quite

Inspecting the layout of a new aerodrome, Goering, in general's uniform, is surrounded by high-ranking Luftwaffe officers. On his right (with mustache) is General Alexander Loehr, the Austrian who later commanded an air fleet in the attacks on Poland, Jugoslavia and also the Soviet Union.

Paying homage to Adolf Hitler, "the great genius," on his return from Czechoslovakia, which the Wehrmacht invaded in violation of the Munich Agreement, Hermann Goering faces his Fuehrer and entourage, who respond with the Nazi salute. With Hitler are Goebbels and von Ribbentrop.

accustomed to take a joke, even at his own expense. He joined in the laughter. The men at Hitler's table, partaking with good grace in the Eintopfgericht (the one-pot meals of German austerity), were still friendly with each other, but an undercurrent of rivalry had already become apparent. Every one of them now controlled his own empire in the State, jealous of interference, each of them anxious to have the Fuehrer's ear. Goering avoided quarrels diplomatically, but Himmler's autocratic handling of police matters, for instance, and police interference in many fields exasperated him. He complained to Himmler about an incident which involved his wife. Frau Goering, somewhat naïvely and anxious to show Germany at her best, had offered to take Karin's sister, Fanny von Wilamowitz, on a visit to a concentration camp to disprove atrocity stories in the Swedish press. Her private secretary, Irene Schulz, had called up Himmler's office for permission, but Himmler himself had taken the receiver and replied: "Tell Frau Goering not to interfere! My wife has never asked to inspect the Luftwaffe rest homes . . ." When Emmy told Hermann about this rude reply, he reassured her, saying that "people in concentration camps are quite well off . . ." and asked her not to bother. But he told Himler acidly to be a little more civil with his wife next time.

Such personal matters were usually discussed at Hitler's table. One day the conversation was of the courage needed by front-line soldiers, a subject which Hitler often discussed, taking the opportunity to talk about his own feats as a soldier, Ernst ("Putzi") Hanfstaengl, his old friend, broke in: "When I was interned in the United States during the World War, I needed as much courage as a soldier!" Hitler was annoyed, and brusquely ended the conversation. What followed has never been fully revealed. According to the version related to me by Bodenschatz, Goebbels, after Hanfstaengl's departure, suggested that his courage should be tested. For that purpose he devised an elaborate "joke." Goering was to hand Hanfstaengl "sealed orders" from Hitler and send him off in a warplane. In the air Hanfstaengl would find out that Hitler had ordered him to be dropped in Franco Spain with a special message to the German General Faupel. When Hanfstaengl had recovered from the shock, the plane was to land in Leipzig. According to

Ernst Hanfstaengl it was no joke at all. Goering gave him sealed orders. But after the plane had taken off, the pilot admitted that he had orders to drop his passenger behind the lines of the Spanish Republicans.

A storm, Hanfstaengl said, forced the plane to land at Leipzig. Convinced that Hitler, Goering, and Goebbels wanted to get rid of him, he made off, travelled to Switzerland, and then to London as a voluntary exile. The flight of Hitler's best friend created an international sensation, suggesting a deep split in the Nazi hierarchy. Goering sent Bodenschatz first to Switzerland, then to London, ostensibly for conversations with the German Military Attaché, General Wenninger, but really to persuade Hanfstaengl to return. British authorities welcomed Bodenschatz in London. They had no inkling of the real purpose of his visit. During a four-hour conversation at a West End hotel, Hanfstaengl asked Bodenschatz to obtain a written guarantee from Hitler assuring his, Hanfstaengl's safety. But Hitler refused, saying, "I shall not give him anything in writing that he can sell to the British press for five pounds." Goering telephoned Hanfstaengl in London, asking him to return, explaining that "it was only a joke." But Hanfstaengl did not think it was funny at all and remained in exile. He was interned in Britain during the war, and is now back on his estate in Bavaria.

The incident may appear to be trivial, but it illustrates the growing tension, the feeling of personal insecurity in the highest Nazi quarters and the increasing strain on the nerves of the Fuehrer. Big things, they knew, were in the offing. Hitler had formulated his policy for the next year and told them of his plan to annex Austria, to free the Sudeten Germans from Czech rule, "and to obtain the return of Danzig and a passage through the Polish Corridor which separated East Prussia from the main body of the Reich. If necessary, Hitler insisted, he would smash Czechoslovakia and Poland. He ordered the General Staff of the Reichswehr to work out plans for every contingency. Goering was in full agreement with Hitler, but he feared that his objectives — beyond the annexation of Austria — might cause grave diplomatic complications, even war. In spite of speeches which glorified the Luftwaffe and were made in menacing tones, he knew that his air force was not as strong as he implied.

When Lord Londonderry visited him at Karinhall, Goering told the British air expert of Hitler's intentions and asked him to tell the British Cabinet that Hitler had no designs on the British Empire, but Britain would have to give up her traditional policy, which was to prevent the emergence to unchallenged prominence of any single Power in Europe. Lord Halifax, Britain's Foreign Minister, went to see Hitler at Obersalzberg and their interview was acid. Goering arrived in time to smooth things over and tell Lord Halifax what he had explained to Londonderry: "We do not want war — but we want Austria!" he said. Austria was very much his own affair, he explained, he had spent his happiest days in Mauterndorf. Now relations between Austria and Germany were such that he could not even visit the widow of his godfather, Frau von Eppenstein. Moreover, the very first paragraph of Hitler's *Mein Kampf* made the Fuehrer's attitude clear beyond doubt. Lord Halifax replied that Britain would be extremely perturbed if Germany moved against Austria, but Sir Nevile Henderson, a frequent guest at Karinhall, who had a real personal feeling [1] for Goering, was not so outspoken. Mussolini, visiting Germany with his daughter Edda and her husband, Count Ciano, Italy's Foreign Minister, told Goering that he had given up his objection to a German penetration of Austria. The war in Abyssinia and the Spanish Civil War had strained Italy's relations with Britain and France, and Hitler was Mussolini's only friend.

It appeared to Goering that he had cleared all diplomatic obstacles. He entertained Dr. Guido Schmidt, Austria's Foreign Minister, at Karinhall and easily impressed him with his arguments. Only Dr. Schuschnigg obstinately resisted — but the Austrian Chancellor would quickly be brought to heel. Goering gave Hitler the assurance that he could proceed undisturbed. On November 10, 1937, Hitler called a conference which was attended by von Blomberg, von Neurath, General von Fritsch, the Commander-in-Chief of the Reichswehr, and Admiral Erich Raeder, the Commander-in-Chief of the Nazi Navy. Bluntly he told them of his plans: "If necessary," he said, "the question must be settled by force." The Austrian problem must be solved within three months.

To Goering it was a great shock when he discovered that the

[1] Sir Nevile Henderson, *Failure of a Mission.*

Reichswehr, that Blomberg and Fritsch, were strongly opposed to quick action such as he and the Fuehrer contemplated. Hitler was in a rage when he heard of this unexpected opposition: "The Army will do as I tell them!" he shouted. He asked Goering to take a hand. But men like Fritsch could not be "talked round" as easily as Balkan leaders or Dr. Guido Schmidt, and Sir Nevile Henderson, for that matter. "I shall have to break this resistance," Goering said, "even if I have to assume command of the Reichswehr myself." This resolution was the beginning of one of the darkest chapters in German internal politics, of a sequence of events which one would expect to find in a sordid thriller rather than in the history books.

In the summer of 1949 I went to Wiessee (Tegernsee) in Bavaria, a beauty spot which had been a favourite romping ground of members of the Nazi hierarchy since the early thirties. Many famous figures of the Hitler régime still live in these parts as retired gentlemen of wealth and owners of villas and estates. One of the people I visited was an attractive blonde in her middle thirties, tall, vivacious Frau von Blomberg, the widow of Hitler's Minister of Defence — or War. Her part in the tremendous developments which led to the last war is little known. It was a part which she did not seek. It so happened that late in 1937 the fifty-nine-year-old Reichswehr general fell in love with her. She was more than thirty years younger than he, but she gladly accepted his proposal of marriage. Blomberg consulted Goering, telling him that he wanted to marry "a lady with a past." "What does it matter?" Goering said; "we are all men of the world!" Then the War Minister asked Hitler for his official approval of the marriage, which was granted. On January 10, 1938, the wedding took place. Hitler and Goering were witnesses.

Three days after the wedding, a storm broke. High ranking officers of the Reichswehr informed Hitler that they took the strongest exception to the marriage which the War Minister had contracted. Goering investigated the matter and, with the help of the Prussian police, probed the current rumours about the morals of the young Frau von Blomberg. From the Gestapo he obtained a dossier containing grave allegations against the lady. In Nuremberg on April 25, 1946, Gisevius, whom I have quoted before, said on the witness stand that the "... file contained the following information: Marshall von Blomberg's wife had been a previously convicted prostitute who had been registered as a prostitute in the files of seven large German cities; she was in the Berlin criminal files. I myself have seen the fingerprints and the pictures. She had also been sentenced by the Berlin courts for distributing indecent pictures. . . ." Goering handed the dossier to Hitler. With that file the two men realised it was possible to ruin the reputation of Blomberg, and with it to damage the prestige of the Reichswehr as a whole — or, if the Generals wanted to avoid a scandal, to bring them to heel.

As the Gestapo files were being searched, another incriminating document was conveniently discovered and handed to Goering. It was an alleged deposition by a convicted criminal, according to which he had been led into immoral practices by General von Fritsch. Goering had the criminal brought from prison and interviewed him at Karinhall. Then he informed Hitler of the result. Hitler, without much further ado, confronted the Army leaders with these two dossiers. If the Reichswehr was obstinate, he would publish the documents. In a dramatic scene he dismissed von Blomberg. Next he called von Fritsch, whom he received in the Chancellery in Goering's presence. Fritsch, when confronted with the sordid allegation, indignantly denied it. Either he was the victim of a plot or there was a terrible misunderstanding, he insisted. At that moment Goering opened the door of Hitler's study and called the "witness" into the room. He had taken the precaution of holding the criminal who had accused von Fritsch in readiness for the great scene. "That's him!" the man said, pointing at von Fritsch, and was quickly whisked away. Hitler dismissed von Fritsch on the spot. The Reichswehr generals hid their heads in shame.

Now the way to reorganise the Army was clear. Goering staked a claim to the post of Commander-in-Chief, but Hitler had other ideas. He appointed General Walter von Brauchitsch, an experienced officer of the General Staff. Goering had too many jobs already, he said. As his special adviser on Army affairs, Hitler called on General Wilhelm von Keitel, who was known to be in full sympathy with his plans. Not much later it became apparent that the files which were said to have incriminated von Fritsch were five years old and actually referred to a subaltern Army officer, Herr von Frisch. But they had served their purpose. Blomberg and Fritsch, who had opposed Hitler, had been eliminated. The other bewildered Reichswehr generals had been brought into line with Hitler and the Nazi Party. Hitler, to distract foreign attention from the Army crisis, took the opportunity to reshuffle his Cabinet.

By mid-February he was ready to move against Austria. He called Dr. Kurt von Schuschnigg, the Austrian Chancellor, to Berchtesgaden, the first foreign statesman to suffer Hitler's shock treatment. Rudely Hitler informed him that he wanted a Nazi Government in Austria — or else . . . Schuschnigg returned to Vienna, sought support from the British and the French Ambassadors, but received only cold comfort. Goering in the meantime was charged with the execution of the Austrian Anschluss. In his palace in the Leipzigerplatz, he lifted up the receiver and proceeded to take Austria by telephone.

In Vienna he ordered Dr. Arthur Seyss-Inquart, a Nazi Fifth Columnist, to form a government and ask for German troops to liberate Austria. He sent one of his economic advisers, State Secretary Wilhelm Keppler, to the Ballhausplatz, the Austrian Chancellery in Vienna, to deliver an ultimatum to Dr. Schuschnigg and the Austrian President, Wilhelm Miklas. The Reichswehr was moblised. On March 10, 1938, Goering attended a gala night at the Haus der Flieger. He took the British Ambassador, Sir Nevile Henderson, aside to tell him that the Fuehrer, incensed by an attempt of Schuschnigg to rig a plebiscite for the independence of Austria, had ordered the Reichswehr to march. When the Czech Ambassador, Mastny, also a guest at the Haus der Flieger, heard of the German move, he hurried to Goering to ask what his intentions were with regard to Czechoslovakia. "I give you my word of honour," Goering said, "that we have no designs on Czechoslovakia. You can rest assured about that." In Nuremberg Goering explained that his word of honour had referred only to the events of the following day. Later that night he was again on the telephone. Three men held themselves in readiness in Vienna to receive Goering's instructions — Seyss-Inquart, Keppler, and General Muff, the German Military Attaché. Here are parts of the conversations which he conducted:

GOERING (to Seyss-Inquart): What's the news? Has Schuschnigg resigned or have you anything else to report?

SEYSS-INQUART: Schuschnigg has cancelled the election. The position is very difficult.

GOERING: The Nazi Party must have complete freedom of action at once. I want a report about execution of this order by 7.30.

SEYSS-INQUART: Yes, of course.

GOERING: I am here in the office of the Fuehrer. I want Muff to call me at once. I also want to talk to Keppler.

Later Goering talked to an employee of the German Embassy in Vienna:

I want a report about the formation of the new Cabinet within an hour!

GERMAN EMBASSY: That is quite all right. Keppler is bringing a list of nominees.

GOERING: I want Fischbeck to get the Ministry of Economics and Trade.

GERMAN EMBASSY: Obviously.

GOERING: Kaltenbrunner shall be Minister of Security; and then the Ministry of Justice — that's quite clear?

GERMAN EMBASSY: Yes, yes.

GOERING: Mention the name!

GERMAN EMBASSY: Your brother-in-law, Dr. Hueber, isn't it?

GOERING: Of course.

There followed a telephone conversation between Goering and Seyss-Inquart, who said:

The situation is as follows — the President has accepted Schuschnigg's resignation. I have suggested to the President that I should be Chancellor. As regards the Party, that will take another three or four hours.

GOERING: Under no circumstances! Things are moving now. Tell the President to hand over government to you at once.

Half an hour later, Goering told Keppler:

Listen, the position is as follows — Schuschnigg has resigned.

Seyss-Inquart has been appointed, the Party, S.A., and S.S. are ready as auxiliary police. . . . The dies are cast.

Later, Goering told General Muff:

Tell Seyss-Inquart to get on with the job quickly. The best thing is for President Miklas to resign.

General Muff: He doesn't want to. He does not give in to force. He remains sitting in his office!

Goering: All right. I hear he has fourteen children. I am not surprised he wants to stay.

A little later, Keppler told Goering:

Now we have a Seyss-Inquart Government.

Goering: Splendid! Now listen! Seyss-Inquart is to send the following telegram to us. Write it down: "The provisional Austrian Government . . . sees its main task in restoring quiet and order in Austria and urgently requests the German Government . . . to help avoiding bloodshed. For that purpose it requests the German Government for earliest dispatch of German troops."

Goering spent a sleepless night. Next morning he was again on the telephone to talk with Prince Philip von Hessen who had gone to Rome to maintain contact with Ciano and Mussolini.

Goering: Listen, Prince. I have talked to the Fuehrer. He is going to write a letter to the Duce. Tell the Duce the German troops have orders not to go beyond Innsbruck. I have talked to the Fuehrer on the telephone. He was marvellous. He feels closely linked to Mussolini.

Hessen: A Swastika is already flying on the Austrian Consulate here. And, incidentally, the King told me that Colonel Beck [the Polish Foreign Minister who was on a visit to Italy] has told him that twenty-five thousand Jews have asked for passports in Vienna. The view here is that it's best to open the frontiers for a while so that the whole scum gets out . . . !

Goering: All right, but not with any foreign currency. The Jews can go, but they will kindly leave their money behind, which they have only stolen.

The next day, March 13, between 9.15 and 9.55 A.M., Goering was on the telephone to London, speaking to Joachim von Ribbentrop.

GOERING: Well, you know that the Fuehrer has entrusted me with the conduct of the Government while he is in Austria. I wanted to inform you there is indescribable jubilation in Austria. You can hear that over the wireless . . .

RIBBENTROP: Yes, fantastic, isn't it?

GOERING: Yes, the march into the Rhineland was nothing in comparison with this jubilation of the people. It is so that, apart from the Jews in Vienna and part of the black ravens, the Catholics, there is nobody who is against us. . . .

RIBBENTROP: So the whole of Austria is for us?

GOERING: The Fuehrer thinks that you should explain matters to the people over there. It is completely false to assume that Germany has issued an ultimatum.

RIBBENTROP: I have explained that to Halifax and Chamberlain already.

GOERING: You can tell them that Schuschnigg wanted to rig the election. Seyss-Inquart has questioned officials who said that even the number of yes and noes had been determined in advance . . . the most shameless manoeuvre ever. . . . Conditions were grotesque! Imagine, only a few days ago there was a house search at my sister's, who is the wife of the new Austrian Minister of Justice. And they have taken pictures of the Fuehrer from her and of myself, her own brother. The British press has not written anything about that, have they?

RIBBENTROP: Was the Fuehrer very moved?

GOERING: Yes — he has gone through difficult days. . . . Incidentally, Ward Price is with him in Austria.

RIBBENTROP: Yes, I have read Ward Price's article this morning.

GOERING: That interests me because he is close to the Fuehrer.

RIBBENTROP: Yes, I know. The Fuehrer has turned to him and asked, "Is that pressure . . . can you call that force, what you see here?"

GOERING: Yes, marvellous! And the weather is beautiful here.

Blue skies! I am sitting on my balcony, wrapped in blankets and drinking my coffee. After that I must make a speech, and the birds twitter. . . .

RIBBENTROP: Marvellous!

The telephone conversations were recorded by the machines which Goering himself had installed in Germany. As he was speaking, German troops completed the occupation of Austria. Hitler had set foot on his homeland for the first time since he had left it as a penniless vagabond. When he returned to Berlin, profusely greeted by his faithful paladin, it was Goering's turn to go on a triumphal tour to the annexed country. In Linz he made his first big speech to the Austrians—his subject an Austrian national characteristic, Gemuetlichkeit, the untranslatable word which connotes the frame of mind of happy, carefree people. "We have great plans for Austria. There will be power stations, a new autobahn, armament works, new industries, harbours, social measures. Unemployment will be banned completely. But the time has come to finish all this Gemuetlichkeit. Now you must work hard!"

By the time Goering reached Vienna, the Austrian Nazis were on the loose; the Jews exposed to terror, grimmer than any to which German Jews had been subjected. Dozens were taking their own lives every day. The foreign press recorded the grim happenings. The London *Times* said later: "We have before us the credible report that since Herr Hitler and his forces entered Vienna, some seven thousand Jews have committed suicide in that city alone." Goering replied to the accusations in a wireless statement in which he said: "We don't like Jews and they don't like us. We will make them glad to go away. I cannot help it if the Jews do away with themselves. I cannot put a policeman behind every Jew to prevent suicides!"

Goering had treated the Austrian problem as if it had been his own private affair. The success of his manoeuvres had strengthened Hitler's hand in his relations with Mussolini. Now the Fuehrer went to Rome to thank the Duce for his support. Ribbentrop had been recalled from London and had taken over from Baron Neurath as Germany's Foreign Minister. Goering took life more easily. He went on a hunting holiday to Rominten, visited Obersalzberg, where his new house had been completed, and left politics alone. His departments carried on without him. His mind was on other things. Although his *Essene National Zeitung* began to show an interest in the Czech question, he was concerned with private affairs — there was the problem of his youngest brother Albert, whom he had met in Austria for the first time in many years. Albert, he told Emmy, had been dabbling in film affairs — "rather undignified," Goering thought. He was not a member of the Nazi Party, which was not, in itself, very important, but there were reports that he had made derogatory remarks about Hitler and the National Socialist movement, and that was embarrassing. "It may suit the Fuehrer to have his half-brother run a restaurant in Berlin," Goering said, "but I neither want a public quarrel with Albert, nor do I want him to lead this sort of life. A job will have to be found for him!"

The next day Magda Goebbels appeared at the Goering home in tears — she could not bear life with her husband any longer, she told Emmy. Goebbels was compromising her with his affairs with other women. The whole of Berlin was talking about his latest girl friend, Lyda Baarova, a Czech actress. Magda had decided to get a divorce. Goering took a serious view of this matrimonial conflict. He implored Magda to hold out — to avoid a public scandal. It was really a matter for the Fuehrer's attention, he said, and advised her to fly to Berchtesgaden and consult Hitler. Goebbels never forgave Goering for this piece of advice to his wife, which involved him in an embarrassing controversy with Hitler. And Goering marked down Goebbels as another immoral character. The relations of the two men received a jolt and they were no longer friendly after that.

Hitler was at this time immersed in the study of documents which Ribbentrop had prepared. They dealt with the problem of Czechoslovakia, which the Fuehrer had decided — to use one of his stock expressions — "to solve in one way or another." Goering knew what was in Hitler's mind, but he was rarely consulted about "Case Green," the General Staff's code name for the invasion of Czechoslovakia. Once an inquiry about Luftwaffe matters in connection with "Case Green" reached him. Absent-mindedly he passed it on to Bodenschatz who, in turn, passed it on to the Air Staff. It was obvious to the adjutant that his chief was not in the mood to discuss either strategy or diplomatic details. A personal matter of far greater consequence held his whole attention. It was a delicate subject in more than one respect. Among Goering's friends it was an open secret that one of his dearest wishes was to have a family of his own. While he was still a struggling politician and married to Karin, they had noticed signs of embarrassment and frustration at his failure to have an heir. Sometimes he had blamed his wife's delicate health. On other occasions he frankly admitted to himself that the injury which he had received in Munich in 1923, his slow convalescence, the pains which he had tried to relieve with morphia during weary years of exile, the morphia habit from which he had only been cured with difficulty, were the real causes. So far it had all been very regrettable — and no more.

But once in power and at the peak of political achievement, he began to look at it from another angle. Hitler was a lonely, isolated figure, difficult to picture as a family man. Eventually the Fuehrer's mantle might fall on him. From this thought it was but a small step to consider further possibilities, the more distant future. One day he might be able to hand over the reins of Germany to his son. One day the world might remember him as the founder of a Goering dynasty. As the years went by, it was more than just an idea to toy with. It became an obsession, a purpose, a mission in life. And now this great dynastic project was about to become reality: Emmy would present him with his first child. He looked up to her with admiration as if she were about to perform a miracle. His gratitude was unbounded. His friends and adjutants quickly realised that they could escape the avalanche of his orders, the fury of his reproofs, as soon as they managed to introduce the subject with a tactful inquiry about the date of the "great event." His secretaries were busy working out plans. They argued that the Goerings were about to accomplish not only a dynastic act, but also a political duty — to provide the country with a "human incident" of which it was greatly in need. The birth of a child to the "First Lady of the Reich" would be a welcome distraction and relief from the pressure of political developments.

Emmy Goering in the meantime was cheerfully expecting the happy event. Her sister Else was with her. Her two sisters-in-law, Paula Hueber and Frau Olga Riegele, were there. Ebba Johannsen, the actress, one of Emmy's closest friends, was in attendance. But the reins of the household were firmly held by the incomparable Cilli who did her best to reduce the anticipation of this "State occasion" to tolerable proportions. "I don't care whether this child will inherit a thousand-year Reich or the whole world — it must be born first, and to that end the mother needs peace!" Cilli was like that. She was not awed by high Nazi dignitaries. She had known Hitler since 1930, and she, at least, had not changed since those days.

In the small hours of June 2, Emmy gave birth to — a daughter. If Hermann Goering was disappointed that she had not presented him with a son, he certainly did not show it. Like any other father, he had paced the floor in his own apartments for hours, waiting, waiting . . . Now that Cilli gave him the news, he cried like the baby who had just been born. Outside the house people had been waiting for hours. It was only with difficulty that Goering was prevented from rushing to the balcony to make a personal announcement. He was as yet blissfully ignorant of the ugly rumours which originated with the gossips in Hitler's entourage. He knew nothing of the tales which swept Berlin, all Germany, and soon penetrated beyond the frontiers of the Reich — that he was not the father of this child.

Almost exactly twelve years later I met his little daughter on the island of Sylt where her mother had spent most summers in her own childhood and where she had taken Edda for her first real holiday since 1943. We had a few days together, swimming in the North Sea, wandering through Westerland. I got to know and like the child. The likeness of this tense, attractive girl and her late father is so striking as to discredit these rumours most effectively. Yet they persisted, and later resulted in an incident of profound political consequences.

Soon after the birth the first presents for the little girl began to arrive. Cradles in prodigious numbers were dispatched to Karinhall. Congratulations came from all over the world. From London, among many others, Lords Halifax and Londonderry ("He was part of the household," Emmy Goering told me) sent telegrams. I think there was genuine joy in Germany. Many people reasoned that the German Government could not be thinking in terms of war if Hermann Goering was preparing to bring up a daughter. The christening ceremony was arranged in the traditional Goering style. The child had three godparents: Adolf Hitler, Cilli, and Pilli

Koerner. She was named Edda — obviously after Mussolini's daughter, the Countess Ciano, who had recently spent much time in the Goering home and whose German friends were mostly good-looking Luftwaffe officers of Goering's staff. History has since turned many somersaults and not the least surprising was the break between the Cianos and the Goerings. After Ciano's deflection from the Axis cause and the publication of his diaries, his name was anathema to Goering's friends. The hatred is so intense that Emmy Goering will no longer have it now that her child was bearing Edda Ciano's name: "Actually," she told me, "I was going to call her Ebba — after Ebba Johannsen; also because of the Ebba tales of ancient German history. But Hermann thought it was a clumsy name and we compromised on Edda."

That same month Goering proudly announced the birth at a meeting of the Goering clan. Two hundred members of the family met in Berlin. Goering delighted in such occasions. Here he was in his best form, more jovial even than usual, even though his bonhomie had a tinge of benevolent condescension such as might be expected from the chief of the clan. Had not one of the Goerings noted in the elaborately produced family history, "Oh, that there may arise at last the hero whom the name of Goering has missed for centuries"?

The Ministry for the Four-Year Plan in the meantime had to work out its own salvation. Hurriedly Goering signed a decree which made all Germans liable for labour service. As soon as Frau Emmy was on her feet again, it was time for a holiday and Sylt was the destination. Photographers hurried to the scene to be sent away by the guards. Hermann was bathing in the sea and quite well aware of the stir which pictures of his tremendous torso in bathing trunks would have caused. From Sylt the couple went for a visit to Denmark where Emmy's old chief and friend, Gustaf Grundgens, was playing *Hamlet* in German on the original site of Elsinore. While Emmy and the baby returned to Sylt, the Czech crisis was developing and Goering thought it would be wiser for him to return to Karinhall. Marshal Balbo came for a short personal visit and Sir Nevile Henderson had asked to be received. Horthy of Hungary, perturbed about rumors of new German plans, was anxious to hear what would be his reward if he acquiesced in the German annexation of the Sudetenland and the break-up of Czechoslovakia. Even Boris of Bulgaria hurried to Karinhall to get first-hand information about the project.

Yet these were melancholy days for Hermann Goering. It was nice of Henderson to have faith in his conciliatory attitude. It was flattering for him to be consulted by Horthy and Boris. But Ribbentrop was handling this matter and Goering had to divert his guests with a hunting expedition into the thickets of Rominten. They went away without knowing much more than before. Goering, distressed, suffered a physical setback. His glands swelled — and his staff showed him a report about the interest which his illness created in England. He was pleased to hear that the *Daily Herald* had published a detailed medical analysis about the lymphatic gland which troubled him. Hitler's doctor, Morell, concocted pills for him which eased the pain.

As the Czechoslovakian crisis moved to a climax, Goering was determined not to remain completely out of the picture. He gathered his strength and, fortified by the pills, was able to get up and take his part in the portentous political moves. His main contribution was an attack against the West to warn them from any interference with Hitler's plans in the East. In Nuremberg he delivered a speech which culminated in the thundering declaration that "our Rhineland frontier defences are impregnable!" He railed against the "pygmies of Prague" and reminded British statesmen that it became them ill to speak about German terror methods while the "whole Colonial Empire was held together only by the lash." He ridiculed the Runciman peace mission to find an amicable solution of the Sudeten problem — poor Lord Runciman was later even attacked from the Allied side for having played into the hands of the Nazis.

Goering's boisterous speeches hid a genuine fear of war. He went to see Hitler and begged to be allowed to go to Munich where the great Four-Power meetings were to take place. He was not only afraid of a serious loss of prestige if he were to be left behind, he was determined to counteract Ribbentrop's incalculable temperament and hatred of Britain. Actually Goering's part in the Munich negotiations was small. German diplomats never had any doubt that Chamberlain and Daladier would buy peace at the price of the

Sudetenland. On October 1, Goering publicly proclaimed his joy at the settlement. He was genuinely relieved. But when the German Army moved into the Sudetenland, he thought that the Luftwaffe should play its part. Into a battle without opponents he sent his crack parachute regiment, the former S.A. Standarte Feldherrenhalle, which descended from the air on Karlsbad, the Czech resort where King Edward VII once took the waters. That was just the right place to try to lose a little weight.

12

"I SAY WHO IS A JEW!"

Much of what Hitler said and did can be traced back to impressions of his early days in Vienna. Hermann Goering often heard him talk about Dr. Karl Lueger, the Austrian politician who forced Emperor Francis Joseph to appoint him Mayor of the great Danube city. Lueger, a devout Catholic, made a reputation for himself with a violent anti-Jewish campaign which gained him many supporters. But he disappointed his followers when, having used their votes to cement his position, he abandoned his anti-Semitism. Challenged about a number of Jews in whose company he could be seen at all times, he peremptorily declared, "It's for me to say who is a Jew!"

Goering did not resent the fact that he was credited with this remark. As Reichstag President, he had signed the anti-Jewish Nuremberg Laws which reduced German Jewry to the status of pariahs. But after the war he declared that the Jewish problem never really interested him. Karin did not like Jews; he did not like them; but he did not share the "acute physical discomfiture" which Goebbels claimed to feel in their presence. Neither did he really appreciate Hitler's constant preoccupation with the problem, and, as to Julius Streicher, the violently anti-Semitic Gauleiter, Goering was certainly not one of his friends. It was customary, indeed obligatory, in the Party to include attacks on Jews in public speeches, and Goering always conformed with this practice. But he had never been hostile, or even unpleasant, in his personal contact with Jews. Erhard Milch he had saved from the embarrassing consequences of his Jewish descent. For Frau von Eppenstein, who had received him in Mauterndorf with open arms, he was full of sentimental affection. Emmy kept asking him to save some of her former colleagues, Jewish actors, from the barbaric provisions of the Nuremberg Laws which threatened their livelihood. At her request he had even wrested Jews from the grip of Himmler's men — however difficult it was to approach the S.S. leader on matters of this sort.

Bodenschatz, who had in the meantime been promoted to the rank of General, and had been put in charge of the ministerial office, Goering's big secretariat, told me that his chief constantly passed on to him requests for intervention on behalf of Jews. Bodenschatz did what he could, but when it became known that Emmy Goering was amenable to such requests, their numbers grew rapidly. "We had better put up a sign that my office will help all Jews!" Goering told her laughingly, after she had tearfully begged him to save an old friend, a famous Vienna actress. "You are going to get Himmler after me!" he added. Emmy told me that she spent many afternoons in consultations with Gustaf Grundgens, plotting, as she said, the rescue of Jewish actors. I have in my possession a dozen sworn statements which testify to the truth of her claim. "In every case," she said, "Hermann did as I asked him — even if I called him out of a conference to help people destined for deportation to a concentration camp!"

Goering actually took a cynical view of the problem — principles did not worry him. But, as he put it, he was a realist. And reality in Nazi Germany was violently anti-Jewish. He was in Munich on November 8, 1938, taking part in the annual meeting of the Nazi leaders in commemoration of the 1923 putsch and in the traditional, ceremonial march to the Feldherrenhalle. At 7.30 P.M. he boarded his private train for the return trip to Berlin. He did not know that in his absence Goebbels had risen at a dinner of the Nazi leaders to announce that a Jewish refugee, Herschel Grynspan, had made an attempt on the life of Ernst von Rath, the Counsellor of the German Legation in Paris. Grynspan's family had suffered terribly from the hands of the Nazi and the young Jew had taken his revenge on the first German official whom he encountered abroad. Von Rath, Goebbels said bitterly, had died of his wounds. In a fierce speech, which was broadcast over the German network, he demanded that the Jews of Germany should be made to pay for this crime. Perfect propagandist that he was, he did not leave anything to chance. The Party and the S.S. were called to avenge the life of the German diplomat. As Goering and his entourage were speeding toward Berlin through the night, General Bodenschatz noticed fires in the city of Halle. The conductor told him that Jewish synagogues were burning all along the route, so were Jewish shops and department stores. Anti-Jewish riots had broken out all over Germany.

In Berlin next morning Goering demanded a report about the savage consequences of Goebbels' orders. In what has become known as the "Crystal Night," the West End of Berlin was turned into a shambles. There was not a shop whose windows had not been smashed. The damage which the S.S. had done was aggravated by the mob, who had used the occasion to plunder the shops — Jewish and others — indiscriminately. To Goering this seemed a shocking waste of the country's economic substance. He was not concerned with the Jews, but he telephoned Goebbels and complained bitterly about this move: "It's easy for you to create riots. But I am responsible for the German economy and the German economy suffers from your reckless speeches and actions." He called a conference to deal with the situation. "The Jews must pay for this . . ." Goebbels demanded. "If they must pay — let them pay in form of a fine!" Goering replied. It was decided to impose a fine of one billion marks on the Jewish community. Goering was told that the insurance companies would be called upon to pay for the damage and were determined to pay in order to avoid general loss of confidence. As the conference wore on, Goering got angrier and angrier until he shouted: "Incredible — the problems you have created! I'd rather you had killed two hundred Jews than allow all these valuable goods to be destroyed!"

Over thirty Jews had been killed, seven hundred synagogues were destroyed. Among the looted shops on the Berlin Kurfuerstendamn was Markgraf's the jeweller who had supplied Goering with many valuables. It had been stripped of all its contents. "I want the police to recover the jewels!" Goering told Reinhard Heydrich, the Chief of the Gestapo. He told the representative of the insurance companies, who bitterly complained that the loss amounted to five million marks: "You pay out — but the Jews will not get the money. The State will take it!" When the insurance man shook his head in despair, Goering cross-examined him and forced him to admit that the companies had made a total profit of six million marks during the last year. "I cannot understand what's bothering you," Goering said. "As things are — you have made six million marks profit and have only five million marks to pay out. Now if an angel in my somewhat corpulent shape appears and allows you to keep a million — you ought to be grateful!" Goering left the conference exhausted. The German Jewish community had received a mortal blow. It was the beginning of the end. Emmy, when he arrived home, confessed that Hitler had sent her an angry letter, requesting her not to intervene on behalf of Jews any more! All communications of that sort would have to be passed on to his office. "Hitler was never very friendly with me after that," Emmy said. "Anyway, after 1938 he seemed to change. I did think a lot of him — but I have come to the conclusion that he was not himself after 1938. Whether he was ill or not — I do not know!"

Hitler, in fact, had undergone the first of three operations to his vocal cords. Dr. Morell, his physician, an expert on venereal disease, whom his friend and photographer, Heinrich Hoffmann, had introduced to him, was in constant attendance. He prepared drugs and injections, used Hitler almost as a guinea-pig. Hitler had implicit faith in Morell, but his staff was perturbed about the influence which the doctor gained over the Fuehrer. Goering himself was not fit as he had been in previous years. The volume of his work had grown so much that he was forced to neglect one branch to deal with another. For weeks sometimes, a Luftwaffe general told me, he would not be available to deal with the air force. Economists and industrialists said the same about the Four-Year Plan. For long periods on end, Goering did not show his face in the Ministry of Economics.

Small things took on big proportions. Emmy had engaged a girl called Martha Maeder as a nurse for little Edda, and received a call from Party head offices requesting her to enter the girl as a Party member. "How can I do that," Emmy asked, "if I am not even a member myself?" Martin Bormann, who often deputised for Rudolf Hess at headquarters, heard of the conversation and challenged Goering. Goering was furious. "I shall not tolerate any interference in my private affairs!" he shouted. But the matter was brought to Hitler's attention. "Goering's wife not in the Party? Incredible!" Goering would not do anything to aggravate his

Fuehrer. He quickly arranged for Emmy to join and get the Party number of an old member who had died. The Party, at the time, had over seven million members. Emmy's number was 744,606.

Such incidents weighed on Goering's mind, which was getting as tired as his body. He tried to keep going with tonics and pills to restore his energy. His hunting weekends began to last longer. He flew to Rominten or to the Vienna Lobau to devote himself to his favourite hobby. His adjutants shook their heads when they found it difficult to arouse his interest in affairs of State which were becoming even more pressing. As Hitler drove inexorably toward "solutions" of the most explosive problems, Goering was not at hand to implement vital Cabinet decisions. He neglected his personal affairs as well as his official duties. He spent much time in his art gallery. For hours he discussed involved art deals with Kunstdirektor (Art Manager) Walter Andreas Hofer, a well-known expert whom he engaged as a full-time custodian of his treasures at Karinhall. With Hofer's help and advice, he acquired new works of art, arranged exchanges with museums in Germany and abroad. He sold pieces which he did not want, bought others. Jewish-owned art treasures were confiscated and objects of "modern art," which he disliked, were exchanged for his beloved Lukas Cranachs and similar works which were more to his taste. The two men gained the reputation of very artful dealers.

But new acquisitions and expenditures on houses and estates exhausted Goering's resources and the State funds. While the world computed the fortune of "the richest man in Europe" — as he was described at the time — the managers of the Deutsche Bank were sitting in conference to discuss how to deal with his overdraft of five and a half million marks. None of them dared to tell the Minister and they decided to postpone action until the figures had reached seven million. It is said that Goering knew about the position, but cunningly let matters slide because he was sure that he would never be challenged. By the end of February, 1938, he realised that not even his hunting expeditions were restoring his vitality. He spent long periods in bed at Karinhall and officials brought papers to his bedside for signature. His glands hurt, his weight increased, his blood pressure rose. His doctors suggested a long holiday and he decided to go to the Italian Riviera. In his special train, accompanied by Emmy and his usual entourage of friends, aides, and secretaries, he went to San Remo.

The sea air quickly restored his vitality. He and Emmy enjoyed themselves bathing and motoring through the Italian countryside. Goering's interest in diplomacy revived. Since his Luftwaffe had helped Franco toward victory, he was anxious to meet the Spanish General, and to discuss with him problems arising out of the new political situation which a Fascist Spain was bound to create in Europe. One of his pet strategic schemes was a German-Spanish alliance which, in the event of war with Britain and France, would enable German troops to march through Spain, rush Gibraltar, and seal off the Mediterranean life-line of the British Empire. "I shall take a boat and travel to see Franco," he told Bodenschatz, whom he ordered to make arrangements for the voyage. Passages were secured and he was already on the high seas when Ribbentrop hurried to Hitler to complain about this threatening interference in his field of foreign affairs, "Please stop Goering!" he requested. Hitler, by now convinced that Ribbentrop was a "second Bismarck," sent a wireless message, requesting Goering to return to Berlin at once; bigger things were afoot! Reluctantly and angry, Goering abandoned his trip and obeyed the Fuehrer's order. Back in Germany, he found the Czech crisis at its peak. He went to Berchtesgaden where Hitler and Dr. Emil Hacha, the Czech President, were in conference — if this repetition of the Schuschnigg treatment could be called a conference. Goering's chief contribution to the tragic interview, which heralded the end of Czech independence, was to produce a syringe and to bring Hacha back to consciousness when he fainted under the impact of Hitler's attacks.

Although "Case Green," the conquest of Czechoslovakia, had been accomplished without his help Goering accompanied Hitler to Prague. He inspected fifteen hundred Czech aircraft which had fallen into German hands, a welcome addition to the Luftwaffe forces. Back in Berlin, he hailed Hitler in an enthusiastic speech: "Mein Fuehrer," he said, "how can we express our thanks for what you have achieved . . . the tremendous, the great power which you have created, we swear we shall never let go — come what may, come what will!" Then he returned to San Remo. Reporters were waiting and he told them, "The Axis is stronger than ever," and, referring to the rising anger of Britain, he added, "Britain is just a barking dog which never bites!" From San Remo he went to Rome on a State visit. With Hitler in control of Austria and Czechoslovakia, Germany's prestige stood high in the land of her Axis partner.

Mussolini and the King united to pay homage to Hermann Goering and his wife. Italian air regiments were on parade. The Italian press described him as the greatest German — after Hitler. The King and Queen gave a dinner for them, and Emmy spent an afternoon in the apartments of the Queen. Mussolini was glad to see Goering; their relations had always been cordial. While the Duce never overcame a lurking prejudice against Hitler, he liked the big, bustling ex-airman and his wife. Emmy told me that her husband and the Duce spent hours in conversation without aides or interpreters. "They talked to each other like two soldier friends," she said. Mussolini's German was near-perfect. He addressed Goering as "Excellency" and Goering called him "Duce." After their consultations they joined Emmy and mostly talked about art, in which Mussolini was as interested as Goering. Often there were new paintings to be admired; often Mussolini had a surprise for Hermann Goering. "With me the Duce chiefly talked of the theatre," Emmy said, "alas, it is the only thing I understand." Once he asked her to recite to him a famous passage from *Nathan der Weise* — the fable of the ring which entitled the owner to one wish, and one wish only.

The Italian trip was one long, almost uninterrupted pleasure. The only disappointment was a hunt which the King of Italy arranged for Goering at his estate in Positano, south of Rome. Goering arrived to discover shooting arrangements which seemed very odd. A dozen high stands had been erected for the hunters and Crown Prince Umberto. To his horror he saw that hundreds of deer had been collected and were being driven past the stands by a company of Bersaglieri, the Italian mountain troops. The King and the Crown Prince shot to their hearts' delight. The King shot one hundred and thirteen animals. The Crown Prince's score was as high. Goering did not fire his gun; that was not the kind of hunting he enjoyed. He was angry when he heard years later that a picture of the slaughtered deer had been published in an American magazine in juxtaposition with a picture of the starved and murdered inmates of Belsen concentration camp — with Goering's smiling face linking the two. "Have I really deserved that?" he asked.

Marshal Balbo, the Governor of Italy's African colonies, invited him to visit Tripoli to discuss the contingencies of desert warfare — just as General Erwin Rommel, travelling as a "tourist," had done the previous year. It was a possibility which Goering envisaged in conjunction with his Gibraltar scheme. He made Marshal Balbo a present of a German Fieseler-Storch observation plane, and in return received a parting gift of ancient Roman vessels. He returned to Germany invigorated and ready for real work.

If, owing to his illness, he had taken little interest in "Case Green," he was soon made aware that Hitler counted on him to play his part in the handling of "Case White," the operation against Poland. On May 23, 1939, in a long private talk with the Fuehrer, the first in many months, Hitler told him that Danzig, which he claimed from Poland and about which the whole world was talking, was not the problem at all. He, Hitler, was determined to smash Poland. Returning home that evening, Goering looked a changed man. "Unless I can perform a miracle, war is inevitable," he told Emmy. Turning to her as he had turned to his mother (in his letter on the eve of the First World War), he was depressed, full of grim foreboding. Emmy Goering, though anxious to show that her husband was determined to preserve peace, was very reticent about this conversation. But I gathered that once more Goering reviewed his whole life. "Surely," Emmy said to me eventually, "he had nothing to gain and everything to lose by war!" All his ambitions had been realised. Hitler, at the beginning of 1939, had promoted him to Field Marshal, the highest rank in the German Army, and presented him with a precious diamond-studded baton. He was, Emmy said, happy at home, among his art treasures; extremely fond of little Edda, for whom he had built a minature house in Sans-Souci style, on the Schorfheide. He had everything in the world a man can wish for — and frankly acknowledged it.

General Bodenschatz, who knew Goering better than most people, explained to me that his chief was in a grave dilemma. As a diplomat he regarded it as his task to avoid conflicts. As an Air Minister and Luftwaffe Commander-in-Chief he felt in duty bound to get the Air Force to the highest pitch of perfection, whatever his personal inclinations and hopes. As a spokesman of the Third Reich he firmly believed that his strong speeches helped to deter potential enemies from interfering with the plans of his Leader, whom he was prepared to follow —even unto death, as he said. But as the country's economic dictator he had his doubts about Germany's ability to wage a long war. From all these conflicting emotions emerges a Goering whom it is extremely difficult to analyse, a man whose words and actions were contradictory and confusing, reflecting the contradictions and confusions in his own mind.

Though he was not present at the long conference in which Hitler developed in detail his plan for the attack on Poland — Generals Milch and Keitel and Admiral Raeder represented the armed forces — he received a transcript of the speech. He called Erhard Milch, Bruno Loerzer, Ernst Udet, and Karl Bodenschatz to obtain the latest information on the state of the Luftwaffe. Relying on Goering's unquestioning confidence, isuing orders in his name, operating through Koerner where the Luftwaffe was dependent on industrial support, Milch, Udet, and Loerzer were the brains trust which advised Goering on Air Force affairs. If his Nazism was a reflection of Karin's sentiments, if his Gestapo activities were the work of Rudolf Diels — the trinity of Milch-Loerzer-Udet represented Goering as the builder of the Luftwaffe; Milch as the organiser, Udet as the technician, and Loerzer as Goering's best friend and confidant.

Behind these men was the growing staff of the Luftwaffe, the reorganisation of which he had approved on Milch's suggestion a little earlier. The young General Hans Jeschonneck was the new Luftwaffe Chief of Staff. The force had been divided into three groups — East, Headquarters Berlin (Commander General Albert Kesselring); West, Headquarters Brunswick (Commander General Felmy); and South, Headquarters Munich (Commander General Sperrle, the former chief of the Kondor Legion). General Zander commanded a group detailed for air-sea warfare. Bodenschatz was in charge of the Ministerial Office of Goering and concentrated on Luftwaffe affairs, and General Ruedel was entrusted with home defence. In the Rhineland a Luftverteidigungszone (Air Defence Zone) had been organised. Goering was convinced and

Goebbels announced that it matched the "impregnability" of the West Wall, the Siegfried Line.

To reinforce the Luftwaffe organisation, Goering called on the German aircraft industry to prepare for production of eighteen thousand first-line aircraft, so that, he said, "Germany will henceforth need no Munich or international negotiations to lay down the law." As this was easier said than done, he arranged a series of conferences to prepare his staff, the aircraft industry, and the ministries concerned in his drive, for the tasks ahead. Here was Hermann Goering at his best — rousing, witty, and cynical at the same time, radiating energy and brooking no contradiction. Behind his harshest words his listeners could detect boyish enthusiasm which was often infectious. But sometimes it went hand in hand with an obstinate refusal to recognise realities. First he addressed representatives of the O.K.W. (High Command of the Wehrmacht), the Luftwaffe, and the economics ministries — Milch, Koerner, and State Secretaries Neumann and Dr. Landfried, the two latter his economic advisers; he called in Captain Tschersich, his old platoon corporal, now a high ranking staff engineer. General Thomas, in charge of the Office of War Economy, and Colonel Conrad, Commander of the Hermann-Goering Regiment of the Air Force, were also present.

His instructions, briefly, were to restrict export of aircraft to Italy and the Balkans, to exploit the Czech industry to the limit. "A considerable change in the political situation has occurred," he explained. To Karinhall he called the leaders of the aircraft industry. "Gentlemen," he told them, "the situation is grave. Jews are agitating for war everywhere. England does not seem to want war, France does not either. But America sees an opportunity of making great profits. You have heard of a great shadow industry in Britain. What's the outcome? They are not even able to cope with current production, far less with the shadows. . . . What about the project of Nuffield, the automobile king? The last report suggests that he is just about to decide where he is going to build a factory. . . . We have achieved great things . . . in quality we are superior. The Luftwaffe is ahead of the British and the French Air Forces. . . . Now I must ask you gentlemen to see that this superiority becomes permanent and definite. . . . Gentlemen! This is my personal opinion: Where-ever it comes to blows, wherever Germany must fight . . . the chance of victory is ours. But it is dependent on our strength, on how we mobilize our strength, on the determination of each of you to accept the advantages and disadvantages of the position."

The German industrialists were not as happy about the prospect of war as was generally assumed. Goering had cut down their profits on armaments deliveries. They preferred to make easy money by supplying the home market. There were even voices which began to doubt the wisdom of the régime and to disassociate themselves from Nazi foreign policy. Such people Goering had in mind when he continued: "Believe me, gentlemen, once Germany has lost another war, it will be no good for you to come and say — 'But I did not want this war, I have always been against it, I was also against the régime, I never wanted to be in this.' They will dismiss such assurances with sneers. You are Germans — whether you want to be in it or not does not interest these people two hoots. . . . And allow me another word — what does your production for the home market mean in comparison with the interest of the nation? Such considerations reveal a very small mind. What the hell does it matter to you whether you produce aircraft instead of bedchambers — as long as Germany is able to stand the test of battle?" With a sneer at Britain, he said: "We must maintain superiority over a democratic enemy without leadership where a Lord Nuffield can say, I build what I like or nothing at all! That can be said in England; thank God, it cannot be said in Germany! And I hope God will preserve our enemy in this frame of mind! One more word about development — I still have no strato-bomber which can bridge space at a height of twenty miles and reach America, if necessary!"

It was one of the many speeches in this vein which Goering made in these days, speeches not recorded in the press and only revealed after the war when Germany's secret archives were found. In the intervals between his conferences Goering received visitors from abroad. His old friend Prince Paul came and he showed him a new ring with six diamonds set in platinum, ideally matching the one which the Jugoslav Regent had given him. In a more serious vein they discussed Jugoslavia's attitude in the event of war. "I can rely on Paul!" he told one of his aides after the interview. His next visitor was Count Ciano, with whom he had a first disagreement when he discovered a reluctance on the part of the Italian Foreign Minister to support Hitler's policy.

Goering went to Berlin to tie up a few loose strings in his private affairs. Frau Elisabeth von Eppenstein came to see him and, at the office of lawyer Dr. Carl von Berg, formally made over Castle Veldenstein to him and his daughter Edda; at last the dream castle of his boyhood was his. To Veldenstein he sent builders to make it ready for early occupation. Then he sent Bodenschatz to Munich to tell the Ballin sisters to learn English quickly. He sent them passports and a large sum in dollars to enable the two Jewish ladies and their families to emigrate. He knew life in Germany would be hard for Jews — even if they had saved his life in 1923.

News reached him that Britain had sent a high Foreign Office official, William Strang, to Russia to hear Stalin's views on the growing German threat to Poland. He also received an unmistakable warning from Lord Halifax that Britain was determined to resist aggression. When Lord Halifax pointed out the tragedy of Germany's failure to understand the British mentality, Goering said: "I'd love to go to England and make them understand! But I cannot risk them throwing a dead cat at me!" New hope rose when President Roosevelt's "Cash and Carry" project was endangered by antagonism in the Senate: "As long as Germany is impregnable in the West," Goering said, "nothing can happen to us!" And he went on a tour of inspection of the Air Defence Zone in the West.

Air General Karl Koller, who became Goering's last Luftwaffe Chief of Staff, discussed the Air Defence Zone with me. Koller, who was captured toward the end of the war and spent over a year as a prisoner in Britain, now runs a small farm near Munich and also works at a big garage. He was present when Goering inspected the Zone. It was a great disappointment to the Commander-in-Chief of the Luftwaffe. Koller and other staff officers felt compelled to point out to Goering that there were many flaws in the scheme which he had all too hurriedly approved. True, a long line of gun emplacements covered the whole frontier, but no single sector could withstand a concentrated assault for long, even if hastily reinforced by mobile guns, for the rapid movement of which new roads had been built by the Labour Organisation of Dr. Fritz Todt.

With good grace Goering accepted the criticism. But the war was already in full swing before the reorganisation could be completed and anti-aircraft defences concentrated near individual targets rather than along the whole line. Undismayed, Hermann Goering changed from his rôle of Luftwaffe Commander to that of economic chief, and went on a tour of inspection of the Ruhr industries. He travelled down the Rhine in his new yacht, *Karin II*, his valet Robert at the wheel. Of course, he did not breathe a word about the newly discovered weakness in Germany's western air defences. On the contrary. On his return to Berlin on August 9, 1939, he made a public report about his experiences. "I have used my trip," he said, "to look after the security of our most important industrial region. . . . I have inspected personally all measures for the defence of the Ruhr territory. I shall look after every single battery which it may be necessary to install. The Ruhr will not be submitted to a single bomb of enemy airmen!"

"*No Bomber Can Reach the Ruhr!*" the German headlines announced. "Yes," added Goering in another speech, "if an enemy bomber reaches the Ruhr, my name is not Hermann Goering; you can call me Meier!" It sounded very funny to German listeners. From his speeches Goering went into conference with Hitler. He told him that he still had hopes of preventing the entry of Britain in the war, even if Poland were attacked: "And if Britain does not march, France certainly will not!" Hitler replied that Ribbentrop had not been idle in the diplomatic field either. Britain's attempts to win Russia over as an ally were doomed to failure: Russia was on Germany's side. Goering, his closest associates told me, was mute in admiration before Hitler's genius when he heard that negotiations for a Nazi-Soviet Non-Aggression Pact had reached an advanced stage. "The Fuehrer is unique!" he said. But he could not hide the grave doubts rising in his mind. In spite of his weaknesses, Goering was a moralist. To see Hitler shake hands with the arch-enemy would be a painful experience. His doubts received a startling support. Hitler called him to a private talk, from which he emerged in acute distress. The Fuehrer told him that Fritz Thyssen had left the country and had published a letter warning Germany of the consequences of Hitler's policy. Thyssen wrote that he would await the end of Nazi adventures elsewhere. It later appeared that

Thyssen had gone into voluntary exile to France. To Goering it was a devastating blow. He regarded Thyssen as one of the builders of Nazi success. In him he had lost a personal friend on whom he had counted in many difficult situations. Thyssen was not only his friend, but also his banker. It was impossible, as Hitler did, to regard him as an enemy of the Reich. Goering was depressed, quiet, and thoughtful. With the determination of despair he pursued his own last diplomatic move to prevent the imminent war against Poland from developing into a world war.

Emmy Goering told me that she was in Wenningstadt, Sylt, where she had a little villa of her own, when, without previous warning, her husband arrived on a hurried visit. Though he seemed preoccupied and under great strain, they spent a few happy hours together and Emmy assumed that he had come to inspect Luftwaffe aerodromes on this most northerly island of Germany, as he had done previously. She bathed in the sea, built sand castles for little Edda while waiting for her husband to return from his work. Not with a single word did he mention the real nature of this work and only much later did Emmy realise that he was engaged — to use his own words — in an attempt to crown his career as a diplomat.

While Emmy was enjoying the hot August summer sun, Goering was in conference with Mr. Birger Dahlerus, a Swedish industrialist and relative of his brother-in-law, Count Eric von Rosen. Some time before, Mr. Dahlerus, who had extensive business interests in Germany and Britain, had offered Goering his services in a last attempt [1] to prevent the outbreak of a world war. The burden of Dahlerus' efforts was to convince Goering that Britain was deadly serious in her determination to stand by her guarantee to Poland. When he first discussed the matter with Dahlerus, Goering developed his own theory that there was no need for Britain to feel threatened by a German move eastward. Danzig and a corridor through the so-called Polish Corridor was all that Hitler wanted. Goering called Mr. Dahlerus as a witness in the Nuremberg trial to prove that he had been actively engaged in negotiations to preserve peace. These negotiations started in Wenningstadt on August 7, when Dahlerus introduced a number of British big businessmen to Hermann

[1] Birger Dahlerus, *The Last Attempt.*

Goering. They were to confirm Dahlerus' contention that the British business community supported the British Government's firm stand. These men could dispel any notion that might have been entertained by Goering's business friends that the "International of Industrialists," regardless of nationality, would always co-operate; that British industrialists would rather continue "business as usual" and give Hitler a free hand in Poland than support their own Government's policy.

Goering, in a white summer suit, hot, bothered, anxious, arrived to shake hands with such powerful, if little known, British magnates as Mr. Charles McLaren of John Brown & Co., Mr. S. W. Rawson, the Sheffield manufacturer, Sir Robert Renwick, Mr. Brian Mountain, Mr. C. Frederick Spencer, another Brown & Co. director, and Mr. T. Mensforth, member of a big electrical firm. The visitors listened carefully to Goering's exposition, although he did not tell them much more than they already knew. They had, of course, informed the British Foreign Office of the Dahlerus project, had been briefed by experts, and were in fact unofficial but trusted representatives of the British cause. Lord Halifax and Mr. Chamberlain never had much hope of Mr. Dahlerus' intervention, but they would not leave any avenue unexplored which might lead to a preservation of peace.

The road which Goering himself travelled in these negotiations was perilous because Ribbentrop looked upon his move as another attempt to interfere with his own conduct of diplomatic affairs. Hitler, though he eventually received Mr. Dahlerus, was contemptuous of Goering's efforts — and of Britain. Goering, harassed, seeing his efforts fail, drowned his fears and doubts in too much red wine. He drank more than he ever had before. The supertonic effect of the pills which he was taking to maintain his strength and to keep awake during long all-night sessions produced a glassy look in his eyes. Sometimes he appeared to be in a state of intoxication. Hitler did not seem normal either, said Dahlerus. With a twisted mouth and staring eyes he shouted that he was not afraid of Britain, that he would build "U-boats! U-boats! U-boats!" and "War planes! War planes! War planes!" Several times Dahlerus flew to Britain to report on the progress of his mission and returned to Sylt and

Berlin to carry on negotiations with Goering, while Bodenschatz flew between Sylt and Berchtesgaden where he reported to Hitler about the latest developments.

At Nuremberg Dahlerus admitted that at the time he thought he could contribute something to prevent a new war. "Had I known what I know today, I would have realised that my efforts could not possibly succeed," he said. What Mr. Dahlerus did not know was that Hitler had made up his mind to attack Poland within a few days. The judgment of the Nuremberg Tribunal includes a passage referring to Dahlerus which said that ". . . it was not until September 26, after the conquest of Poland was virtually complete, that he first realised that Goering's aim all along had been to get Britain's consent to the German seizure of Poland."

So what? Goering's surviving friends asked me bluntly when I discussed the incident with them. Of course he knew that Hitler was intent on attacking Poland. Of course he carried on conversations, even after August 22, when Hitler issued his final instructions for the attack. But Goering's aim, they say, was simply to prevent German-Polish conflict from developing into a world war. Was that not an honourable endeavour on the part of a man who was committed to his Leader and his country? The negotiations, they add, were begun before Hitler had finally made up his mind. The conclusion which can be drawn from the Dahlerus incident is a sad one for Goering. Whether he played Hitler's game or was genuine in his negotiations, his last major diplomatic intervention was a failure. Ribbentrop, on the other hand, with whom he competed for diplomatic honours, registered a success. In negotiations in which Goering had no part, a German-Russian understanding was reached.

On the morning of Tuesday, August 22, 1939, the German people picked up their copies of *Der Voelkischer Beobachter* which announced in two-inch black streamers underlined in red: "*Non-Aggression Pact Germany-Soviet Russia. Reich Foreign Minister Ribbentrop in Moscow on Wednesday*." Underneath were pictures of German troops manning the Siegfried Line. "Those who want to storm the West Wall," said a caption, "run into death." If Goering had failed to free Hitler's hand for the conquest of Poland, Stalin had succeeded. Himmler provided Polish uniforms for a number of concentration camp inmates who were ordered to "attack" the

Goering as a diplomat regarded himself as one of the architects of German-Italian friendship. Here he is with Count Ciano, Mussolini's son-in-law and Foreign Minister. The Goering-Ciano friendship came to an end during the war when the young Italian began to oppose the Duce's German policy.

Near Berchtesgaden, during the war, Goering takes a walk with members of his Luftwaffe entourage. With him is Colonel von Brauchitsch, his military aide (extreme left), General Karl Bodenschatz, then Chief of his Ministerial Office. On the right, General Karl Koller, at the time Chief of Operations.

German radio station at Gleiwitz on the Polish frontier (and who were immediately killed by S.S. men, once they had carried out their mission). Seizing on this manufactured incident, Hitler ordered the Wehrmacht to move against Poland. Goering had his private train fitted out as mobile headquarters and travelled to Potsdam. The train was put on a siding near the Luftwaffe Headquarters. There on Sunday, September 3, at noon, he was still in conference with Birger Dahlerus when Koerner arrived with a transcript of Mr. Chamberlain's speech. It put an end to whatever hopes Goering may still have entertained about keeping Britain out of the war. As units of the Luftwaffe in lorries passed his train, he could hear them singing in the distance: "Leb' wohl mein Schatz — wir fahren gegen Engelland" (Farewell my treasure — we are driving against England). War was upon the world.

13

WAR

London was under a hail of German bombs when I escaped the shrapnel of the barrage into King's Cross underground station, where hundreds of people patiently waited for the All-Clear siren. An old Cockney next to me was saying to his friend: "Have you heard? They have brought down Goering!" The reply was instantaneous. "You bloody fool! That wasn't Goering what they brought down; that was a barrage balloon!" The cryptic conversation conveyed a little of the general British attitude toward Goering. To most people his name was synonymous with that of the Luftwaffe, which was no joking matter in these days. At the same time he was the ideal subject for wisecracks such as the British invariably produce at the tensest moments of their lives. Goering was not really hated in Britain — can the British hate at all? His girth, his big round face, his medals and uniforms, were a godsend to the cartoonists. But even the wicked brush of David Low suggested good-humoured banter rather than deep-felt anger with the Commander-in-Chief of the Luftwaffe. His private photographer, who accompanied him on most trips to the front, failed to present him as a really martial figure.

Withal, Goering and his Luftwaffe were Britain's main concern as soon as war broke out. Yet Goering's part in the war was greatly overrated. Unlike Winston Churchill, for instance, who emerged from the clash of arms as a world figure, Goering's stature shrunk — yes, even physically — as the war went on. In victory and in defeat, he seemed to disappear against the formidable background of world-shaking events. Of all the estimates which I sought from knowledgeable British statesmen, only that of Sir Archibald Sinclair, the wartime Air Minister, and as such Goering's British counterpart, conforms with the result of my own investigation: "Goering," Sir Archibald said to me, "seems to have been at the summit of his achievement when war broke out and then to have been eclipsed by the German High Command. . . ."

War, as it did to all of us, rudely tore Hermann Goering from the groove in which his life proceeded. It came at a time when his health was deteriorating. At the meeting of the Reichstag which was called to launch Hitler on his Polish adventure, he made a brave show, saying in a concluding speech that his "faith in victory in this war, which has been forced on Germany to end the injustice of Versailles, was unshakable!" Hitler named Hermann Goering as his successor in case he himself should meet a soldier's death in battle — but the announcement was chiefly designed to impress the German people with the hint of the common danger which Hitler was ready to face. The public appointment as Germany's Number Two, however, officially confirmed the position which Goering held in practice. It flattered him, but it also soon involved him in bitter intrigues. Heinrich Himmler, Martin Bormann, Joachim Ribbentrop, Joseph Goebbels, had long been watching Hitler's health, speculating on his stamina, secretly preparing themselves for the rôle of Germany's future Leader. Goering's designation was a setback to their hopes. Before he went off to war, he reviewed the Luftwaffe regiment which bore his name and which he had developed from a small beginning of five hundred men. He confirmed Colonel (later General) Conrad as Commander of the unit which he decided to enlarge into a full division. A company of the regiment under Major (later Colonel) Waldemar Kluge became his military guard, additional to the Begleitkommando (personal guards) of civilian security officers, drawn from the S.D. (Sicherheits Dienst — Security Service), an offshoot of the S.S. He engaged a nurse, Christa Gormanns, to accompany him in his streamlined, armour-plated train and keep a check on the tonics and medicines which he took in increasing doses. Emmy, he decided, and the child should live at Haus Goering, his villa at Obersalzberg, or at Veldenstein.

The Air Force organisation had been brought to a pitch of perfection by Erhard Milch, who now combined the office of a Secretary of State in the Air Ministry with that of an Inspector-General of the Luftwaffe. General Stumpff was put in charge of home defence. Goering's favourite "young man," the Chief of Staff Hans Jeschonneck, was promoted to Major-General, although not yet forty years of age. Lieutenant-General Ernst Udet became Generalluftzeugmeister (Luftwaffe Production Chief). The new Air Fleet IV was put under the command of General Alexander Loehr, former chief of the tiny Austrian Air Force. Like Kesselring and his air fleet, he was attached to the German armies mobilised against Poland. Bruno Loerzer commanded an air division under Loehr, but spent little time with his unit. He was almost inseparable from Goering, whom he accompanied everywhere. Goering's heart was not in the novel technique of Army-Air-Force co-operation, which became the key to the sweeping success of the German attack. An old horse does not easily learn new tricks and he had his doubts about the strategy which Panzer General Heinz Guderian had developed from the theories of the French General, Charles de Gaulle.

Hitler did not go to the front at once, as he had said in the Reichstag, but stayed in Berlin. When the Fuehrer Headquarters was finally established, he accepted Goering's advice about the location and chose Rastenburg, in East Prussia, not far from the Rominten hunting lodge. Goering entrusted General Bodenschatz with an important mission — to be his personal liaison officer at the Fuehrer Headquarters to listen to all conferences and to pass on Hitler's instructions to him. When I visited Bodenschatz at Erlangen, near Nuremberg, where he now lives with a friend, he came to meet me on his bicycle. "I wanted to order a car for you," he said, "but I have no telephone. Funny, ten years ago I had two cars and a Junkers plane at my disposal; I was talking on half a dozen telephones at the same time. . . ." Bodenschatz remained in his new liaison job, and close to Hitler, for the next five years. It was a difficult position which virtually forced him to serve two masters at the same time, even when they were no longer in harmony. Whatever Hitler expected of Goering and the Luftwaffe, he told Bodenschatz. The bluff, jolly officer did not cherish his new duties, although they placed him in an envied and privileged position in the higest councils of wartime Germany. As his personal aide Goering chose the young Colonel Bernd von Brauchitsch, whose father was Commander-in-Chief of the Army.

Goering spent much time travelling between Potsdam and Berlin, between Berlin and Karinhall, or the Obersalzberg at Berchtesgaden. He left routine office work to Koerner and Dr. Gritzbach, but still managed to interview people from many walks of public life. In 1945 Goering's desk was ransacked and parts of his diary and correspondence relating to this vital period were found. But Goering, unlike Goebbels, who meticulously recorded his every move and word in a diary, was not making many notes. Stenographers took down the salient parts of official conversations, but his personal diary contained little except names or dates, official and private business mixed in happy confusion. But he did make a note of such incidents as, for instance, the request from the former Polish Military Attaché, Major Schimanski, to save his wife who was cut off in Poland and afraid of falling into the hands of the advancing Russians. Schimanski approached Emmy Goering. "You must get her out," Emmy pleaded with her husband. A passage was arranged for Madame Schimanski, who travelled through wartime Germany in a sealed compartment and safely reached Switzerland. "It's worse than treason, what we are doing!" Goering remarked to Emmy, who was not sure whether he was joking or angry with her.

Next day, as the Allied press recorded the progress of the German Army, using the name of Goering as a substitute for that of the Luftwaffe, saying that "Goering" attacked a Polish aerodrome here, a Polish tank formation there, Goering was in Berlin in heated arguments with Alfred Rosenberg. Hitler relied on Rosenberg for advice on Eastern affairs, but Goering disliked and distrusted the man. For a time during the First World War, Rosenberg was a student at Moscow University. "I would give anything to know," Goering commented when he heard about it, "what this fellow Rosenberg did in Russia in 1917." But now Rosenberg was in charge of special units, called "Einsatzstab Rosenberg" (Action Staff Rosenberg), which were organised to travel in the wake of the Wehrmacht, with the task of safeguarding enemy art treasures. "We must get a list of everything that falls in the hands of your staff," Goering demanded of Rosenberg.

For some time the distribution and disposal of objets d'art in Germany had occupied Goering's interest. The State had taken over art collections belonging to Jews as ownerless objects. Goering for a time had a virtual monopoly on these art objects.

Many of them found their way to Karinhall until Hitler decided also to collect paintings, sculptures, tapestries, for a new museum to be built in his home town Linz "after the war." Hitler's competition had been a constant worry to Hermann Goering, even when only German art objects were under discussion. But now Rosenberg would be able to put his hand on inestimable Polish treasures. Goering wanted to make sure that Karinhall should get its proper share.

In the meantime, the Wehrmacht, including Goering's Luftwaffe, in a Blitzkrieg such as the world had never seen before, rolled across Poland. The clockwork precision of the German operations impressed the Western world. But General Loehr wrote of this first real war test of the Luftwaffe: "At the outbreak of war, we felt tense, torn between confidence in victory and the torturing question whether we would employ the right methods at the outset and how much we should have to pay in losses to learn our lesson!" In a similar staff treatise about the Polish campaign, Goering eventually underlined a passage which recorded that the Luftwaffe had launched out into terra incognita, and that only victory in Poland had dispelled apprehensions and doubts about the wisdom of this strategy.

Wondering whether the Luftwaffe would stand up to the test, Goering studied a report about the strength of the Italian Air Force — twenty-seven hundred front-line planes and twenty thousand officers, N.C.O.'s and men. If there was trouble in the West, he would have to call on them in an emergency. The emergency did not arise — and Italy was as yet not prepared to enter the war. Loehr's doubts, anyway, were unjustified. Stukas (Sturzkampflieger — dive-bombers) played havoc with the Polish factories, with troop formations and aerodromes. The German Panzers moved inexorably forward. Long-range reconnaissance Dorniers (Do 17) ranged deep into Polish territory. New Heinkels (He 111) and Dorniers (Do 215) carried destruction into Poland. Junkers (Ju 87) joined in the battle, the standard Me 109 fighters and a new twin-engined type (Me 110) harassed the Polish troops. Luftwaffe experts noted with satisfaction that the Polish Air Force of roughly one thousand front-line machines had been distributed over the whole country — in a way very similar to the original false conception of the German Air Defence Zone West. At no single point was it able to withstand the massed onslaught of the German formations. The tranquillity on the Western Front encouraged Goering. In a long talk with Hitler, he came to the conclusion that the war in Poland may be over quickly enough for him to approach Britain with another peace proposal before the Luftwaffe had clashed in real battle with the R.A.F.

On the Polish front it was an unequal fight. On a visit to the Fuehrer Headquarters, Goering was in high spirits. Revelling in his technical knowledge and tactical experience, though by no means infallible in his strategic views, he lectured the Army generals on matters which were really outside his province. Keitel, Reichenau, and Blaskowitz, who were in command of the ground forces, did not like it. But as a Field Marshal, he was their senior. He wore a simple uniform. The big three-tiered cupboard where he kept his decorations in Karinhall was locked. ("How many?" Bodenschatz retorted laughingly to my question: "Who can say — I had over a hundred and fifty myself.") Goering, during the war, only wore his Pour le Mérite, the Iron Cross First Class, and the Golden Air Medal. "Good job, too!" commented Robert. As I talked to him he picked up a German newspaper with a reference to Goering's medals. "It was not as easy as all that," he explained. "I was responsible for the decorations he used to wear. Now say, for instance, that he went to a ceremonial dinner and I did not know that the Swedish Ambassador was there. If I forgot to pin his Swedish decoration on, there was bound to be a diplomatic incident. They might think that the Marshal had left it off purposely because he was angry with Sweden. I could not risk that sort of thing, so I always demanded a complete list of guests at any dinner which the Chief attended."

Goering's idea of an airman's conduct was still founded on his concepts of 1918 — he must be ruthless in combat, but chivalrous to his opponent. "My boys," he jovially told the German war pilots, "when I was engaged in a dog-fight, I fought to the finish; but when I had my opponent on his knees, I helped him up and shook hands with him!" It was not idle talk on Goering's part. On September 8, only five days after the outbreak of war, he tried to prove his sincerity in an unusual conversation. A British Whitley was hit on a leaflet raid and the crew bailed out near Gotha. The two pilots were Pilot Officer Tommy Thompson and Squadron Leader "Wank" Murray.

"Wank," now Group Captain S. S. Murray, in command of an R.A.F. station in the Midlands, told me what happened next. Though he was not named, his experience has already been described.[1] After a night in the cells at Gotha Aerodrome, he and Thompson was driven to Berlin. Next day they were told that they would be taken to meet an important personality. Passing a wood, they came to a siding, were led past railway carriages to a clearing, and into the presence of a figure whom they recognised at once — Field Marshal Hermann Goering. Goering got up, returned the salute of the British airmen, and offered his hand. Group Captain Murray said that he was impressed. Goering was extremely friendly. Speaking through an interpreter, he said at the outset: "I am not going to ask you questions of a military nature. I know you are not permitted to answer them!" He was most anxious to know what the people of Britain thought about the war, what Murray himself thought about it.

Murray was noncommittal. Goering smiled as he told him that Russia would join Germany in the conquest of Poland. "The war will be over soon; you will be home by Christmas!" The Luftwaffe, he said, would look well after the R.A.F. prisoners. "I know that men who fly are, by nature, least adaptable to imprisonment." When Murray asked for his flying jacket to be returned, Goering promised to see that this was done. (Twenty-four hours later he was handed his jacket.) With a salute Goering ended the interview which had lasted half an hour. He seemed pleased that he had been able to demonstrate to British airmen how he felt about the encounter of the Luftwaffe with the descendants of his World War I opponents. He wanted to convince these boys that they could expect every consideration.

No such consideration was required, or even thinkable, in any other sphere of action. If refugees crowded the roads — why, the obvious thing was to create panic among them to obstruct the retreat of the enemy and facilitate complete destruction of its armed forces.

[1] Lieutenant Paul Brickhill and Conrad Norton, *Escape to Danger*.

If a vital target was in a densely populated area — too bad! These Poles should have thought of that before they challenged the might of the Luftwaffe.

That was Goering's view when Warsaw was encircled and Hitler asked him for a supreme Luftwaffe effort to end the siege quickly and thus save costly and lengthy ground operations. The main target was the Okecie Airfield, from which Polish fighters operated in the defence of their capital. Next in importance were the railway stations. Goering approached the job in a familiar manner. "I think," he said, "if we threaten to bomb them to bits they will give in!" He ordered that a warning be given to the diplomatic corps in Warsaw to leave before the German attack. It would also impress the Poles, he thought. "Let's give the commander of the city one more chance to surrender or else tell him to evacuate the civilian population!" he suggested. While Goering made public fun of British "leaflet raids" on Germany, he asked Goebbels to reinforce his demands for the surrender of Warsaw by a leaflet campaign of his own. It was of no avail. Polish airmen fought heroically against an overwhelming superiority and the morale of the Polish people stood up against the worst punishment. They were determined to fight to the last drop of blood, and when the war of nerves failed, Goering gave General Kesselring the order: "Attack!"

Former Field Marshal Kesselring is now serving a long-term prison sentence as a war criminal at Werl in the British zone of Germany. The terror bombing of Warsaw was one of the charges against him, but his conviction was for atrocities against Italian civilians three years later. The Luftwaffe operation against Warsaw which he directed served another useful purpose. To Goering it seemed an ideal opportunity of showing the British what to expect if they insisted on continuing the war. Kesselring himself was up in the air after every attack. He maintains that the attack was designed to knock out Warsaw as a centre of communication and to destroy large stocks of war material in the railroad freight yards. He insists that the main damage to Warsaw was done by Army shelling at which his airmen, just as Goering had done in the First World War, operated chiefly for the purpose of reconnaissance.

From a visit to Hitler's train which was the nerve centre of the Fuehrer Headquarters, Goering returned to Berlin because the imminent victory over Poland brought economic problems with it. He knew about Himmler's plans to Germanise the conquered country, to destroy the Polish nation as a whole and to obtain living space for German settlers in the rich agricultural areas. These plans he regarded as long-term theory which he might study at some later date. For him it was more important to get Polish workers for the German industries, which the armed forces had drained of man-power. "We must get a million Poles to work in Germany," he declared. With General Thomas, the Reichswehr economic expert, he also discussed plans for the exploitation of the Polish economy. "We shall get their factories and their agricultural produce. We shall have plenty to eat soon!" He signed an order giving the Wehrmacht power to sequestrate all economic resources of Poland. "We must get every ounce out of this war!" he said.

Economic decisions were forced on him at a rate which would have confused even a trained expert. Goering was signing documents so fast that at the day's end he often mopped his brow trying to remember what he had decided in the morning. Nazi Party officials, some of them old friends, queued at his office, all anxious for a share in the spoils. Germany would have to administer Poland; the country would be divided into districts; industries would have to be revived — there were hundreds of lucrative jobs going and Hermann Goering could dispense them among his friends. Among the Gauleiters (district leaders) and State secretaries, he had now only friends. Pilli Koerner dealt with the avalanche of requests and most other problems, often as bewildered and overwhelmed as his chief and by no means his equal in the quick grasp of unfamiliar problems. He worked his fingers to the bone for Goering. Koerner's decisions were sometimes even more haphazard than Goering's, and while overimpressed outsiders admired the apparent efficiency of the German administration, in Berlin it was often impossible to get order into the chaos of day-to-day measures and orders. The left hand of Goering did not know what the right hand of Rosenberg was doing. The Wehrmacht operated in competition with the S.S., who were entrusted with all-embracing security measures. "Foreign exchange experts," "economic trustees," vied with each other to put their hands on the Polish resources. But if there was chaos and dissension inside the Nazi hierarchy, the effect of these disunited operations was the same as if a swarm of locusts had descended over poor Poland. While the Nazi heads disagreed about who should have what, they were most careful, one and all, to leave nothing behind.

In the Nuremberg trial Goering gave an account of his economic policy in Poland, but in this account he actually described the measures which were only taken many months after the surrender of the Polish Army. Only then did his experts find time to sort out all details. He said that his plan was to strengthen rather than to weaken Poland's economy — for German use, of course. He intended that Polish raw materials should be converted into manufactured goods on the spot, but as Polish factories could not produce what Germany wanted, steel, copper, tin, and other raw materials were taken to Germany to be used for the war effort.

While his ministries and his staff dealt with these questions, Goering kept a wary eye on the Polish art treasures which the Einsatzstab Rosenberg was taking over "to safeguard them"; that is, to prevent wanton destruction and small-scale looting. An agreement was reached between Goering and Rosenberg according to which collections abandoned by owners who had fled the country, valuables found in churches, objects confiscated from Jews or museums, were taken to Koenigsberg in East Prussia or to Berlin. "We must wait for the Fuehrer's decision about their final destination," Goering said. He asked Rosenberg's expert, Dr. Kajetan Muehlmann (who was eventually attached to the staff of Hans Frank, the Nazi Governor-General of Poland), to report to him about all details. He wanted, truly, to be in the picture when it came to the distribution of the loot. Muehlmann showed him the order which he had prepared and which was eventually published (Verordnungsgesetzblatt G.G.P. II S. 61) and pointed his attention to Paragraph 2, which ordered the Poles to report all objects of artistic, cultural-historic, historic importance, originating from 1850 or earlier. "To be reported are," said the order, "(*a*) paintings; (*b*) sculptures; (*c*) antique furniture, porcelain, glass, gold and silver objects, Gobelins, carpets, embroidery, lace, etc.; (*d*) drawings, copper engravings, woodcarvings; (*e*) rare manuscripts, musical scores, autographs, bookbindings, miniatures, prints, covers; (*f*) weapons and armour; (*g*) coins, medals, seals, etc." Paragraph 4 provided that "scientific experts are to be entrusted with the execution of this order." Muehlmann's decree became the pattern for the Nazi campaign of cultural conquest all over Europe.

On September 27, 1939, Warsaw surrendered and victory in Poland was assured — if it had ever been in doubt. The Luftwaffe had employed less than fifty per cent of its front-line strength, about fifteen hundred aircraft, and had been aided by perfect flying conditions — "Goering weather," an expression which became familiar among Luftwaffe and R.A.F. pilots alike. Losses were negligible — about two hundred front-line aircraft — but so was Polish opposition if feats of individual heroism are discounted. Already, after the first week of battle, Goering approved the withdrawal of many Luftwaffe squadrons for resting and re-forming. The Luftwaffe had proved its might in war; it had lived up to the formidable reputation which it enjoyed. Goering and his advisers were optimistic, but as yet uncertain about the outcome of a contest with an opponent of equal strength.

On October 6 Hitler announced the end of the Polish War. The swift conclusion was a signal for Goering to resume his peace negotiations. Through his brother-in-law in Sweden, he tried to get in touch with the British Government once more to find out if German peace proposals would be entertained. Though Hitler was indifferent, Goering engaged him in lengthy discussions about his plan, working out suggestions which might be acceptable to the Western Allies. Finally the Fuehrer conceded to Goering that he would be prepared to give Czechoslovakia greater freedom; to reconstitute the Polish State on a smaller scale, so long as there was enough living space for surplus Germans. Goering pointed out that the Russian advance from the east had gone faster and farther than anticipated and the common frontier with the "traditional enemy" was a strategic contingency which he did not cherish. Unless the West was prepared for peace, he said, Germany would have to be prepared for dangerous possibilities. Hitler did not expect much from Goering's intervention and nothing came of it. It was more important, Hitler said, that he should travel to Rome to negotiate with Mussolini about Italy's attitude. Italy, were the Fuehrer's instructions, would have to hold herself in readiness to March with Germany.

Goering's relations with Mussolini and Ciano were approaching a severe testing time. Young Count Ciano no longer saw eye to eye with his father-in-law or Hitler and Goering. Emmy Goering told me that her husband often said he would prefer Italy to remain neutral. Evidence does not confirm her impression. If Goering conveyed this impression purposely, he was not telling the truth. From Italy he returned exasperated and annoyed with Ciano, who had a habit of speaking as freely as Goering himself. During this visit the Goering-Ciano friendship came to an end. When, not much later, Ciano visited Germany and came to Karinhall for a courtesy visit, Emmy had to tell him that Hermann was indisposed and unable to receive him. "I shall never forget the angry sneer on his face," Emmy Goering told me. "It was as if Count Ciano had dropped his smooth mask. He fumed, turned on his heel, and made to leave with hardly a word of greeting. Just then my husband, in slippers and dressing gown, came down the stairs to see him, after all. . . ." It was a short, cool conversation.

On November 8 the Nazi Party, as usual, assembled in Munich for the putsch anniversary celebration. Goering was unwell and did not attend the meeting. But every other member of the Nazi leadership was in Munich. Among those present were Alfred Rosenberg, Max Ammann, Dr. Ley, Dr. Goebbels, Dr. Frick, Rudolf Hess, Martin Bormann, Heinrich Himmler, General von Epp, Heinrich Hoffmann, Hitler's aides, Brueckner, Schaub, and Schmundt, and many other prominent Nazis. Goering's absence from such a gathering was striking. There was a feeling of apprehension in the beer cellar where the meeting took place, and Hitler, who usually made a two-hours' speech on these occasions, spoke only for eight minutes. After the speech he abruptly left the meeting. No sooner had he left than a bomb exploded under the platform, shattering the room and killing a number of "old fighters." In Britain there were rumours hinting that Goering had engineered a plot against Hitler in order to succeed him in the leadership of Germany. The rumours were as unfounded as the official German reports that the British Secret Service was responsible for the attempt on Hitler's life. It did not take the Gestapo long to arrest the man who had planted the bomb — Georg Elser, a brave German anti-Nazi. For Goering the event had consequences, the significance of which was soon to reveal itself. One of them was that Artur Heinecke, the young detective and S.S. man who was responsible for Elser's arrest, was decorated by Hitler and on Himmler's advice appointed chief of Goering's Begleitkommando, the Field Marshal's civilian Security Service Bodyguard. From that day, though he did not know it, Goering was not only being guarded; he was also being watched. Hitler certainly did not see anything suspicious in Goering's absence, but Himmler, as I was told after the war, never trusted Goering again.

We knew in London that relations between Goering and Himmler were not happy, and I wrote a story to that effect for the *Daily Herald.* Ten years later in Munich one of Goering's aides showed me a faded copy of *Das Schwarze Korps*, the weekly paper controlled by Himmler and the S.S. My story about the "Nazi Chiefs' Duel" was reproduced in facsimile on a page wholly devoted to an attempt to disprove it. The Nazi Government was very sensitive about such reports when they came too near the mark. It was decided that Goering should write a letter to Himmler for publication. "My dear Himmler," he wrote," as I have just read in the *Daily Herald* about our quarrel and hatred, it is a great pleasure to extend my greetings to you and the whole S.S. . . ." Himmler replied with a telegram: "Field Marshal Goering, Karinhall, Schorfheide — Dear Party Comrade Goering: — Please be convinced that I shall always be honoured to call myself your faithful comrade." Both messages were reproduced in the copy of *Das Schwarze Korps.*

But Himmler's men were not only in constant attendance on Hermann Goering alone. Emmy Goering told me that the bodyguard which Himmler assigned to her became a veritable menace. When she visited the theatre, these S.S. men rudely pushed everybody aside to clear her way. "It gave people the impression that I was aloof, conceited, and responsible for these brutal security measures. Why, friends with whom I wanted to shake hands were moved on before I could approach them. I am convinced Himmler was trying to discredit me and, through me, my husband," she concluded. But the dissension, the tension among the men around Hitler subsided as they basked in the glory of the victory over Poland. If Britain and France did not accept it as a signal for peace, Germany was ready for total war.

14

"GOERING WEATHER"

MILLIONS of people in Western Germany, and not a few in Soviet-occupied East Germany, revel in the memory of the blows which the Wehrmacht inflicted in Russia in 1941. But the Nazi-Soviet Pact of 1939 is a sore spot which they prefer to forget. If it is mentioned in conversation, Germans still describe it as an ingenious political move, a temporary device to wrest the initiative from the Soviet. But they did not like the pact while it was in force. "Honest Hermann," as they called him, could never hide his real feelings. Angrily he flung aside Nazi newspaper supplements produced for the occasion, in which many pages were devoted to articles and advertisements in the Russian language. "If we get a million tons of wheat from the Ukraine as they have promised," he said, "I shall certainly take it. But I doubt if we shall ever get it . . . !"

He left his bed to attend his first wartime Christmas party for needy children, but refused a request from his officials to adapt its cost and style to current conditions. Goering was very fond of these occasions. He lavished gifts on the children, chiefly toy aeroplanes and tin soldiers, but also cakes and sweets. Reluctantly he allowed himself to be dissuaded from appearing at the party dressed up as Santa Claus. His staff, however, soon found him sitting on the floor, surrounded by children, and playing with the toys to his own heart's delight. At Goebbels' Christmas party, the one-pot meal was the main attraction. Goebbels remarks about Goering's exhibitionism and extravagance were not complimentary. When the Ministry of Economics organised a collection of scrap metal and asked for surplus pots and pans from every household, Goering stormed into Veldenstein and began to weed out the metallic contents of the house. "He nearly cleared out my kitchen," Emmy said. "He wanted to give an example to all Germany."

From such personal preoccupations Goering returned to Berlin for vital conferences. General Bodenschatz told me how Hitler and his military advisers, Generals Wilhelm Keitel, Alfred Jodl, Walter von Brauchitsch, Hans Jeschonneck, and Grand Admiral Erich Raeder spent hours deliberating about the next move. It was obvious that Britain was not prepared to enter into peace negotiations and Germany was forced to devise a new strategy to bring the war to a speedy conclusion. Hitler had great faith in the U-boat campaign to cut off Britain's life-lines in a counter-blockade, but Admiral Raeder explained that it was a lengthy process and that more and better bases were required if such a campaign should be successful. "Where do you want bases?" Hitler asked, and Raeder produced maps to show that the coast of Norway would offer the greatest advantages. General Bodenschatz was present at these conferences — "only as a listener," he said, "to keep Goering informed." "So we must have Scandinavia," Hitler replied with a sweeping gesture, and ordered a quick survey of existing staff plans for an invasion of Denmark, Sweden, and Norway.

In his Nuremberg trial Goering said that the Norwegian project came as a surprise to him, and that, strangely enough, he was not informed about it for a long time. He knew of Hitler's plans through Bodenschatz, of course, but it was not strange at all that Hitler delayed an official approach until the last moment. He was well aware of the fact that Goering had been in touch with King Gustav of Sweden. Goering had assured the aged monarch that, wherever Germany would strike, Sweden would be safe. "Sweden is my second country!" he said to the King. "I shall never take up arms against you!" The danger of a German-Swedish conflict had always weighed heavily on his mind. He was convinced that Sweden would resist a German attack, which meant that his stepson, Thomas von Kantzow, would have to fight against Germany. There were Count Eric von Rosen and many other relatives of Karin, who would inevitably be involved if there was a conflict. It was unthinkable! Goering made no secret of his sentiments, although he clothed them in reasoned arguments about the advantages which Germany would derive from Swedish neutrality. When the General

Staff plans for an all-out attack on Denmark, Norway, and Sweden were submitted to him for approval of the Luftwaffe part in these operations, he rushed to see Hitler. He told the Fuehrer that he could guarantee to secure Swedish ore deliveries for Germany; he would go to Sweden, he said, and counteract British influence; he would get Swedish consent for German troops to pass quietly through the country. Anything! Denmark, Norway — of course, they would have to be conquered, but Sweden — never!

At one point Goering threatened to resign if Hitler should persist in his plan. While the British Foreign Office and the Service Chiefs worked day and night to counter the new formidable German threat, Hitler and Goering were locked in their first serious personal quarrel. There were harsh words: Hitler hinted that "Goering had gone soft." Later it became apparent that he blamed Emmy Goering for her husband's "weakness." Karin, though Swedish-born, Hitler insisted, had she been alive, would not have hesitated to make the sacrifice for Germany's sake . . . In the end Goering prevailed on Hitler, who ordered a revision of the General Staff's plans to exclude Sweden. But when Goering requested him to give the King of Sweden a written assurance to that effect, Hitler delayed it until he was sure that his Scandinavian plans would work out without an invasion of Sweden. "The King of Sweden never knew what he owed my husband," Emmy Goering told me. "Without Hermann's intervention, there would have been war between our two countries. . . ." As soon as he had saved Sweden, Goering checked the Luftwaffe plans for the Norwegian campaign. "As Commander of the Luftwaffe," he said, "I welcomed the addition of Norwegian bases as much as the Navy!"

In the meantime, he seized on a new thin thread of hope to promote peace even at this late stage. Sumner Welles, the American Under-Secretary of State, arrived in Germany. President Roosevelt had requested him to tour Europe, to assess the political situation and the chances of a settlement. In Germany Sumner Welles saw Hitler, Rudolf Hess, and Joachim von Ribbentrop. Goering, whom he visited at Karinhall, showed himself in his best light, and Welles regarded him as the Nazi leader most likely to be amenable to sensible suggestions. When Welles appeared at Karinhall, he was treated to a most reasoned exposition of Germany's aims and objectives.

Welles later described Goering as a more congenial personality than Hitler, Hess, or Ribbentrop, but said that he also merely followed the official line of German arguments. Goering took the American on a tour of Karinhall and showed him his collection. He would have been surprised had he known that Sumner Welles would "find it hard to imagine an uglier building or one more intrinsically vulgar in its ostentatious display." Welles said that Goering's hands were shaped like the digging paws of a badger, but "his manner was simple and unaffected and exceedingly cordial and he spoke with greater frankness than any other German official. . . . He had at least some conception of the outer world and of the psychology of other people." [1] He recorded that "Goering's face gave the impression of being heavily rouged, but since at the end of the conversation the colour had vanished, the effect was probably due to some form of physical maladjustment."

Nothing came of the three-hour interview. Goering returned to the study of strategic problems. He put General Stumpff in charge of a new Air Fleet 5, to conduct the campaign against Norway and Denmark, the Luftwaffe's first long-range operation. Special anti-shipping experts were recruited. The first Luftwaffe objectives were aerodromes in Denmark, from which aircraft could operate more conveniently over Norway. A large fleet of Ju 52's was assembled to employ the lessons of the air transport operations in Spain. They carried units of German infantry across the North Sea. Luftwaffe documents found after the war and interrogation of Luftwaffe officers revealed that approximately eight hundred German aircraft were employed in the Norwegian campaign: about half of them bombers, over one hundred and fifty seaplanes and flying boats, and about seventy tactical and strategic reconnaissance types. Few fighters were deemed necessary as opposition in the air was expected to be negligible.

The Luftwaffe was given credit for the swift success of the operation. Goebbels fully exploited the propaganda opportunity gratuitously provided by Prime Minister Neville Chamberlain's rash statement that "Hitler had missed the bus!" Before the end of the campaign, Goering had to take to his bed, and only returned to active participation in the war when Luftwaffe operations against

[1] Sumner Welles, *The Time for Decision.*

the Low Countries began in May, 1940. Presiding over a staff conference in his headquarters at Potsdam-Eiche, he was more than satisfied with the prospects. Spurred on by Erhard Milch, the aircraft industry had equipped the Luftwaffe with a formidable force. Five thousand front-line aircraft were available for the operation which was to develop into the conquest of France. "That is the end of the Sitzkrieg!" Goering said, coining a new word to describe the tranquillity on the Western Front to which the British people referred as the "Phony War."

While his relations with the Luftwaffe generals were excellent, he was at loggerheads with the Army commanders. His ideas of strategy were utterly opposed to their attempts to get closer Luftwaffe co-operation. To ward off their constant demands, he produced alternative schemes and used his authority as the senior officer of the Reich to dismiss their criticisms contemptuously. Like Hitler, he was suspicious of the General Staff. He was irritated by the cool, aloof, superior attitude of men like Rommel, whom Hitler first employed as military commander of his field headquarters organisation because, Hitler said, "he is temperamentally and ideologically the only reliable Reichswehr officer to whom I can entrust my personal safety!" He left it to his staff officers to work out plans for co-operation with the tanks of Rommel's division which would be the spearhead of the attack on France.

Goering's entourage noticed signs of strain. He was tired and weak when he returned to Potsdam, leaning heavily on Christa Gormanns, his nurse, with the big medicine cabinet always at hand. Whenever he seemed to be tiring, Christa hurriedly and unobserved slipped a packet of his pills into his hand. Years of life in comfort had left their mark on Hermann Goering. "He was difficult to please," Robert Kropp said, "although he never flared up in a bad temper with me as he did with others!" Robert had learned to anticipate his chief's every wish. With the pride of a professional valet, he told me that the Marshal only caught him out once. "He was thirsty while we were flying over Germany," Robert mused, "and I offered him a choice of beer, whiskey-soda, champagne . . . I had everything with me, even orange and lemon juice. . . . But he wanted iced water, and I had to confess that it was the only thing I could not give him!" "Well, if I can't even have water . . ." Goering sighed. "He made the most unusual requests," Robert summed up sadly. Henceforth he always had iced water available. Goering never asked for it again.

On the eve of the attack on Holland, Goering pulled himself together. In the map room of his headquarters in Potsdam he took charge of the operation. On a pad he noted the questions to which he had not received satisfactory answers. He bombarded Colonel Bernd von Brauchitsch with requests and Brauchitsch was constantly on the telephone to Bodenschatz, who was with Hitler. Goering's pet plan was the employment of a large force of parachutists, two divisions of approximately seven thousand men each. From over-all supervision during the first three days of the campaign, when weak Dutch air forces and small units of British Hurricanes put up a brave but hopeless show of resistance, Goering really went into action when his Fallschirmjaeger (parachutists) under General Kurt Student were let loose over Holland.

With the expert touch of a man with much experience in secret police work, he studied reports from Nazi agents in Holland, drawn from a large Fifth Column. Holland, to him by that time, was an open book. His plan was to drop the parachutists in the rear of the Dutch Army, where they could make contact with the Fifth Columnists. Not only would the Dutch forces be cut off and encircled, but it would be possible to capture leading Dutch personalities, perhaps even members of the royal family. With his ear glued to the telephone, he followed the operation and eagerly noted down front-line messages while junior staff officers, whose duties he usurped, stood by idly.

The parachutists were dropped according to plan. Three vital Rhine bridges were attacked and two, near Moerdijk and Dordrecht, were quickly captured. General Student jumped with the unit whose objective was a bridge near Rotterdam. It was the only one to meet heavy opposition. On landing, Student hurt his ankle and became technically a prisoner. But as the German operation was nearing sucess and with a large Panzer formation making headway in an effort to link up with the parachutists, he began negotiations for peace and surrender of the Dutch Army.

After the war Goering was closely questioned about the terror bombing of Rotterdam, which was the next move of his Luftwaffe.

Displaying the workings of his extraordinary memory, he gave a detailed description of the operation. There was a misunderstanding, he said, with regard to the peace negotiations; flare signs which had been agreed upon were not noticed in time. As they had no heavy artillery, he had promised his parachutists support from the bombers. When they were under heavy pressure, he ordered an attack against a block of houses which was obstructing their progress. A butter factory went up in flames; the bombs started vast fires which, according to his version, were really responsible for the extensive damage. It was the First World War observer pilot in him who spoke when he said six years later: "To this day I could draw an exact picture of the situation." In response to the call for help from the parachutists in Rotterdam, he dispatched about thirty Heinkels. The system of communications between headquarters and front in these early days, he said, was not as well developed as it was in the later stages of the war. If the Heinkels had duly received the information about the peace negotiations in progress, they would have returned to base without dropping their bombs. Owing to the misunderstanding, over a square mile of Rotterdam's heart was flattened. So confused was the situation that General Student, looking out of a window during the negotiations, was shot and wounded in the head.

The main operation concluded, Goering hurried to meet Hitler. He had heard a rumour that a decision, long agreed, to reward Seyss-Inquart for his part in the Anschluss with the appointment as Reich Commissioner for Holland was in danger of being upset. He had promised Seyss-Inquart this job, even negotiated with him about details of the economic measures to be taken in Holland in the light of experience in Poland and Norway. The question of foreign exchange was uppermost in his mind and Seyss-Inquart suggested the formation of foreign exchange Kommandos on the lines of Rosenberg's cultural Einsatzstab — a useful, practical idea which Goering readily adopted. And now it seemed that Hitler, as so often in Goering's absence, had listened to other counsels. Hitler, however, double-tongued in dealings with friends and ministers, rarely faced up to Goering, whose show of faith and loyalty often disarmed him. Denying blandly that he had considered any change of plan, he confirmed Seyss-Inquart's appointment on the spot. Both

Hitler and Goering were tense but exhilarated by the success of the Dutch attack. Goebbels joined them at a private talk of which Goering gave his aides a hurried summary.

In London Neville Chamberlain had resigned and Churchill had taken over as Prime Minister. Goebbels said that this was welcome fuel for his propaganda machine because it was easy to represent Churchill as a wicked enemy of the German people. Chamberlain, whom he had once been forced to describe as a peaceful man and friend of Germany, was not such a good target. When Goering was given a translation of Churchill's famous speech about blood, toil, tears, and sweat, he remarked laughingly that he had made many speeches of that sort himself. But when an aide told him that Britian was launching a new production drive and that Lord Beaverbrook had been appointed as Minister of Aircraft Production, he commented: "Eine gefaehrlicher Bursche! [A dangerous fellow!] I have often discussed him with my English friends. We must keep an eye on him. . . ." On May 15, Holland was in German hands. The bulk of the Luftwaffe operational force was now employed in Flanders. The German campaign against Belgium and France was proceeding according to plan.

Goering professed himself surprised at the weakness of British Royal Air Force resistance, but, although Jeschonneck reported to him daily about the progress of the campaign, he did not take part in the actual conduct of operations as he had done in Holland. Touring German aerodromes, however he indulged in his favourite wartime occupation — meeting the Luftwaffe pilots and discussing with them the problems of a fighter pilot. There was Major Galland and Werner Moelders, who both surpassed his own record of twenty-two air victories. "Conditions are different nowadays," he was fond of saying. When he first went into action, he said patronisingly, he had only a revolver or rifle. It was a long time before he had a machine gun installed in his plane, and, as to synchronisation which made it possible to fire machine-gun salvoes through the revolving propellers — well, that was something which made it child's play to shoot down the other fellow. . . !

While he thus basked in the glory of old times, he received news which showed that Hitler's opinion of him was not as high as that of the young Luftwaffe pilots. He had already been disturbed when the generals failed to invite him to the extensive Army manoeuvres along the river Weser, which were held before the attack in the West. Bodenschatz had handled the situation tactfully. He had only complained that "the Luftwaffe had been excluded . . ." But what he meant to convey was his chief's annoyance at the personal rebuff. Halder, Jodl, and Keitel wanted none of Goering's unsolicited comments. Now Hitler called in Student, Kesselring, and Richthofen to report to him personally and omitted the obvious courtesy of inviting the Commander-in-Chief, his friend Goering, to attend the conference. Moreover, General Blomberg, in retirement at Wiessee, told a mutual friend that he had suggested Goering as his successor as Commander-in-Chief in 1938, but Hitler had replied that "Goering was too lazy!" So that was what the Fuehrer meant when he told him "he had too many jobs already"; that was what Hitler thought of him in 1938! No wonder Emmy had noticed at the time that Hitler had changed. Goering was also told of the Fuehrer's casual remarks about his "softness." As usual, they had spread quickly beyond the intimate circle of Hitler's staff, who always passed on his views, frequently embellished with their own comment. Like other Nazi leaders, Goering had his "contact men" to keep him informed about his ministerial colleagues. Was he in disgrace? Quickly he seized an opportunity to show his real fibre when he received a report that a German airman had been lynched after coming down behind the French lines. "We shall take five French lives," he threatened, "for every German airman killed on landing. . . . He saw to it that full publicity was given to his statement.

He visited Brussels which held many memories of his own fighting days and returned to Berlin anxious to bridge the indefinable gap in his relations with Hitler. At the conclusion of the Battle of France, he rhapsodised about the Fuehrer. "As the greatest leader of of our times," he said, "the Fuehrer first increased the strength of the Reich without the use of arms. Now that war is upon us, we find that in his person are united unique political leadership with the art of a general. I am qualified like no other German to explain this" — and later made sure that this passage was emphasised in the report to the press — "for," lifting his voice, "I have the confidence of the Fuehrer to such an extent that I was allowed to know all his thoughts and plans!" Alas, it was no longer true, but Goering concluded his speech with the greatest praise he could bestow: "In Frederick the Great, Germany once had such a personality. In Adolf Hitler, Providence has given us again such a genius!" What pleased him most was that Goebbels could do nothing else but plug this felicitous phrase for many months to come.

Mussolini, Churchill's "jackal," who had stabbed France in the back, conferred on Goering the Annunziata Order, Italy's highest decoration. The award was made to celebrate the victory in the West, but also to smooth over the strained relations between Goering and his son-in-law. Goering only later familiarised himself with the details of the Luftwaffe operations in the French campaign, in which the air force was chiefly employed in support of the German armies. Fifteen hundred sorties were made every day, apart from mine-laying operations against northern French ports. Wing-Commander Asher Lee, the R.A.F. intelligence officer, noted correctly that "the employment of the German long-range bomber force was a novelty at the time. But, though the full galaxy of German Air Force talent and resources was employed, the Luftwaffe did not escape without substantial losses." [2] They amounted to some two thousand aircraft lost or badly damaged. The battle lasted for six weeks, the limit, a German staff officer confessed, to which it could go at that rate. While Hitler and his staff worked on new ambitious plans, the Luftwaffe experts were relieved that the end of the battle had come. But only Goering's closest advisers knew that. In Germany and abroad the reputation of his very own war weapon was supreme. The weapon itself was blunted and needed repair.

Goering was back in Karinhall when a personal matter of utmost gravity intruded on his full enjoyment of the Luftwaffe triumph. For several months past Bodenschatz had repeatedly told him about acute unrest in Nuremberg, where most of the General's friends lived. It had spread, he said, beyond the Party to important people on whom the régime and, moreover, the armed forces, relied for full moral support. Bodenschatz told me that Herr Martin, Nuremberg's Police President, had come to Berlin to put the complaints before him. It appeared that the antics of Julius Streicher,

[2] Asher Lee, *The German Air Force.*

Gauleiter and owner of the anti-Semitic *Der Stuermer*, and the undisputed Nazi lord of the district, had become intolerable.

Streicher's sadistic and often pornographic campaign against the Jews had gone too far. But that was not all. The people of Nuremberg were talking about his corrupt practices, about motor cars which he confiscated and sold to his friends for a song. Streicher had collected golden wedding rings from minor party officials "for the war effort," but had them melted down and made into a cigarette case for his girl friend. Previously Goering had listened to Bodenschatz's tales, but his answer had invariably been that Streicher was a personal friend of Hitler, and that, as Gauleiter, he was responsible only to Rudolf Hess or Martin Bormann. If he had committed a criminal offense, it was Heinrich Himmler's affair. I do not want to be mixed up with this," Goering said.

When Goering returned from France, however, Police President Martin arrived with a startling piece of news. Streicher, he told Bodenschatz, had sneered at Goering during a drunken skittles party, and when conversation turned to his daughter Edda had shouted loudly: "His daughter? Ridiculous! She is not his daughter at all . . . at best she is a synthetic baby. . . ." Bodenschatz felt that Goering should know about this public insult, made within the hearing of many people. He reported the incident to his chief and caused an explosion. Banging the table with his fist, too exasperated to say a word, Goering jumped up, reached for his coat, ordered his car, and went to see Hitler at the Chancellery.

It is not known in detail what ensued between the two men, but Goering told Bodenschatz that he had demanded Streicher's instantaneous dismissal — or else he, Goering, would be forced to resign. Hitler was in a difficult position. Though he often tolerated, even encouraged, quarrels between his principal aides, he knew that Goering was hurt beyond repair. He ordered the Party Supreme Court to inquire into Goering's allegations — not only about the personal insult, but about the charges of corruption and other irregularities which Goering for good measure had enumerated. And he consented that Bodenschatz, though not a member of the Party, should attend the inquiry as Goering's personal representative. Bodenschatz told me the rest of the story. The Party Court had supreme supra-legal powers in Germany. Witnesses were called. Streicher was questioned. The result of the investigation was such that Rudolf Hess apologised to Bodenschatz, a non-Party member, about the despicable practices which had come to light. A report of the findings was sent to Hitler, who showed it to Goering.

The allegations have been proved correct, Hitler admitted, but, for high State reasons, he could only take limited action: "I feel like having the fellow shot!" Hitler said, but if news of dissension among Hitler's friends leaked out, it would encourage France and Britian and all enemies of Germany who were now prostrate. Hitler ordered Streicher to relinquish his position as Gauleiter and to retire for the rest of the war to his private estate in Franconia. He was forbidden to set foot in Nuremberg. From then on Streicher led the life of a rich retired gentleman. But his political career was at an end.

The incident added to the strain under which Goering was labouring; he felt overwhelmed. History had moved at breakneck speed. The Battle of France lasted only twenty days. Hitler accepted the complete surrender of the traditional enemy. With unusual gaiety he danced a jig of joy. On the new French Government formed by Marshal Pétain he imposed the indignity of choosing Compiègne and Marshal Foch's famous coach as the scene for the signing of the armistice. What did it matter if General de Gaulle, over the radio from London, made his idle threats? Mussolini, more impressed by the German victory than by Goering's previous arguments, was now his firm ally. When the two dictators met to demonstrate the unity of the Axis, it looked as if a personal friendship was springing up between them, after all. Commenting on the alliance with Italy, Goering said to Emmy: "Italy is a mascot — they're always on the winning side! And, you know," he added laughingly, "Italy is like Schnitzel — the more she gets beaten, the bigger she becomes!" Another Churchill speech provoked him to a new sneer. When he heard that the British Prime Minister had asked the people to face "their finest hour," he said, "Very fine hour this, when forty thousand British are captured . . .!" But he knew that the escape of a quarter of a million men from Dunkirk was a serious disappointment to the Wehrmacht, who had planned the complete annihilation of the British Expeditionary Force.

After a short holiday in Gastein, Goering went to Amsterdam to see General Christiansen, his old friend and collaborator, the first Luftwaffe officer to be appointed Supreme Military Commander of a German Army of Occupation. It was while he was staying at General Christiansen's house that Bodenschatz arrived with the best piece of news he had ever had. Hitler, after the French campaign, had promoted scores of his generals. Erhard Milch, Sperrle, Kesselring, Stumpff, were now General Field Marshals. Pondering how Goering's seniority could be preserved against such a galaxy of supremes, he decided to create a new, unique title for him. Bodenschatz heard the news at Hitler's Headquarters. "Congratulations!" he said, once again. "Congratulations, Herr Reichsmarschall!" The official citation, dated July 19, 1940, read: "As a reward for his mighty contribution to victory, I herewith appoint the creator of the Luftwaffe to the rank of Reichsmarschall, and award him the Grand Cross of the Iron Cross." Signed, "Adolf Hitler." A few weeks later the official Army magazine, *Deutsche Wehrbeitraege*, published a description of the insignia of Goering's new uniform: "It has two different collar tabs. On the left are two crossed gold-embroidered Marshal batons on a silver brocade base; on the right a gold-embroidered Reich Eagle, also on a silver brocade base. The collar is lined with thick gold braid. Colour of the uniform and blouse is grey-blue." Victorious Germany received the news about Goering's new uniform with great hilarity, but rumours which made fun of the new Reichsmarschall's choice of these striking colours did him an injustice. It was not his choice. When the uniform was ready, he did not like it: "Robert," he said, "get Stechbart to make me another one in plain white."

Robert was worried. One white uniform would never do; it would have to be two or three. "Herr Reichsmarshall," he pleaded, "could we not leave it as it is?" He received an indignant reply: "If I say white — it's white!"

15

BLITZ

On the eve of the Luftwaffe all-out assault on Great Britain, Goering decided to inspect an advance Luftwaffe command post at Angers. A small cavalcade followed his armoured car. There were two heavy mobile anti-aircraft guns, two lorries with his military guard under Colonel Kluge of the Hermann Goering Division, and two cars with members of his personal staff. A quarter of an hour after his arrival, three British Hurricanes cruised over Angers. Next minute there was pandemonium. An unobserved British aircraft dropped a casual bomb which exploded not more than a hundred yards from the post. With a deafening noise the post's own anti-aircraft batteries and Goering's mobile guns opened up in a barrage. "You fools!" Goering shouted. "Call them off! Stop them! Do you want to advertise that I am here? Do you want to kill me?"

With the instinct of an old war pilot, Goering, quicker than the others, realised that "show of strength" at this isolated spot would only arouse suspicion. The British airmen missed the chance of a lifetime. Unaware of the target below them, they flew on to perform whatever task they had been given. Goering lost interest in the strategic problems which he had come to discuss and returned to his own headquarters, situated in a small forest near Beauvais, northeast of Paris, a location where his armoured train would be safe. Half the train, including the carriage with his bedroom and private office, was inside a tunnel, secure from air attacks. A strong anti-aircraft gun formation guarded the other carriages. High oak planks formed an impenetrable wall around the siding. A second train housed the troops of the Guards Regiment, carried wireless, telephone, and teleprinter installations. Of his big staff only General Bodenschatz and Colonel Bernd von Brauchitsch lived in the Chief's train. Robert was with Goering, so was Christa Gormanns. As a cook he had engaged Fedor Radmann, of the Mitrope, the German wagon-lits. "I want good home cooking — understand?" Goering told him. Radmann, in conversation with me, was emphatic that Goering never consumed the gargantuan quantities of food with which his girth might be associated. "And what he did not know about wine," Radmann said, "was not worth knowing."

A bottle of wine before him, leisurely reclining in his easy-chair, Goering studied reports about the preparations for the battle to end all airbattles of this war. Nearby were the headquarters of his Chief of Staff, Colonel-General Hans Jeschonneck, and his two senior staff officers, Colonel von Waldow and Colonel Josef Schmidt. Two air fleets were ready for a massive assault on Britain. Field Marshal Kesselring, the victor of Warsaw, commanded Luftflotte II with headquarters at the Central Hotel in Brussels and an advanced post at Cap Gris Nez. Field Marshal Roman Sperrle, commanding Luftflotte III, had moved from St. Cloud, where he had supervised the preparations for the battle, to Deauville. The rear organisation of his air fleet was at the Luxembourg in Paris. Chief of Operations of Luftflotte III was General Karl Koller, with whom I discussed this critical phase of the war in detail.

A survey, which Koller compiled after the failure of the initial attack, throws some light on the emotions, hopes, and doubts of the Commander-in-Chief as he braced himself for the historic occasion. During his last visit to Berlin, Goering had taken part in discussions about "Operation Sea Lion," the plan for the invasion of Britain. Official German papers found after the war do not convey Hitler's half-hearted approach to the plan. "I am on safe ground where my Army goes," he said to Goering. "I can follow them — but these naval operations . . ." He did not admit what the men around him knew only too well — that he had a strange aversion to water. Hitler could not swim, had never experienced bathing in the sea, had never been on a voyage in his life. Goering was equally sceptical about the operation. Koller's report mentions significantly that "now the Luftwaffe had to try and end the battle against Britain alone." Goering, in fact, was convinced that there would be no need to attempt an opposed landing; that, once the Luftwaffe had completed its attack, Britain would sue for peace.

In this conviction he disregarded most of the inquiries from Admiral Raeder's staff about the progress of the Luftwaffe preparations. He encouraged both Kesselring and Sperrle to take their time. From Brest to the north of Holland the ground organisations were installed with meticulous care. The two commanding Field Marshals never expected them to be complete before the beginning of August, 1940. When they were completed, Sperrle's forces were distributed over twenty-six aerodromes; Kesselring's air fleet occupied twenty-four. Air Fleet III installations stretched from the extreme west to the mouth of the Seine, Air Fleet II from the Seine to Northwest Germany. The two fleets were reinforced with five air corps and several fighter groups. Britain, on Goering's map, was divided by a long line, separating the spheres of operations of the two air fleets.

The aircraft on which Goering and his staff relied was of a vast variety of types. Standard models had been improved and modified in quick succession. They were equipped with new engines as the battle progressed, adapted to carry heavier armour and more machine guns. While most people still had notions about the traditional German inflexibility, there were, in fact, constant changes and much improvisation. In many instances Goering's own impatience and impetuosity were responsible for changes which complicated the operations and imposed a heavy strain on the combatant airmen. The single-seater Messerschmitt, Me 109, its double-engined cousin, Me 110, Heinkel 111, Dornier 17, 17Z, and 215, Junkers 88, and dive-bombing Junkers 87, represented the core of the attacking force. This force, Goering was sure, could bring Britain to her knees. More than once, when the Fuehrer Headquarters dispatched a signal dealing with the combined air-sea operations of the invasion, Goering handed it to Brauchitsch, "Read it — and tell me all about it later. Anyway, it'll never happen!" The movement and assembly of the barges for the invasion he regarded simply as a useful side-show of the operation: "The Englaender will waste a lot of aircraft trying to bomb them — that's all these play-boats are good for!"

Impatiently he studied reports about the initial reconnaissance operations, about Luftwaffe thrusts, designed to test the British defences. He was anxious for the day when the battle would reach a climax. Day after day he paced the ground, walking up and down by the side of his train. Bodenschatz was with him; Bruno Loerzer, though not actively engaged in the operation, was there to help sooth his nerves. Ernst Udet came for a visit, but was more and more irritated by Goering's constant criticism of technicalities for which Udet as Production Chief was responsible. For years the two men had met on equal terms just like old war comrades, but as the great test approached, Goering often, and unpleasantly, exerted his authority as Supreme Commander and the Reich's senior officer. On the eve of a great battle there is little a commander can do: the plans are ready, his work is done. Goering's nerves suffered as he spent the last few days waiting, waiting. He had asked the meteorologists to advise him when to expect a period of four fine days during which he could carry out the first phase of his plan. He flew into a rage when he heard of a delay in allocating a number of Kondors (Focke-Wulf 200's) to the meteorological units which ranged the air around Britain, flying from Stavanger to Bordeaux and back. At last, on Monday, August 12, the meteorologists signalled that the weather conditions were favourable for the operation to start on the next day. General Jeschonneck, at Goering's request, checked with the chief meteorologists of the two air fleets, both of whom concurred.

The plan was for the Luftwaffe to smash the advance defences of Britain, to destroy the British economy, and prevent supplies passing through the main ports. It was at this stage essential that targets should be seen from the air. It seemed certain that these conditions would prevail on Tuesday, August 13. The Luftwaffe zero hour was 7.30 A.M. The whole coast of France reverberated with the drone of the engines, Luftwaffe pilots were ready for the sign to take off. But at 7.15 A.M. reconnaissance aircraft reported sudden fog formation at Calais. Air Fleet III received information that mist was hiding the region of Brighton. Goering insisted that the attack should proceed. "The attack of Air Fleet II," Koller's report sadly states, "failed completely. The success of Air Fleet III had to be registered as moderate." Bodenschatz had difficulty in keeping his chief from the meteorologists. "These fellows ought to be shot!" Goering screamed. Then he said sadly, "It's a bad beginning." He was full of evil foreboding. "When can we move?" Goering asked. He was near tears, I was told. It was decided to fix the date for August 16. But again the blessed British weather frustrated his plans. It was impossible to see a single target. A few squadrons went up and flew over Britain, dropping their bombs haphazardly through the mist. The rest returned with their bomb loads unexpended. On the seventeenth the whole operation was cancelled. "This failure at the outset of the great battle against England," Koller records, "shook the confidence of the High Command in the meteorologists."

Goering was not prepared to wait and risk another disappointment. After consultation with Kesselring and Sperrle, he ordered a change of tactics. Never again would he rely on these long-range prognostications. He ordered the bomber squadrons to move against Britain in individual daylight operations. "Impossible," Sperrle objected. The monocled, big-boned, tough-looking Field Marshal was no great friend of Goering. As a senior officer in the First World War, he had once rebuked the exuberant fighter pilot, Lieutenant Goering, for an act of indiscipline. Goering could never forgive him; he always felt that Sperrle was still addressing the young lieutenant in him and not the senior Marshal of the Reich and Commander-in-Chief of the Luftwaffe. "What's the matter; why impossible?" he asked.

It took Sperrle, supported by Kesselring, only a few minutes to explain. Daylight raids in big style were impossible in the face of determined British defence. Owing to the limited fighter range, attacks would have to be restricted to targets near the coast. Goering, who had only a rudimentary knowledge of night operations and only a short personal experience of night flying, was not happy as he approved a switch to night operations which were started with an attack on Liverpool. Two days later a raving Goering was calling his staff together. They came forward with great reluctance. His aide, Colonel Brauchitsch, kept away as long as he could. Goering was in a state of almost maniacal fury. "Didn't I tell these fools!" he shouted. It appeared that the Luftwaffe's crack squadrons had unloaded their bombs on a dummy replica of Liverpool Harbour. The first major night operation was a complete flop.

Goering suffered insult to add to the injury. From Hitler's Headquarters came contemptuous reproofs. To his consternation, it was Goebbels who advised Hitler on how to overcome the difficulties with which Goering was obviously unable to cope. Goebbels produced material for a speech which Hitler made on September 4, threatening reprisals against indiscriminate British bombing of Germany. The emphasis was on "indiscriminate." If the Luftwaffe could not reach its targets by day and could not find them by night, let them drop their bombs, anyway. "The Fuehrer speech," said a staff report cynically, "eased the tasks of the Luftwaffe; it cleared the way for night attacks in every respect."

For those who experienced the Blitz on Britain, the attacks on London, for the people who lived in the vicinity of the coastal aerodromes from which British fighters flew in the defence of the country and which were the first targets of the Luftwaffe, for the relatives of the heroes who laid down their lives in these days, it is, perhaps, small comfort to be told ten years later that there was less precision, less certainty, less efficiency in the Luftwaffe organisation than the grim effect of German bombing seemed to indicate. But it is true that, during the whole period which followed Hitler's speech, there were divided counsels on the other side. Hitler was the chief advocate of the terror bombing on London. The Luftwaffe Marshals were determined to eliminate the fighter defence over Britain by attacking the front-line aerodromes. Goering's economic advisers bombarded him with requests to harass the ports so as to intensify the blockade of the U-boats. The invasion plan was sinking into oblivion as time went on.

Goering himself was near nervous exhaustion. He could only sleep with the help of severe drugs, with the result that he was not at his best in the early morning when the final touches were put on the plans for the day's operations. A Luftwaffe staff doctor, Ondarza, was in constant attendance on him. Christa Gormanns supervised the tonics which he was taking. Slumping heavily in his easy-chair, nothing would move him — except the regular telephone calls from Hitler's Headquarters. When Hitler was personally on the telephone, he would rouse himself quickly in a burst of energy. Torn between many doubts and his anxiety to please the Fuehrer, he gesticulated, bowed, and even cringed in the face of the receiver, over which the voice of Hitler reached him. "We knew when he was talking to Hitler," a captain of the Hermann Goering Guards Regiment told me; "he was acting as if the Fuehrer was standing in front of him!"

The might of the Luftwaffe with over thirty-five hundred front-line aircraft, over a thousand long-range Dorniers, Heinkels, and Junkers bombers, five hundred Ju 87 Stukas, twelve hundred Messerschmitt fighters, and all the supplementary aircraft which make up a striking force, were at his bidding; he could send nearly two thousand aircraft into battle any day, but Goering did not feel supremely confident any longer. At the height of the battle, Field Marshals Kesselring and Sperrle showed much better nerves. As events moved faster every day, they operated according to their own designs, cool scientists of modern warfare, paper and pencil in hand, treating the operation like a mathematical formula which had to be solved. The avalanche of orders from the Commander-in-Chief were put at the bottom of the documents which reached them from his headquarters. The temperamental outbursts of their Commander-in-Chief were strange interludes in the calculated business of war. As Goering rallied in the course of the morning, he would drive to the advanced command posts, visit Kesselring at Cap Gris Nez or Sperrle at Deauville. But the commanders were working twenty hours per day, and there was little time for conversations even with the Reichsmarschall. Goering spent more time than was necessary listening to the exciting, but often long-winded tales of combat pilots about their individual actions. There were tears in his eyes as he decorated some of them with the Knight's Cross of the Iron Cross — eventually with the diamonds added to this decoration, the new equivalent of his own Pour le Mérite. How much pleasanter it is for a man of action to fight, he told Brauchitsch, than to sit at a desk and to contemplate strategy and organisation.

As his hopes of forcing a surrender on Britain receded, he gave the order for a violent knock-out blow to be delivered. "Hit the head — and you need not worry about the body!" he said. It was the signal for the first mass daylight attack on London on September 7. Five hundred aircraft battered the East End and the port of London. Fires were raging in the city. They warmed Goering's heart for the first time since the abortive initial assaults of mid-

August. British observers kept an eye on the invasion barges, which were now massed along the coast of France. From British General Headquarters the code word "Cromwell"—Invasion Imminent—was flashed to Eastern and Southern Army Commands, and all London formations. Goering's optimistic reaction to the concentrated attack on London encouraged die Seeloewen (the sea lions), as he called the naval staff officers, to get ready for a try after all. Any day now! In Berlin Goebbels took full advantage of the situation. His propaganda broadcasts assumed a triumphal ring. Hans Fritzsche, his chief assistant, went to the microphone every day to introduce members of the "propaganda companies" who had flown with the Luftwaffe and gave graphic word-pictures of the inferno that was London. Over the German wireless, for all the world to hear, came the strains of the inevitable "Wir fahren gegen Engelland!" "Any day now, mein Fuehrer," Goering told Hitler.

On September 9 the German press, in a communiqué from the High Command of the Wehrmacht, announced that the Luftwaffe had begun "to repay the continuous enemy attacks on civilian targets by the British Air Force. In a first blow," the communiqué said, "the Luftwaffe attacked on Saturday and in the night of Sunday military targets in the inner city districts of London. The attacks were continued in the course of Sunday. The action is under the personal direction of the Reichsmarschall." A press report added: "In uninterrupted sequence up to now over a million kilogrammes of bombs of all types were dropped on harbour installations, merchant ships, docks, storehouses, power plants and waterworks, gasworks, factories, arsenals, and transport installation were hit and partially destroyed. Big fires are raging in the neighbourhood of the docks. In powerful thrusts fighter planes cleared the bombers' way to London."

The Munich *Nueste Nachrichten* had this to say: "On Wednesday, after a night of terror for the population of London, six day alarms kept the people of London in a constant state of apprehension." The *Voelkische Beobachter* wrote: "How serious the position of British reserves must be emerges from a spiteful attack on Reichsmarschall Goering, delivered by Sinclair, the British Air Minister. Losing all control and confidence in their own forces, the battered British are sliding into a blind rage. Nothing could surpass in its venom the attack which Sinclair delivered. This insignificant fellow, who never had the joystick of an aircraft in his hand, went mad standing on the roof of the Air Ministry, as he said, and witnessing the fate that has befallen London." Sir Archibald Sinclair, of course, had a fine record as a front-line officer in the First World War. The paper made fun of his solemn declaration that Britain would not rest until "the criminals of Berlin and London have been exterminated." Hitler's own paper poured scorn on Sir Archibald Sinclair's comparison between the "precision bombing of British pilots, who attacked from low altitudes, and the indiscriminate assaults by the pirates of the Luftwaffe."

The Commander-in-Chief of the "pirates" was no longer interested in the selection of targets. Whether his men hit East End dwellings or Buckingham Palace was quite immaterial now. It was simply a matter of knocking out the capital of the Empire. But every evening during the fateful week that followed there were sobering moments when General Hans Jeschonneck arrived at Beauvais and boarded Goering's train with an estimate of the day's losses. "Four hundred out on operations — fifty down. It is more than we expected!" "Incredible!" Goering said, comparing the figures with the total strength and available reserves. "How long can they hold out . . . how long can we go on?" he asked. As the days went by, as the strength of the British defence did not weaken, the very mention of "Sea Lion" produced beads of perspiration on his forehead. Goering waving his crumpled handkerchief, calling on Robert for a change of shirt and collar in the middle of a conference, was now a familiar picture. "He has not the nerves for this sort of thing," said Kesselring, though he had never criticised Goering before.

In Britain on September 15, Mr. Churchill was on a visit to the Uxbridge Headquarters of Air Vice-Marshal Park, Commander of the Fighter Group 11, the glorious few to whom the world owes so much. "I do not know whether anything will happen today," Marshal Park told the Prime Minister. "At present all is quiet." [1] At that very moment Goering received the report that his squadrons had just been launched on a new final all-out attack. "They

[1] Winston Churchill, *The Second World War: Their Finest Hour*, Vol. II.

must be reaching the limit of their resources," said Colonel Brauchitsch, who maintained contact with advance headquarters and had just received the latest signals from Colonels Schmidt and Koller. "Today's assault should complete the operations!" He was not far off the mark. Air Vice-Marshal Park had to ask for reinforcements from other groups, which had been kept in readiness for a switch of the Luftwaffe attack. But "The Few" rose to the occasion. The Luftwaffe was turned back with a bloody nose. It was the Luftwaffe and not the R.A.F. which had reached the limit of its resources. "We cannot keep it up at this scale," Kesselring telephoned; "we are falling below the standard of safety."

Next morning Goering was informed that the R.A.F. claimed to have brought down over one hundred and eighty planes. "I want an authentic report," he said. "Losses below fifty," he was told, "but even that is more than we can afford." (The actual figure was fifty-six.) "My order is to carry on the attack with the utmost strength," he said. "Emphasis now on night bombing. We cannot be squeamish!" "For sixty-five nights without interruption we bombed London," Koller said to me, still proud of the achievement ten years later. But Goering gave the order for his train to be ready for immediate departure. "I agree with the Fuehrer that these attacks on London were necessary — if for no other reason than to stiffen the morale of our people back home," he said. "But I could have told him that the British would not easily give in. . . . " Not a single member of his entourage took his statement very seriously. Goering had been sure that nobody could take such punishment. He believed so implicitly in the ability of bombing to win the war that the failure of the Luftwaffe superefforts was a grave disappointment to him. Though he always appeared reluctant to look unpleasant facts in the face, though he never admitted mistakes, in his heart he was realist enough to know that, at best, it would be a long time before the Luftwaffe could register real success. He did not comment on Hitler's decision to postpone an invasion attempt until 1941. The events of the past few weeks had a profound psychological effect on him. His staff noticed another great change in his mental make-up.

From Berlin came news of Hitler's acute embarrassment. Goering's confident assurances had strengthened him in his hopes of an early British surrender. Goebbels had publicly fixed a date for total victory over Britain. Now he blamed Goering for the awkward position in which the Luftwaffe failure had placed him. Though, by a cunning propaganda manoeuvre, he gave this failure the appearance of a great German victory, he lost all respect for the Luftwaffe Chief. In Goebbels' eyes, Goering henceforth was a complete flop, a nuisance, a useless drag on the German war effort. Bodenschatz told me that Goering was a much-chastened man when he complied with a request by Hitler to see him at Berchtesgaden and to report personally on the situation. They talked in private and Goering returned to Paris the next day for a conference with the Army commanders. It took place on September 20 at the Luxembourg, the headquarters of Field Marshal Sperrle. Though outwardly still clinging to his theory that the Luftwaffe would eventually triumph, he was subdued. The generals were relieved to be spared his customary criticisms. It was clear to them that the Reichsmarschall was about to escape from the harsh realities of the abortive air battles into another friendlier and more rewarding sphere of his activities.

16

ART UNDER THE COUNTER

SOMEWHERE in the deep dark jungle which I traversed in my quest for information about Hermann Goering's life, I came across a bulky bound volume containing more words than this whole book. It was a complete, detailed record of Goering's art deals compiled by the United States Army authorities. Five years after the end of the war, this document (Office of Strategic Services, Art Looting Investigation, Consolidated Interrogation Report No. 2, dated September 15, 1945) was still on the secret list, classified or restricted in the official parlance. The reason for this secrecy became apparent to me only after a long study of material from other sources. It was forced on the American authorities, the State Department's Monuments and Fine Arts Division, by an avalanche of requests for restitution, many of which were simply speculative and spurious. The transactions by which Goering acquired paintings, sculptures, church ornaments, antiques, were so complicated that it often took years to trace the rightful owners. In some cases the trail was completely lost.

Many of these treasures changed hands a dozen times before they landed in Karinhall or Veldenstein, in Rominten or in the Leipzigerstrasse. Scores of intermediaries were involved in the deals. Reputable art dealers and blackmailing Nazi functionaries had a hand in them. Some had been left behind by European Jews who had hurriedly fled their country as it was occupied by the Wehrmacht. Others had been freely offered to German agents with foreign exchange which Hermann Goering, in his capacity as Germany's economic leader, had at his disposal. Some had been acquired by exchange; others simply stolen in the chaos which accompanied the collapse of countries battered by the Luftwaffe. Again — Quisling

Ministers, without the right to dispose of their country's property, had curried favour with the Germans by presenting Goering with the show-pieces of their national museums.

Only Kunstdirektor Hofer perhaps knows the details, but the transactions in which he had a hand bear the stamp of scrupulous legality. The whole time of Fraeulein Gisela Limberger, Goering's second secretary, was taken up by the extensive correspondence in connection with these deals. She has tried to explain them to the American authorities as best as she could. Since the end of the war she has been staying at the house of the famous Munich art dealer, Bornheim, whose professional services Goering frequently employed in the acquisition of valuables. But no single person can really penetrate the thicket of these transactions. Experts from many countries still search for lost or missing objects. France, Italy, Holland, Belgium, Greece, Jugoslavia, and other European governments have sent delegations to recover some of these treasures. Officially restitution is complete, but few weeks pass without new requests reaching the American "Collection Point" at Wiesbaden, where officials have worked for years to sort out this invaluable mess. Only the large collection of Goering's favourites, the voluptuous women on the canvases of the German painter, Lukas Cranach, are still stored in Amerika Haus, the former Fuehrerbau, in Munich. Most of them were originally in German hands before they became part of Goering's collection. To add to the confusion, a few odd, if valuable, West European objets d'art remain behind in Germany, as their owners will not claim them, because they were, as it was the practice in many countries, acquired against cash payments to disguise illicit profits or to evade payment of taxes. At the other end of the scale there are cases like that of the city of Cologne, for instance, which had made a present of one Lukas Cranach to little Edda Goering. Now the city is claiming it back, but by the end of 1950 no decision had been made on this claim.

The events which led to this confused situation started in Holland and France in the autumn of 1940, when Goering tried to escape from the depressing preoccupation with Luftwaffe affairs into his favourite realm of art. He hurried to Amsterdam when he was given details of the art treasures which Rosenberg's organisation had found in Holland. One collection, in particular, "ownerless," he was told, demanded his immediate personal attention. It was the famous Goudstikker Collection, whose owner had perished in an accident during his escape from Holland to Great Britain. It would have been easy for Goering to order the confiscation of this collection, but he decided that it should be acquired legally in a way which was as cheap as confiscation. His experts, as economists of most conquering countries, introduced German "cash certificates" as legal tender in Holland, to be accepted in lieu of Dutch currency. Their value was to be set off against the cost of the German occupation, which Holland had to bear.

A German trading company was established, furnished with the requisite number of cash certificates, and entrusted with the acquisition of the Goudstikker Collection and other objects of artistic value. Herr Alois Miedl, who is still active in Bavaria, was asked to carry through this deal. Although important pieces of the collection found their way to Karinhall, it was not a transaction which Goering ordered on his own account or for his own benefit. There were over a thousand items. Most of the paintings were sent to Berlin to be stored. Hitler earmarked a number for his gallery in Linz. Eventually they were found intact and restored to Holland. Goering, during his stay in Amsterdam, inspected many other collections. He immersed himself in the study of art catalogues, and his heart beat high when he saw the glorious Dutch masters which graced the museums of Rotterdam, Amsterdam, and the Hague. Forgetting the problems of the war, he sat down to write Hitler about them in his own hand, "All these works of art must be secured." Hitler replied briefly, "We shall deal with them after the war." Permission was, however, given for Seyss-Inquart to make a present of one painting to the Vienna Kunsthistorische Museum.

In the meantime, the Dutch were well aware of Goering's personal interest in these matters. Intermediaries presented themselves with attractive offers. Goering did not ask many questions about origin or ownership. Herr Hofer insists that whatever was bought was duly "paid for." Collectors who feared confiscation sought out the art dealers who were able to establish contact with Goering's representatives. From a new fund of foreign exchange Goering paid out fantastic sums. Among paintings which he bought for himself were a Van der Meer and a Franz Hals, a sale negotiated by the Dutch artist, Hans van Meegeren. When van Meegeren, after the war, was indicted in the Dutch courts and accused of trading with the enemy, with Hermann Goering and other Nazi leaders, he declared in his defence that he had only cheated the greedy Germans. The paintings, he said truthfully, were forgeries. He had painted them himself. Van Meegeren, who made a fortune from these forgeries, was sentenced to a term in prison and died later. Goering only found out after the war that he had been one of many victims of the cleverest forger of the century.

From Amsterdam Goering went back to Paris where he moved into a large apartment at the Ritz Hotel in the Place Vendome. Poincaré's offices at the Quai d'Orsay were made ready for him and its big mirrors reflected his still powerful figure, but a weary face and idle hands toying with the elaborate inkstand in which Talleyrand once dipped his pen. His own pen was not put to papers of State. It was ticking off items in the catalogues of French museums, which aroused what he later called his "collector's passion." He gave orders that art treasures of importance should be brought from all parts of France to the Louvre in Paris where he could conveniently inspect them. After a week there was not enough space in the Louvre and an exhibition hall, La Salle du Jeu de Paume, was taken over for the rapidly growing collection. Though many pieces would have to go to Linz, Goering noted those which he was determined to get for Karinhall.

According to Goering's explanation, he was anxious to pay for them. "Fraeulein Limberger can testify to this," he said. The money, he added, was available in his bank. He called in a French expert to value the objects and a price was eventually fixed. But Herr Schwarz, the Nazi Party Treasurer, could not understand why Goering was so anxious to expend hard cash. Permission for the transfer of his money, Goering said, was refused. He did not explain how the Party Treasurer came to override the decision of Germany's economic dictator, but the money was never transferred to France. One object in particular roused Goering's fancy. It was a statue, La Belle Allemande, which was of German origin. Once it had actually been in Goering's possession. He had traded it and it had come to France. Now he wanted it back. Other Paris art treasures had been removed to castles along the Loire to protect them against bomb damage. Goering offered the museum managers the suggestion that they should be taken to Germany where they would be secure. It was genuine concern for art which motivated him. Many paintings and statues were removed from France and later found in the shafts which had been driven in the Bavarian mountainsides or in the salt mines of Salzburg where German and looted art treasures were stored.

France was rich in modern art, but Goering detested artists who painted in the manner of Pablo Picasso. Though the Spanish artist, who, with a mammoth painting, had engraved the German bombing of Guernica in the memory of the world, was left unmolested in Paris during the war, Goering regarded him as the exponent of "degenerate art." His work, that of Braque and other contemporaries, was confiscated and exchanged for the works of French impressionists, which went to Germany. The memory of the Edelweiss Chapel perpetuated in Goering a predilection for church ornaments and it was in these days that he heard of the famous "Basle Altar," one of the most beautiful masterpieces, dating from the eleventh century, a gift of Emperor Heinrich II to the Cathedral in Basle. France had acquired the altar in the nineteenth century. It was crowned by the figures of Jesus Christ, Archangels Michael, Raphael, and Gabriel, and St. Benedict — the pride of the Musée Cluny. Goering's negotiations for this altar continued over many years and the patriotic French employed many ruses to keep it from him. But the mere view of it, a French art expert told me, drove Goering "into a frenzy." It moved him so much that he knelt for hours in front of it and could not tear himself away.

His emissaries soon made a discovery to console him over the delay and eventual failure to get the Basle Altar. They found Van Eyck's "Mystic Lamb," an equally famous altar piece from the Ghent Cathedral which the Belgians had transferred to France in 1940, to be held in safe-keeping, in a village in the Pyrenees. To get it in his possession, Goering started negotiations with the Pétain Government and Abel Bonnard, its servile Minister of Culture. The details of the transaction are still obscure, but the "Mystic Lamb" during the second half of the war graced a special room of Karinhall.

Goering's collector's passion ranged wide. He made large funds available to enable the Reich to acquire the world-famous collection of Baron Henry de Rothschild. The invaluable eighteenth-century French masters were sent to Germany.

For weeks Luftwaffe signals to the Commander-in-Chief remained unanswered; Koerner, single-handed, shouldered the burden of organising the German economy. Hermann Goering was unapproachable by all except Hofer and the agents and dealers who were offering new paintings, tapestries, and valuables of every description. By now there was no country in Europe with which Karinhall Museum was not negotiating for purchases or exchanges. French masters went to Jugoslavia and old German paintings came to Germany in exchange. Italy produced some of her finest pieces to get objects in which Goering was not interested. In almost every city a privileged dealer could boast that he was the representative of the Marshal of the German Reich. There was no limit to the amounts which could be expended for the right object.

Yet, curiously, every single dealer with whom I spoke emphasised that it was not easy to deal with Goering. He was not only well advised but also had the profound knowledge of a connoisseur. And he resented attempts to take advantage of his irresistible urge to buy. He drove hard and astute bargains, paid as little as possible. His meanness in business became as proverbial as his generosity in private affairs. "If Hermann Goering," one dealer said, "had wanted to prove that he was spending his own hard-earned money, he could not have gone about it in a more impressive manner." Goering had another explanation for his meanness. "Wherever I went," he said, "before or during the war, in Paris, Florence, Rome, or Amsterdam, as if people had known in advance that I was coming, I would always have, in the shortest of time, a pile of written offers from all sorts of quarters — art dealers and private people. And sometimes I was rather deceived. As soon as it was known that it was me, the price was raised by fifty, or even a hundred, per cent." They never got that price.

That Goering had become a hard-bargaining, down-to-earth, practical businessman was soon apparent when he turned his attention again to larger economic issues. The officers of the Wehrmacht Economic Department and the official buyers which Germany sent to France, Holland, and Belgium were equally harassed by the tremendous prices which patriotic French demanded of them. The next step was for the Western patriots to let movable goods disappear altogether rather than allow them to fall into German hands — paid or unpaid. But the Wehrmacht and the German economy as a whole had counted on French produce. They went to Goering for advice and help. "Everything," they said, "is available — but only on the black market. Officially it is impossible for us to get raw materials, foodstuffs, butter, meat, or any of the things we need . . ." Goering laughed at the helplessness of his officers and economic envoys. "If things are available on the black market only — why, we shall simply go into the black market to get them!" An old airman friend, Colonel Veltjens, was put in charge of a German undercover organisation to buy raw materials, copper, tin, agricultural produce — everything in the black market. His agents ranged the West of Europe. From the canals of Holland where they were hidden, from the soil of France where they were buried, came materials which the German economy needed and of which France, Belgium, and Holland would have deprived the invaders had it not been for Veltjens and his big organisation of collaborators, Quislings, and unscrupulous agents.

"You know what the German economy needs," Goering told the Colonel. "Get it! Where it comes from is immaterial to me!" Goering did not realise what he had started. In the reckless scramble for materials in which a dozen German departments were engaged, agents of several ministries and of private German firms bid against each other — none knowing that the other also served a German master. Prices rose with the demand until they became prohibitive. The Wehrmacht employed Quislings to outbid the Ministry of Economics; the Todt Labour Organisation faced competition from Krupp's emissaries and sub-agents of the Hermann-Goering Works forced some of Goering's most privileged private intermediaries to pay three times over the odds. When he tried to stop the rot by giving Veltjens a monopoly on black market deals, it was too late; when even Laval asked him to put an end to these German practices, his attempts to return to legitimate business methods failed. The black market had replaced the regular economy of Western Europe.

It was inevitable that this type of German policy should create an atmosphere of treachery, corruption, a general lowering of moral standards, and outright crime. Honest Frenchmen were tempted into deals with operators whom they knew to be in German employ. Germans, Dutchmen, Belgians, scrambled to pick up profits from deals which involved millions of francs and guilders. The agents resorted to bribery to get on the track of hidden stores for which the Germans were prepared to pay fabulous prices.

Goering's own entourage, under these circumstances, could not keep their hands clean. Whether it was art or ore, commissions often amounting to hundreds of thousands were always on offer. The ear of the Reichsmarschall was worth a million. The Wehrmacht was cleaning out the shops of Paris. There were no nylons as yet, but silk stockings, lace blouses, lingerie, were in every parcel which went to Germany. Goering's adjutants bought trunkloads of valuable furs and silks. Sometimes they did not pay. When, a few months later, Emmy Goering told her husband that the wife of one of his aides had lost everything in an air raid on Berlin, Goering asked her not to be too sorry for her. "Whatever she had," he said, "her husband bought in Paris — and charged it to my account!"

The central figure in the midst of these crazy, criminal happenings did obviously not remain unaffected either. One of Goering's fiercest enemies in Germany pondered about him: "You cannot help feeling," he reluctantly admitted to himself, "that temptation of this sort does not come in the way of an average person. Opportunities for such transaction are luckily rare. A man whose bidding is done by everybody must fall easily!" It was not so when the position was reversed after the defeat and occupation of Germany. Though there were a few minor dark spots on the shield of the Allied armies who conquered and occupied Germany, not a single officer at the higher levels of the military and civilian administration soiled his hands. The German friend of Hermann Goering would have expressed himself more succinctly with the familiar dictum: "Power corrupts. Absolute power corrupts absolutely!" Hermann Goering, who started out as Goebbels' "upright soldier," was corrupt.

His legitimate income had risen to fantastic proportions. His salary as a Reichsmarschall, as President of the Prussian State

Council, as Air Minister, Reichstag President, Commissioner for the Four-Year Plan, Reich Chief Hunter, together with separate expense allowances for each job, plus his income from his newspapers, the book of his collected speeches, and the shares in the aircraft industry and the Hermann-Goering Works amounted to one and a quarter million marks per annum (1,285,200 marks, to be exact and according to his income-tax return). In captivity he was questioned about his financial affairs, but it was agreed that the subject should not be raised at his trial in Nuremberg. But what he told the interrogators made it clear that, even so, he was living far beyond his income. His income tax was owing. His bank overdraft reached the limit of seven million marks. Private firms like Reemtsma, the cigarette manufacturers, advanced money for his use. He invested only small amounts in insurance which he took out in almost every neutral country. But money had lost its meaning for him; the exact value of the Karinhall art collection was a matter of little concern to him. He personally no longer carried cash. "Brauchitsch, pay!" was his standard order to his personal adjutant.

Having reached the dizzy height of a position to which only few men of our age ever aspired, Goering, living in Paris in the style of Louis XIV, had every reason to feel great. He was forty-seven now, still young enough to enjoy the fruits of his life's struggle. But his friends noticed that he was neither happy nor satisfied. Freud would have said that he was still yearning for the satisfaction of his infant desires, which had been transformed into an insatiable hunger for everything within his apprehension. Professor Trevor Roper, whose penetrating analysis of the Nazi mind [1] almost always hits the mark, is however wrong when he assumes that Goering, like Hitler, relaxed in the confident expectation of early or inevitable victory. Ailing, suffering from nervous exhaustion, relying on drugs, weakened by glandular complications, Goering, once an inveterate optimist, was tormented by fears. In a letter to a friend, he wrote from Paris that "things are too good to be true!" He had risen so high that even the remote possibility of a fall terrified him. Somehow he felt that he could not forever remain on the high peak of absolute and unrestricted power. How right he was!

He was too astute to overlook the ill-disguised hostility of many

[1] Trevor Roper, *The Last Days of Hitler.*

eminent men he met; he had no illusions about the feelings which the German invasion had aroused in Western Europe. Goebbels never believed his own propaganda about Germany's "European Mission." Goering knew that it was sheer humbug. He was such an intense patriot that, though he treated and entertained them royally, he had little personal respect for Pierre Laval and the Dutch Quislings. He did not even regard Marshal Pétain as a worthy member of the military profession. How could these men be real patriots?

More than ever before he relied on the small circle of his personal friends, whom he could trust implicitly. He would not let Bruno Loerzer from his side; he called for Bodenschatz; he wanted Koerner to be with him. The only Nazi functionary with whom he was on friendly terms was Philip Bouhler of the Party Office. Though he attended many functions and appeared good-humoured and talkative, he felt lonely. In a hostile world he became sensitive and intolerant of every hint of criticism. After discussing his frame of mind with people who knew him well in these days, I have come to the conclusion that the failure of the Luftwaffe had hurt his pride, even though he was still hoping for, even counting on, a victory over Britain. One of the mental pillars on which his self-assurance had rested was cracked and crumbling. Hitler's disappointment, Goebbels' reproaches, made him suffer. What Hitler really thought of him was a constant preoccupation. If there was the slightest suggestion of disapproval from any quarter, he would flare up: "Is that what the Fuehrer thinks?" He felt Hitler's shadow darkening the sun which seemed to shine on him as on no other mortal of his age.

17

UNDER A CLOUD

WHEN I drove to the Obersalzberg after the war, to Hitler's Berghof high above Berchtesgaden, tourists from a dozen countries were inspecting the ruins of the Third Reich Olympus, where the Nazi gods used to dwell and no ordinary man or woman was allowed to tread. They inspected the shell of the once fortified block which housed the Leibstandarte, and the little villa reserved for Hitler's numerous adjutants, the outhouses, staff quarters, and farm buildings which made up Hitler's mountain retreat. The climax of their sight-seeing tour was the Fuehrer's famous study, now bare brick and mortar, and the yawning gap, once the world's largest window, looking out onto the Austrian mountains.

An elaborate hydraulic press operated the huge, thick pane of glass, there were deep carpets, silent footmen and orderlies, sparkling flames in the red-brick fireplace, when Hermann Goering visited the Fuehrer in the early days of 1941. Dressed in his hunting outfit, wide-sleeved shirt under a mediaeval, long leather garment, belt with dangling dagger, he walked the half-mile from his own villa across the mountain, passing the house which Martin Bormann, with symbolic significance, had built on an empty plot between the residences of Germany's two leading men. Hitler was awaiting him in the study and Goering settled down in one of the deep, green-leather chairs for a long, long talk with his Fuehrer. There was a shadow over his cheerful face, revealing the fears and doubts which had possessed him since his return to Germany. As usual, he had been able to hide them when, from a public platform, reviewing the events of the past year and speaking like a man without a care in the world, he had said, "In 1940 we have achieved the most brilliant successes in the history of the German people!"

But away from the crowds, Goering showed signs of his physical deterioration. He was either extremely tired or unnaturally buoyed-up by a new drug, paracodein, of which he had ordered large stocks. Hitler was also in a state of artificial exhilaration as he dealt with a hundred new plans at the same time. Deferential as usual, Goering, a little petulantly, complained to him that he had been left out of important political moves. While he had been fiddling in Paris, the wild fire of war had rapidly spread. German troops had moved into Hungary and Rumania, where General Antonescu had deposed King Carol. King Boris had been in Berchtesgaden to receive Hitler's orders. Twice Hitler had seen Mussolini trying in vain to dissuade him from a prestige move against Albania and Greece where his troops soon got into difficulties. Field Marshal Milch had been to Rome to install the Luftwaffe in Italy.

At the year's end, Hitler had travelled to meet General Franco at Hendaye. Goering only later told General Koller the full story of the Fuehrer's failure to persuade Franco to enter the war, a grave disappointment about which he wrote to the Duce: "Franco's decision . . . is particularly regrettable as German forces were ready to enter Spain with a view to attacking Gibraltar." According to Goering, Hitler had refused to give Franco a written confirmation of his promise of a free hand for Spain in Africa: "If I give him that in writing," Hitler said, "he will only go to the Allies and get a better bargain from them." Goering said that Hitler never intended to keep his promise, anyway; and Franco, wisely, stayed out of the war. One of Goering's strategic ideas had come to nought.

When the United States signed the Lease-Lend Agreement with Britain, Hitler told Goering: "War with America is now a possibility. It makes it necessary for us to get a firm hold on North Africa; we may have to try and conquer the Atlantic Islands. Long-range bombers will have to be developed to carry the war right into America." It was an unpleasant prospect. Goering had a personal request. His only diplomatic engagement had been to see Molotov in Berlin for a short and frigid conversation. He did not want to fade out of the political picture and he asked Hitler to strengthen his position. The Fuehrer obliged with a speech to celebrate his birthday and said that "the Reichsmarschall's merits are unique!" But their conversations inevitably turned to a subject which Goering was not at all anxious to discuss. The R.A.F. had probed deeply into Germany, bombed Berlin, Bremen, Cologne, and attacked Essen in the Ruhr, which had been guaranteed immunity by Goering: "Well, Herr Meier . . . ?" Hitler asked with undisguised irony, recalling Goering's unfortunate promises. Goering did not as yet know, but all Germany was referring to him as "Herr Meier"; "They even called us the 'Meier Division,' " Bernhard Hoffmann, a former staff captain of the Hermann Goering Division, told me laughingly in Munich. It was no laughing matter to him then, nor did the troops of the division like it.

Goering tried to pacify Hitler. "They cannot do to us what we have done to Coventry," he retorted, although after the war he took great pains to explain that he had ordered the attack on Coventry because he regarded it as the heart of the British aircraft industry and as a legitimate target. He felt sure, he told Hitler, that the psychological effect of that Luftwaffe operation would soon make itself felt. It would also give him an opportunity to impress the German people. However much he had changed, he still had great personal courage and agreed to address a meeting of Ruhr miners. "I know," he told them, "that it is unpleasant for you to suffer all this damage, to worry about your families . . . but remember that for every twenty or thirty British bombers which come over here, five hundred to seven hundred Luftwaffe aircraft are attacking Britain." The Ruhr miners were not concerned with retaliation. Close acquaintance with a shooting war shook their confidence in victory.

Hitler's faith in the Luftwaffe and its chief was equally shaken — the real cause of their creeping estrangement. Their relations received a further jolt when General Simovic's swift revolt in Jugoslavia ousted the pro-Nazi Premier, Cvetkovic, and drove from power Goering's friend, Prince Regent Paul, forcing a rapid and awkward change of Germany's plans to aid Italy and Greece. The vicious bombing of Belgrade, as the Wehrmacht attacked Jugoslavia, was one way in which the Luftwaffe avenged the hurt feelings of its commander-in-chief. With the campaign in Jugoslavia under way, the subject of Hitler's plans for the attack on Russia loomed large in his discussions with Goering. Here, for once, he had to oppose Hitler. Was the Fuehrer undoing his own "master stroke" in concluding a pact with Russia? Now that Hitler went to the other extreme, Goering protested. What about *Mein Kampf*, the long passages describing the dangers of a war on two fronts? "There will be no war on two fronts," Hitler retorted. "My Atlantic Wall will protect us in the West while we quickly knock out Russia." Goering gave a very complete version of this conversation. "We are," he said to Hitler, "fighting against a great world power, the British Empire. . . . I am definitely of the opinion that sooner or later . . . the United States will march against us. In the case of a clash with Russia, a third great world power would be thrown into the struggle and we would again stand alone against practically the entire world. . . ." But he could not shake Hitler's argument that Russia was planning an attack on Germany and that Russian re-armament would reach a climax in 1942 or 1943. "The plans for 'Case Barbarossa' [staff code word for the attack on Russia] "are ready," Hitler said. "The Luftwaffe will receive my instructions." Goering left as doubtful about Hitler's genius as Hitler was of Goerings's ability as a Luftwaffe Commander.

To escape the tension of such dramatic conversations and to avoid the Fuehrer's unmistakable displeasure, the reproachful look in his eyes, Goering fled to Veldenstein. Though he took his staff with him, he did not concern himself with affairs of State and sought relaxation in long hunting expeditions.

On Sunday, May 10, 1941, Bodenschatz was on the telephone from Hitler's study in Berchtesgaden.

"The Fuehrer wants you to come to the Berghof at once."

"What does he want?"

"I cannot tell you . . ."

"Give me a clue, please, a clue . . ."

"I am afraid I cannot . . . Fuehrer's orders!"

Bodenschatz, chief witness of the day's events, told me the full story. He was present when an orderly announced the arrival of one of Rudolf Hess' adjutants with orders to hand Hitler a personal letter from his chief. "It's Sunday," Hitler said; "I don't want to see him." When the orderly explained that the man would not be turned away, Hitler eventually asked him in. He stood at attention. "A letter from Rudolf Hess, mein Fuehrer," he said. "Open it,

Bodenschatz," Hitler ordered. As he glanced at it, his mouth opened and he slumped into a chair behind him: "Bodenschatz . . . imagine . . . this crazy idiot . . . he has flown to England!"

Hitler's consternation and surprise, Bodenschatz said, were supremely played: "Bodenschatz," he said again, "he is crazy . . . he has gone to England . . . call Ribbentrop . . . where is Goering . . . I want him at once . . . telephone Bormann. You must not say a word about this . . . Hess has flown to England . . . I want you to find out how and from where . . . the Luftwaffe, die verfluchte Luftwaffe [the damned Luftwaffe] again . . .!"

Within half an hour, Bodenschatz established that an unscheduled Messerschmitt had been seen flying out toward the North Sea; it was obviously identical with an aircraft which had taken off from the aerodrome of the Messerschmitt Works in Augsburg. Bormann came from his house, only a few hundred yards away. Albert Speer, Hitler's favourite architect and armaments expert, came in. Ribbentrop motored from his castle in Fuschl, Salzburg. Goering, after a four hours' drive from Veldenstein, was the last to arrive. Hitler informed every one of his lieutenants in turn of Hess' flight: "He says in his letter that he is trying to make peace, but will not disclose my plans to attack Russia. . . ." At Goering, Hitler hurled insults: "Your Luftwaffe has flown Hess to England! You will pay for this!" Changing his tune, he asked Goering: "Can he make it . . . ? You are an airman, tell me . . . can he get there on his own?" "It's a fifty-fifty chance!" Goering replied, using the English expression. "So you are already speaking English," Hitler flared up. "If Mussolini hears about this, he will think I have been trying to make a separate peace . . . Ribbentrop, get the Duce on the phone . . ."

There was pandemonium. "If he gets there, it will give Britain a unique propaganda opportunity," Goering said. "We must issue a communiqué, we must come out before they can say a word." "But, maybe, he has fallen into the sea," Hitler retorted, "then nobody will know . . ." As Goering insisted, he consented to prepare a communiqué in any event. Bodenschatz wrote to Hitler's dictation: "Tear it up!" Hitler said after he had read it. Seven versions were written as Ribbentrop and Goering suggested alterations. "I shall arrest his adjutants and question his wife!" said Bormann, Hess' ruthless, ambitious deputy. He was the only man in the room who was happy about the event. If Hess had gone forever, he would succeed to the most powerful position in the Party and would make good use of it. He would be able, at last, to face men like Goering on equal terms . . .

In the early hours of the morning, Goering left the Berghof arm-in-arm with Bodenschatz. He winked at his old friend: "The Fuehrer has slipped up, hasn't he?" It was clear to all that Hitler, faithful to his wartime practice of discussing top secrets only with the people immediately concerned, had hatched a plot with Rudolf Hess, his closest associate. If Hess could convince Britain that Germany was about to attack Russia, peace in the West might, after all, be possible. He could bring off the coup which Goering had failed to achieve with diplomacy and the Luftwaffe.

Mr. Churchill sternly rebuked Stalin when the Soviet leader doubted his description of the Hess episode as the action of a crazy individual. Though they hardly agree on anything else with the Soviet dictator, every single surviving member of Goering's entourage, including General Bodenschatz, shares Stalin's doubts. They are convinced that Hitler not only hoped to make peace with the West, but also hoped to persuade the British Government to join in Germany's attack on Russia. Hitler's bewilderment in Berchtesgaden was due to fear that his plot had failed. Hess was supposed to send a message on his arrival, and Hitler realised that something had gone wrong when there was nothing but silence, tormenting silence, from Britain.

Hitler sent Ribbentrop to Rome to discuss the "affaire Hess" with the Duce. Two days later he was at the Palazzo Venezia in conference with Mussolini and Count Ciano. "We were flabbergasted," he told them, on Hitler's instructions, "when the news of Hess' trip reached us. It is the action of a madman." Goering was on the telephone from Germany and lent support to Ribbentrop's explanations. He, too, explained that Hess had been suffering from a disease and had fallen into the hands of nature healers, who only damaged his health further. "We are investigating all these things now," Goering said. "We are also dealing with his adjutants who know that Hess has been practicing secretly with an Me 110. Anyway, Duce, you can judge for yourself that it is the move of an infantile mind, the result of a mental state caused by illness." Hitler, he added, took a very serious view of the affair. Hess had been deposed and would be shot if he ever returned to Germany. Mussolini thought the consequences were not serious. "It all depends on what Hess will spill in England," he said. Goering was pleased that he was "back in diplomacy," and when Count Ciano came to Germany, he gave him a grand reception. "I met Goering at his home in Berlin," Ciano noted[1]: "The form observed was that used for sovereigns; the guests, lined up in the entrance, awaited his arrival which was announced in a loud voice by a Master of Ceremonies . . . Goering gave the conversation a really friendly character such as I had not encountered in him for a long time. . . . "

Another consequence of this incident affected Goering in a personal and more serious manner. Though, in a new decree, Hitler confirmed him as his deputy, he also appointed Martin Bormann, his worst enemy, to succeed Hess as Party Chancellor. With Goebbels contemptuously aloof, Himmler suspicious, and Bormann downright hostile, Goering's position in the Nazi hierarchy was shaky. He could not now very well shirk his duties as a military commander and turned his mind again to the Luftwaffe. The Wehrmacht had scored in Greece and inflicted a defeat on the British diversionary force. Goering worked on staff plans for a parachute assault on Crete. But although his Fallschirmjaeger eventually conquered and Hitler boasted that "there are no unconquerable islands," the losses were so heavy that the effective strength of the Luftwaffe's crack parachute division was destroyed. As the Wehrmacht massed against Russia, Goering was forced to withdraw Kesselring's air fleet from the West. He realised that his ambitious plans to win the war against Britain by bombing had failed.

The nerve centre of Hitler's Government and war strategy was the Wolfschanze, the Fuehrer Headquarters in Rastenburg, in East Prussia. There Hitler lived in his train, while barracks were adapted as offices and other improvised buildings housed the S.S. Leibstandarte, his military guard, the offices of the Wehrmacht High

[1] *Ciano's Diplomatic Papers,* edited by Malcolm Muggeridge.

Command and the Army General Staff. Luftwaffe Headquarters were a few miles away at Goldapp, in convenient proximity to Goering's Rominten shooting lodge. At the Wolfschanze, Hitler was in constant conference with Field Marshal Wilhelm Keitel and General Alfred Jodl, his personal military adviser. His entourage included Staff Officers General Buhle and Major Buechs. Bodenschatz was there, so was Press Chief Dr. Otto Dietrich, the Fuehrer's Luftwaffe aide, Colonel von Below, and his personal adjutants, Colonel Rudolf Schmundt, Julius Schaub, and Wilhelm Brueckner. Ribbentrop and Himmler came for occasional conferences. Every day at 1 P.M. there was a Lagebesprechung (Situation Conference) at which the Chiefs of Staff of the three services reported about the events of the preceding twenty-four hours and received Hitler's instructions. Goering attended only occasionally. Bodenschatz kept him informed of all topics under discussion and General Jeschonneck reported to him on official matters concerning the Luftwaffe.

Goering lived in a world of his own, drawing the circle of his personal friends closer around him. He appointed Bruno Loerzer as Luftwaffe Chief of Personnel to see that only officers loyal to the Commander-in-Chief be put in key positions. The man who had made an airman of him, his old First World War comrade, was with him day and night. It was almost inevitable that he should soon gain a dominating influence on the Reichsmarschall. Goering called for his advice on everything he did. He would listen to few other voices. As his own influence on Hitler waned, he became ever more anxious to exert himself as a leader in his own sphere and insisted on reserving all decisions to himself. The Fuehrer principle, the exercise of which he had enjoyed so much in the years after 1933, became his last anchor of personal authority. In Luftwaffe matters he insisted on it rigorously. The range of his personal preserves grew. The volume of work which he took on became bigger until he was quite unable to cope with it. The number of decisions which he deferred and of matters which he neglected increased rapidly.

Bruno Loerzer was the kind of "adviser" who usually attaches himself to a person of prominence. Goering also attracted one or two other "friends" who tried to impress him with spirited contradiction in details while anxious to please him with indiscriminate agreement on larger issues. Such men know how to flatter a bigger personality in his moments of weakness, but invariably in the end desert, betray, or lead their idol on a course of fatal consequences. Inevitably, too, Goering allowed them a free hand. While they relieved him of the minor unpleasantnesses of his duties, they eventually led him into greater dilemmas. At the time, as always in such instances, he was not aware of the sins committed in his name.

Problems of great magnitude confronted him in these critical days. The Wehrmacht swept into Russia and Luftwaffe resources were strained to the limit. Hitler, who could quickly familiarise himself with technical problems, criticised Luftwaffe production methods and Goering passed on the criticism to General Udet, his old friend, whom he had entrusted with a responsibility far exceeding his capability. The old warhorse had remained a happy-go-lucky fellow, always at hand with a funny story, always thinking out practical jokes, wisecracking, doodling, drawing, even during important conferences and causing much amusement with his funny pictures and caricatures. Udet was popular, although he irritated serious, anxious generals and production experts whose train of thought he often interrupted with his pranks. On this gloriously uninhibited character Goering unloaded the full force of his complaints which Hitler heaped on his head. When the cold Russian winter caught the finest types of German aircraft unequal to the barbaric weather conditions, Goering's accusations of "inadequacy" rudely tore Udet from a world of happy fantasies and brought him back to catastrophic realities. He was obviously unequal to his task, but he never expected his friend Goering to put all the blame on him. After a violent argument, Udet disappeared from Goering's presence. On November 18, 1941, the official Deutsche Nachrichtenburo (German News Agency) reported: "Colonel-General Udet, in the course of testing a new weapon, suffered a grave accident and died of his injuries. . . . In recognition of his services in the development of the Luftwaffe, the Fuehrer has decided to name Fighter Group III after him. . . ."

In Munich, when investigating the sudden death of Ernst Udet, I almost became fair game for the scores of ex-Nazis engaged in their favourite and profitable business of selling "secret documents" and information about the mysteries of the Hitler period. The "truth about Udet" rated many thousand marks. I found out more cheaply that it was no secret in Germany in 1941 that Colonel-General Udet had committed suicide. Goering was badly shaken. He called on one of Udet's lady friends, who had been with him during his last days. Angrily he threatened her with arrest, even with death, if she revealed the facts. For reasons of public morale, he told her, the unforunate truth must never become known. Goering attended Udet's funeral, crestfallen, grey in the face, shaking. Hitler walked with him silently. There was another shock in store for them when, in a real accident, Werner Moelders, Goering's favourite war pilot, was killed at about the same time. A wave of rumours swept Germany. They all centred on Goering. His nerves greatly affected, he was given to violent explosions, continually shouted at his staff, threatening even generals with Erschiessen within the hearing of junior officers. The scenes in which the once so smooth and perfect gentleman was involved could no longer be hidden from wider circles.

Everything was going wrong. Emmy had been insulted again. When, in view of the official petrol-saving campaign, she refused to use her car, went by underground or walked through Berlin on foot, her bodyguard reported to Martin Bormann, who told Hitler. From the Fuehrer she received a rude letter, saying in effect that she was damaging the prestige of Germany. If it appeared that there was not enough petrol for Germany's First Lady, the Russians and the British would soon guess that his Luftwaffe and his Panzers were running out of fuel! Whatever they did, neither Hermann nor Emmy Goering could escape Hitler's criticism. Even the General Staff took a tilt at the toppling Goering Empire. General Halder demanded that the Luftwaffe ground organisation and regiments be pruned and whole units be transferred to the Army. Goering felt the ground slipping from under him.

"There is no discipline in the Luftwaffe, anyway," Hitler said when Goering complained to him. Hitler, in his prejudice, picked on a minor incident, but Goering took up the cue. When Luftwaffe court-martial sentences against airmen were submitted to him for approval, he flew into a temper. "Five years for cowardice in the face of the enemy!" he bellowed at the Judge Advocate: "I order erschiessen!" The culprit was not yet eighteen years old, a mere boy, Bodenschatz protested. "Erschiessen!" shouted Goering. But the ink on his signature was not yet dry when he changed his mind. "Bodenschatz," he called, "tell the Judge Advocate to let the Court's original verdict stand." This happened time after time.

The blows were falling hard and fast. Stung at Pearl Harbour, the United States of America ranged themselves on Britain's side in the battle against the dictatorships. The Russian winter, with icy, iron fingers, gripped at the heartstrings of the Wehrmacht. In the face of disaster, Goering could still rise to the occasion. His speech about the débâcle of the unprepared and ill-equipped German Army in Russia was a masterpiece of demagogic oratory. For two hours he harangued a vast crowd, rousing their sympathy for the soldiers in Russia, treating them to a long list of German achievements. "We are thousands of kilometres deep in the Russian land . . . " he said — but he did not mention that Hitler had expected to take Moscow before the winter. "The worst winter in a hundred years!" he said. "Remember Napoleon and his retreat . . . but our front stood firm. And what is Napoleon compared with the strategic genius of the Fuehrer?" He had to admit, however, that "some of our troops, attacked by the icy cold, did not see it through and had to be sent home." The Russian plains were littered with the bodies of frozen, mutilated Germans. "The Fuehrer's faith in his soldiers and officers is unshaken!" he said, although he knew it was no longer true. "And the Fuehrer himself suppressed all feelings of weakness," he added. "He was hard; his mind was clear; he was superhuman. If it was possible to hold out and return to the offensive, the credit belongs to one man only — the Fuehrer!"

While defending Hitler in public, however, he had to defend himself against Hitler's accusation that the Luftwaffe dared not venture into Leningrad. Goering, according to his own account, replied: "As long as my air force is ready to fly into the hell of London, it will equally be prepared to attack the much less defended city of Leningrad. But I lack the necessary forces . . . mein Fuehrer, you must not give so many tasks to my air force . . . !"

The Luftwaffe was stretched out along a two-thousand-mile front in the East, it faced the R.A.F. and the first units of the American Army Air Force in the West. "Hold out, my friends!" Goering asked the German people, whose cities were being battered by bombs; "all they want us to do is to divert fighters from the front and to let our fighting men down!" He was still adept at producing a popular twist. On a tour of aerodromes in Russia, he visited towns and villages. "I saw such abject poverty in Vinitza that I could hardly believe people could live under such conditions!" What he saw in Russia staggered the lord of many manors, but his statement was chiefly designed to refute accusations that the Wehrmacht had plundered even these poverty-stricken districts.

From the cold of Russia, Goering sought refuge in a warmer climate. He took his wife to Vienna. It was an untimely visit. Germany was feeling the strain of war and shortages, but Baldur von Schirach, the Nazi Youth leader, arranged a gala performance at the Opera in honour of Reichsmarschall and Frau Goering. There were rumblings in the audience when the Goerings, exquisitely dressed, appeared in their box. Emmy looked like a queen, Hermann, in his fine white uniform, like an Eastern potentate. "But it is not true that I wore an ermine-lined coat," Emmy said, "though I had three at home!" The Marshal had to take a telephone call during the interval and Schirach insisted that the beginning of the second act should be delayed until his return to the box. It was three-quarters of an hour. For the first time the Reichsmarschall heard the slow clapping of a crowd whose anger, he knew, was directed against him. As the lights went out, ugly remarks came from the darkness of the auditorium. Gestapo agents failed to locate the shouters. There was no mistaking the fact that the Goerings were not popular in Vienna.

Angrily he cut short his visit, and departed for Italy where the news was better: Rommel had taken Tobruk and twenty-five thousand prisoners; German prestige was high in Italy. With Mussolini he discussed another hopeful sign — of quarrels and dissensions in the Allied camp. Russia was publicly clamouring for a

"Second Front"; Lord Beaverbrook supported Stalin in a speech in Washington. The Wehrmacht was poised for the conquest of Stalingrad. But Germany was in a grim mood, public morale was low. Criticism of the régime spread to the highest quarters. When Goering returned to Berlin, he went into conference with his legal advisers and asked them to draft a new law. "The powers of the leadership must be supreme! We must have a law of totality. Whether we are dealing with civilians or soldiers — we need blind obedience to deal with a different situation!" The law reflected the growing uncertainty in Hitler's mind and Goering's own refusal to allow criticism. Once before, in 1933, he had promulgated a decree abolishing individual freedom. His new law, when he introduced it, put this early version in the shade. Every single person was at the Fuehrer's disposal. It was formulated to apply specifically to the restive generals. "Nobody," it said, "is allowed to leave his post without permission!" Generals and privates alike were affected. Rumours of an Army crisis spread when Hitler dismissed General von Brauchitsch and personally assumed leadership of the Army. Word went round in Germany that Field Marshal von Reichenau (who actually died of a stroke) had been shot. Goering faced the storm and said threateningly: "We have not yet shot any generals . . . but that does not mean that generals cannot be shot!"

The Luftwaffe generals suffered the full impact of his attitude. Every encounter with them ended in a clash. General Karl Koller told me of an incident which was typical of this phase in Goering's life. Summoned by his Commander-in Chief to discuss a technical problem, Koller ventured to contradict Goering. "You are trying to sabotage the Luftwaffe," Goering accused him. "You are a traitor!" His veins swelling, his fingers gripping as if to strangle Koller in the next second, standing face to face with the unfortunate general, Goering seemed to lose all self-control. Koller told me: "I was wondering what to do if he should touch me. After all, I was a general . . . and we were not accustomed to such behavior. . . . I decided, if he moved another inch toward me, to kick his fat belly with my knee. The thought of this seemed so funny that it relaxed my tension. I turned on my heels, left the room, and wrote out my resignation."

Reading Koller's letter, Goering regretted his impetuosity. He answered with an apology in the most humble terms, assuring Koller of his complete confidence. "Amazing fellow," Koller commented. He really liked Goering. "He was ein saugrober Lackel, aber ein guter Kerl," he summed up in his Bavarian idiom—a piggishly rude guy, but a kind fellow withal. Goering still had many faces. When Hitler promised Rommel greater Luftwaffe support which was really not available, Goering was asked to pacify Germany's most popular general. Accompanying Rommel on a long train journey, he cunningly avoided the subject of the missing Luftwaffe. Rommel spoke about air support in Africa, Goering talked about art in Italy. When I later told Frau Goering that Frau Rommel [2] had quoted the General's highly uncomplimentary comments about this conversation with Goering, she shook her head sadly. "I was present. We got on so well. My husband was fond of Rommel and I was so proud to meet him . . ." she said, but she did not really know the background of Rommel's disappointment and anger.

Though Goering could not send Rommel air reinforcements, he agreed that his Hermann Goering Division should be shipped to Africa together with an S.S. division and a Regular Army division. What an opportunity for Keitel and Himmler to get in a blow at Hermann Goering, the fallen idol! The Hermann Goering Division was duly dispatched to Africa; the S.S. and Army units were delayed. The Reichsmarschall's troops walked straight into Anglo-American captivity! Goering's pride had disappeared in the enemy's bag. Captain Hoffmann told me how acutely the Luftwaffe officers felt that they had been sold down the river by the Wehrmacht. The toppling Nazi Colossus was already beginning to cut off his nose to spite his face.

Defeat was as yet not a possibility even contemplated in Germany, but the prospect of a drawn-out conflict, with all the attendant uncertainties and difficulties, oppressed the Nazi leaders. France did not co-operate as expected and total occupation became necessary. Among the thousands of unfortunate anti-Nazis in Vichy France who fell into the hands of the Gestapo was Fritz Thyssen, who was

[2] Desmond Young, *Rommel, The Desert Fox.*

quickly whisked off to a concentration camp. For Goering, the sentimentalist, who was always looking over his shoulder into the past, this was too much. He implored Hitler to release him. "We must not forget what he has done for us!" he said. Hitler protested that leniency would only encourage enemies of the régime. Goering, world-wise, had an answer: "Everybody thinks we have sent Thyssen to France as our agent. If he is released, it will only seem to confirm this view and no damage will be done." Thyssen was released.

The Luftwaffe involved Goering in a new conflict with Hitler. General Karl Koller told me about one of his own schemes to save the lives of German airmen who came down in the Channel: "We were always in touch with the R.A.F. and advised them when we saw airmen in the water and in distress," he said. "Sometimes they were R.A.F. men — but what did it matter as long as we could save our fellows!" During one of the R.A.F. sweeps over France, Squadron Leader Douglas Bader, the great legless airman, was shot down, but managed to save himself in a parachute descent. Hitting the ground hard, he damaged one of his artificial legs. His reputation stood already high in the Luftwaffe, and when he told his captors that he had a pair of spare legs at his own aerodrome in Britain, Koller signalled the R.A.F. that the Luftwaffe would hold its fire if a British aircraft flew over their lines to drop Bader's spare limbs! The operation was carried out according to his arrangements, but as the legs floated down, Bader was already on the first of his many daring attempts to escape.

His disappearance was reported to Hitler personally, who called for a report from the responsible Luftwaffe officer. "How come that you let him escape?" he asked; "Mein Fuehrer," was the reply, "we never expected him to make an attempt before he got his legs. . . ." Hitler gathered from this innocent reply that the Luftwaffe and the R.A.F. had been in communication. "That's treason," he shouted, "I shall have you shot . . . !" He called Goering, who, as always, concurred with Hitler. He threatened Koller on the telephone; proceedings for high treason would be taken against him and all concerned, "Surely, you understand why we have maintained these communications," Koller appealed to Goering, ". . . surely you approve of our attempts to save our own men?" His arguments prevailed, Goering was mollified. "Marvellous fellow, that Bader," he said eventually; "I'd like to meet him!" Even Koller thought that Goering actually summoned the R.A.F. hero, as he had asked to see Squadron Leader Murray early in the war. But Group Captain Bader told me that he never met Goering or any of the Nazi chiefs.

Goering, these days, did not visit the front very often. He was again operating chiefly over the telephone from Veldenstein or from the Obersalzberg. Frequently, as far as the conduct of the war was concerned, he did not operate at all.

18

APPROACH TO DEATH

DURING the last night of May, 1942, there was music in the air over Britain. Acute ears heard the drone of aircraft engines in the dark sky. Years of experience told the people that they could keep their heads high. These were not Luftwaffe Heinkels and Messerschmitts. It was the R.A.F. flying toward Germany in a never-ending stream, wave after wave, squadron after squadron, from a hundred aerodromes all over the country. Steadily they passed the shores of Britian, inexorably they flew across the continent. Cologne was the target for tonight. Fifteen hundred tons of bombs were dropped; alas, thirty-nine aircraft failed to return. But on this night in Cologne the R.A.F. smashed more than German factories, warehouses, railway yards, and Rhine shipping. They tore a breach in the unity of the German High Command, a gap in the relations between Hitler and Goering which was never closed again. With this raid, a friendship which had lasted exactly twenty years came to an end.

Goering was not present at the Lagebesprechung in the Fuehrer Headquarters at Rastenburg the next noon. Hitler seemed calm as he listened to his naval spokesman, who told him about the trouble into which German shipping had run off the coast of Africa. He made no comment when he was informed about the details of the situation around Kharkov, where the Wehrmacht was trying to relieve strong Russian pressure with a counter-offensive. "The Luftwaffe . . . ?" he asked with a studied quietness which should have told the gathering of staff officers and aides that a storm was brewing: "General Jeschonneck, I am waiting . . ." The slim, youthful Chief of Staff of the Luftwaffe gathered his papers. "Cologne, mein Fuehrer . . . there was an R.A.F. attack on

Cologne!" Bodenschatz gave me a description of the scene. Hitler, he said, was looking at the air force officer, waiting for details. "A pretty heavy attack," said Jeschonneck. "How heavy?" Hitler asked, cold as ice. "According to preliminary reports," Jeschonneck replied, "we estimate that two hundred enemy aircraft have penetrated our defences. The damage is heavy . . . we are still waiting for final estimates!"

"You are still waiting for final estimates" — Hitler's voice rose — "and the Luftwaffe thinks that there were two hundred enemy aircraft!" His shouts turned into a shriek: "The Luftwaffe has probably been asleep last night . . . but I have not been asleep. I stay awake when one of my cities is under fire. And — " screaming — "and I thank the Almighty that I can rely on my Gauleiter, even if the Luftwaffe deceives me! Let me tell you what Gauleiter Grohe has to say! Listen — I ask you to listen carefully — THERE WERE A THOUSAND OR MORE ENGLISH AIRCRAFT — you hear — A THOUSAND, TWELVE HUNDRED — maybe more!" he ended, exhausted by his exertion.

"Herr Goering, of course, is not here; of course not . . ." Hitler said, pointedly omitting the title of the Reichsmarschall. Bodenschatz thought that this was his cue to slip out of the room and to the telephone. Over Hitler's own line he called Goering at Veldenstein: "Chief — you'd better come here. There is TROUBLE!" In a few words he told him what had happened. "But I have a staff report here saying that there were only two hundred British aircraft," Goering said; "I am coming at once!"

"It was pitiable!" Bodenschatz commented, shuddering in retrospect. When Goering arrived, stretching out his hand to Hitler in greeting, the Fuehrer ignored him. Rudely, in front of junior officers, he cut the Reichsmarschall. A stammering, bewildered Goering was lost at the Fuehrer Headquarters, where he had few friends. Jeschonneck, his favourite Jeschonneck, could hardly look him in the eye. The young Luftwaffe general was an ardent Nazi who could not resist the spell which Hitler cast over many members of his entourage. The dispersal of the Luftwaffe, the weakening of the once all-powerful force which he represented, had thrown the Chief of Staff off his balance. Hitler's contemptuous references to the air force hurt him deeply. From Goering, who was himself downcast, prostrate, he received very little comfort.

But Goering, at least, stepped in when Jeschonneck told him about a new, peremptory request from the Fuehrer that "the Luftwaffe will have to supply my armies at Stalingrad until my Panzer formation can break through the Russian ring and relieve them!" Yes, Goering promised, the Luftwaffe will assemble an adequate transport fleet. "If it takes two weeks, three weeks . . . the Luftwaffe will drop food and ammunition." Hitler was in conference with Colonel Werner von Stauffenberg, the Chief of Staff of General Fritz Fromm, the Commander of the reserve army, whose task it was to form new Panzer units. But it took more than two weeks, or three weeks, to assemble the new divisions. Four weeks passed and the effort of the Luftwaffe was weakening. The Russians shot down the cumbersome Junkers like sitting ducks. "Tell the Fuehrer that we cannot go on!" Goering told Jeschonneck. He did not like to give Hitler the bad news, but Jeschonneck was not anxious either to invite the Fuehrer's torrential displeasure. Nothing was said. Nothing was done, as the Luftwaffe, before Stalingrad, faded out completely.

When the end came at Stalingrad, the generals blamed Hitler for his obstinate refusal to face strategic realities and to abandon the attack while there was still time to withdraw. Hitler, in turn, looked for a scapegoat: "The Luftwaffe has failed again . . . it's best to carry on this war without them. I do not want these cowards . . . Finished! They ought to be shot!" Bodenschatz was sure he meant Goering whenever he mentioned the Luftwaffe. "It was not a pleasant situation!" he recalled. He was not with Goering to observe his reaction to the catastrophes which befell the Wehrmacht in quick succession. Even control of the Luftwaffe was slipping from Goering's hands. He was in Karinhall with Emmy when a report from Headquarters warned him that large enemy air forces were flying in a direction not as yet determinable. "Concentrate fighter attacks around Stettin!" he ordered. "Come to the shelter!" Emmy pleaded, but Goering could not be persuaded to leave his desk. Once more he picked up the receiver: "Supreme concentration at Stettin!" he ordered again. "Why Stettin?" Emmy asked. "What makes you expect an attack on Stettin?" "It's difficult to say," he answered, "but when I am faced with these emergencies, I simply put myself in the position of the R.A.F. Command. Now, my dear, if I were the R.A.F., I should go for Stettin tonight. . . . Considering the pattern of their attack . . . why, they are bound to go to Stettin!"

He went down to the shelter. "They were a lonely couple, sitting quietly by themselves," Fedor Radmann, the cook, told me: "I almost stumbled over the Chief in the dark!" As soon as the all clear sounded, Goering was on the telephone again. With weary satisfaction he told Emmy: "I was right . . . it was Stettin! How glad I am that I was able to protect these poor people!" He fell into a deep sleep to be awakened by a call from Bodenschatz: "Terrible damage at Stettin . . . " Emmy Goering told me what had happened. Countermanding Goering's orders, Hitler had changed the disposition of the Luftflotte Reich, the home defence force, and ordered concentration of all defences at Berlin. Stettin was almost defenceless when the blow fell. Goering made a brave show. He took the opportunity to insist that henceforth he alone should be entitled to control movements of Luftflotte Reich. But Jeschonneck neither had the will nor the strength to maintain his Commander's authority against Hitler's interference.

Goering retired to the Obersalzberg where he received an unexpected visit from Joseph Goebbels. It was their first intimate conversation for many months. "It seems to me," Goebbels noted in his diary, recording the visit, "that Goering has been standing aside too long from the political factors which supply the real driving force!" Goebbels really meant that there was no other popular figure in Germany who could face the people as successfully as Goering. Goebbels had plans for a new approach to Hitler. Heinrich Lammers, the Minister in charge of Hitler's Chancellery, Martin Bormann, and Field Marshal Keitel, the inveterate yes-man, were paralysing the Fuehrer's great qualities. To break through this ring of the "Three Wise Men from the East," as Goebbels called them, he wanted to enlist Goering's help. They discussed the war situation. Goebbels complained that Goering had never called a meeting of the Council for the Defence of the Reich, of which he was Chairman. ("It was only a name," Goering explained at his Nuremberg trial; "it never really functioned.") "You must come out of your shell and act as a leader," Goebbels concluded. It was balm to the open wounds of Goering's injured pride.

It never materialised. When Goering's name was mentioned in the conversation between Goebbels and Hitler, the Fuehrer broke into wild accusations against the Reichsmarschall. Goebbels noted in his diary that "the moment was not opportune" to raise the subject he had discussed with Goering. Typically he changed his tune and went further even than Hitler. He turned finally against Goering. In a public speech he flayed those "prominent personalities in the Reich who still lead a life of idle luxury while the people are suffering." It was an unmistakable reference to the Reichsmarschall. The next day he ordered that all luxury restaurants in Berlin should be closed — "including Horcher's," he emphasised — knowing that Goering, wherever he was, received regular food supplies from Horcher's, even by air. As soon as Goering heard of the order, he put through a call to Goebbels at the Propaganda Ministry. In a telephone conversation taking three-quarters of an hour, Goebbels insisted on the complete execution of his order. Goering, raging, finally replied: "If you close Horcher's today, I shall open it tomorrow as a Luftwaffe Club!" To that Goebbels had no answer except to order a "spontaneous demonstration" outside Horcher's. Nazi rowdies smashed one of the restaurant's big windows. The next day Luftwaffe sentries with fixed bayonets were drawn up at the door.

A lone figure, Goering carried on, half-heartedly, one objective in mind — to escape from the insoluble problems of war into the comfort of peace. Better than Hitler, who would never admit defeat, better than Goebbels the fanatic, he knew now that the war could not be won. He chose an Army audience to prepare another peace campaign, aiming at the same time to get the ear of the Western Allies for his favourite argument. "Let me tell you," he said to a gathering of high ranking officers, "about a piece of information which I have just received, a report of a private conversation in which Stalin said that 'Europe is just a province of Russia and that only Germany bars our way into Europe. If we defeat Germany, Europe is ours . . .' That's Stalin's view and that is why we are fighting — not only for Germany, but also for Europe!"

Quickly he tried to cash in on whatever effect his words might have if they were to reach Britain and America. At Veldenstein he received a mysterious visitor. "He even sent *me* away," Robert told me, "but I knew it was one of his Swedish friends!" Goering was determined to find a way to end the hopeless conflict, to save Germany, to save himself. Knowing that it was a very hazardous venture to undertake single-handedly, he arranged for a meeting with Goebbels and Himmler to tell them about his secret conversations. If they would accompany him to Fuehrer Headquarters, he would put his peace plan before Hitler. Unexpectedly, they both agreed with his reasoning. But the encounter with Hitler was grimmer even than they had expected. Hitler would not let Goering finish his explanations; "One more move in this direction, Goering, and I have you shot." Goering hurried away. "Erschiessen . . . !" was all he heard before he closed the door. Hitler was no longer listening to his old friends. Martin Bormann had become his closest, inseparable companion. "There is treason around you, mein Fuehrer," Bormann whispered in his ear, "treason in the highest quarters!"

Robert told me that he and the whole domestic staff knew full well that Martin Bormann hated Goering; "I warned the Reichsmarschall that Heinecke, his civilian guard, was writing weekly reports about him, about us, about everything that went on in the house. Every visitor, every telephone conversation, was reported!" Robert said that Goering called Heinecke and challenged him openly, and Heinecke admitted frankly that he had been writing these reports for years. "The Chief was a funny person," Robert concluded. "He simply told the fellow he could go on reporting, as there was nothing to hide. And left it at that!" The telephone conversations of the Goering family were recorded by the Gestapo. "Martin Bormann himself was listening in to me!" said Emmy Goering. She could no longer contain herself and ended every telephone conversation: "Have you heard all that, Herr Bormann?" There was never a reply.

She knew that her husband suffered under the constant threat of Bormann's hostility and they discussed it frequently. Once, when he became aware of a particularly nasty intrigue, he explained in despair, "Better a quick Genickschuss (shot in the neck) than this slow murder!" "Why don't you do something about it?" Emmy asked him. She told me how he reacted. "Hermann was too trusting." Apparently Goering decided to have it out with Bormann. At the lonely marble table on a hill facing his house on the Obersalzberg — they called it the "Adolf Hitler hill" — he talked to Bormann for two hours. The British Ambassador had sat at his table, every important visitor to Haus Goering had been in conference with the Marshal in this elevated spot. An R.A.F. bomb eventually hit it squarely, and all that was left of it were a few marble splinters, the last of which I picked up. From a window, Frau Emmy was watching; the servants kept an eye on the two enemies. But Goering returned from the interview to the house and smiled. "I cannot understand what you have against Bormann," he told Emmy. "He is really a very nice fellow, concerned only with the Fuehrer's well-being." No wonder both Bodenschatz and Koller said that "Goering was really a big little boy."

A powerful man on the decline is a pitiful spectacle. "Goering was in a bad condition," Koller said. "We knew he was taking too many of these pills!" Members of his entourage often whispered that "the high chief is under the influence again. . . ." There was not a week without new complications. The Allies were advancing in Italy; Mussolini had been extricated from a humiliating imprisonment only by a daring exploit of the S.S. Leader, Otto Skorzeny; the Russian Front was crumbling and the German High Command was in several minds on the strategy to prevent a Soviet breakthrough at Kursk, aimed at opening the way to Kiev and eventually to Rumania. The Luftwaffe at Kursk was inadequate to support a German counter-offensive. From Goering's Headquarters Jeschonneck received instructions for a change in the disposition of the air fleets on the Eastern Front. From the Fuehrer Headquarters, post-haste, came a different set of orders. The Chief of Staff of the Luftwaffe was breaking down under the confusing, contradictory tasks which he was set; "Mein Fuehrer," he told Hitler, "I suggest that you personally take over the command of the Luftwaffe, as you have done with the Army. You, alone, can restore the prestige of our Air Force. . . . The Reichsmarschall is never available for consultations. If I could serve you directly as your Luftwaffe Chief of Staff . . ."

It took only two days before the Nazi bush telegraph had conveyed the gist of this conversation to Goering. So Hans Jeschonneck, the youngster whom he had promoted over the heads of others, his favourite Luftwaffe general, was turning against him! Goering flew to Goldapp: "Call Jeschonneck!" he ordered. I have received an account of their conversation from a close friend of Goering. With unusual calm, Goering told Jeschonneck that he regarded his suggestion to Hitler as a clear case of insubordination. It was a stab in his back: "I shall have you indicted for insubordination . . . unless you find a way out of the situation which you have created!" Jeschonneck understood. Obviously, in the conflict of Hitler and Goering, he had become the whipping boy; he would be blamed for the failure of the Luftwaffe.

The Lagebesprechung next day was one of the few which Goering attended in person. The Navy reported, the Army said its piece. The Chief of the Luftwaffe Staff was missing. "Find Jeschonneck!" Hitler ordered. Half an hour later an officer orderly arrived from Goldapp. He called Colonel von Below, a liaison officer. Below, pale, trembling, approached Hitler: "Colonel-General Jeschonneck has been found at his quarters at Goldapp — with a bullet through his head!" Jeschonneck, caught in the net of the poisonous Nazi relations, had taken his own life. At the burial near the Fuehrer Headquarters Goering laid a wreath, and his voice sounded cool and hard as he said in a short funeral oration: "Our young Chief of Staff had no peace, no rest. In all the efforts of the Luftwaffe he played a big part. A hard fate, incomprehensible to us, has called him away. Or perhaps" — he ended with a double meaning of which few were aware — "perhaps it is understandable after all — because he would not spare himself!" The official announcement said that the Chief of Staff of the Luftwaffe had died suddenly. The leaves were falling fast from Goering's tree of life. He went to the Lagebesprechung again once or twice to keep in touch with Hitler. It was an exasperating, humiliating experience. "When he came back from the 'Lage,' " Robert said, "he was completely zerschlagen" (completely "beat" conveys his meaning best). He had to change quickly and dropped into his chair exhausted, unable to eat more than a sandwich or take a glass of beer: "He was down and out," Robert summed up.

To keep the threat of an all-powerful, ever-present Gestapo firmly before the eyes of the grumbling and despairing German populace, Himmler, in a reshuffle of the Government, was appointed Minister of the Interior. There were no new plums for Goering, who was just good enough to stump the country in a last attempt to give heart to a people dazed by the concerted bombing campaign of the R.A.F. and the American bomber squadrons. His trip across the country was really mapped out in the briefing rooms of R.A.F. bomber stations in Britain. Cologne, Duesseldorf, the Ruhr, and Berlin were attacked — Goering rushed to speak at the most harassed localities. Nuremberg, Munich, Stuttgart, Bochum, Wilhelmshaven, Kiel, Mannheim, Paderborn — he could no longer follow the trail which British bombs were blazing. The Mohne and Eder Dam was breached; seven major attacks brought down ten thousand tons of bombs on the Ruhr. Sixteen thousand tons rained on Germany the next month, nineteen thousand in August. There were eighteen night raids by Mosquitos in one month alone, seven of them on Berlin. Even when the weather deteriorated in October, 1943, the R.A.F. still mounted nine big attacks and dropped thirteen thousand tons. In one November night, particularly, Berlin trembled under a devastating assault concentrated in thirty minutes. There were not enough fire fighters, ambulance men, anti-aircraft gunners; prisoners of war, foreign labourers, Russians, Hungarians, Italians, had to be recruited to man the defences. "Some of my batteries," Goering said, "looked like the League of Nations. . . ."

Raids on power stations paralysed production. The vital ball-bearing factory at Schweinfurt was hit and the interruption in production affected a dozen industries. One by one the oil refineries on which the Luftwaffe depended for fuel were pounded; one by one aircraft factories were attacked — the Focke-Wulf Works, the Messerschmitt plant in Augsburg were picked out for special attention. After a few months of experimental runs over France early in 1943, the United States Army Air Force gradually brought its whole terrifying strength to bear on Germany. By 1944, flying serenely and exerting their tremendous fire power, the famous Flying Fortresses, in full light of day, ranged into the most distant corners of the Reich. That was what Goering had feared for years — an opponent superior in productive capacity and technical skill, propelled, as he put it in his own flowery language, by a death-defying courage such as only a great, young, pioneering, fighting-fit people can muster if it wants to finish a tough job. As the American attacks grew in intensity, his staff told him that it was impossible to assign more than a thousand fighters to the defence of the Reich. It was approximately a fifth of the total front-line strength of the Luftwaffe, which was not only deeply involved in the East, but burdened with the hopeless task of defending Western Europe from Trondheim to the Bay of Biscay.

Specially trained night-fighter units met the R.A.F.; swarms of Messerschmitts pitted themselves against the majestic Fortresses. They inflicted heavy losses — but it was only a rear-guard action against an ever-increasing stream of Allied Air Forces. Was there nothing to stop this avalanche from the air? Goering knew already from the experience of his own family that the limit of the people's endurance was being reached. Those who did not suffer from direct bomb damage were soon parted from their familiar surroundings, forced to flee from the hail of bombs. Emmy's sister, Else Sonnemann, had to abandon her Berlin flat. Goering ordered her furniture to be stored in the cellars of the Reichstag, which were of little other use these days. With his friends he devised a scheme to raise volunteers to meet a glorious death by ramming the irresistible American heavy bombers in the air. General Koller, Chief of Operations since General Korten had taken General Jeschonneck's place as Chief of Staff, spent hours trying to dissuade Goering from the ramming project. But not until one of Goering's nephews had sacrificed his life to comply with his uncle's instructions — one of five Goerings to be killed in the war — did he give up the costly and futile project. If every Luftwaffe fighter plane had crashed in a successful ramming attack, there would still have been enough Allied bombers left to destroy a defenceless Germany.

Goering's long holidays had hitherto only roused the Nazi leaders, economic chiefs, and senior Luftwaffe officers to acid comments. Wider circles now reflected the shadow of his decline. When he went to Gastein, in the Austrian mountains, the local people grumbled audibly: "He has brought his own cow; our skimpy milk is not good enough for the fat boy!" He was no longer as fat as he used to be. Sick at heart and in body, he dragged himself to Munich for the putsch anniversary. Martin Bormann presided, an evil eye on the deflated Reichsmarschall as he rose to speak weakly, meekly, about defence in the air. "If everybody remains in his place," he said, "we shall hold out — and we shall win!" He did not believe what he said. Nobody believed him. Bitter irony at this hour — he was shown Allied press reports saying that he, alone among Nazi leaders, had retained his popularity. "Laugh, Pagliacci," he hummed bitterly, "make the craziest grimaces . . ." But people were beginning to suspect how he felt deep inside.

Many who had previously applauded his extravagances, his colourful uniforms, criticised him now. He went to the front line at Leningrad only to be rebuked by Hitler about the elaborate arrangements which accompanied his visit. No tears were shed at Goering's house when Count Ciano was executed, but the grim fate of his former friend seemed to lower the sword of disaster hanging over his own head. There were still a few faithful soldiers of the Luftwaffe, such as the platoon which "captured" the altar of the Cassino Monastery in Italy and transported it to Germany as a present for the Reichsmarschall: "Plunderers, looters, criminals . . . !" he shouted at them and refused to accept it. In secret council with Bruno Loerzer, he fashioned plans for the Luftwaffe. In the middle of intricate operations in Jugoslavia, Loerzer, on his instructions, changed the air commander. He did not bother to tell Headquarters. "Imagine my surprise," General Koller told me, "when I asked for General Froehlich, the commanding general, on the phone, and General Fiebig answered and told me that he was in command now. I, the Chief of Operations, was not even informed. In Veldenstein or on the Obersalzberg they had decided to swap horses in midstream. . . ."

Individual action, desperate expeditions, were discussed in the close circle around Goering. But even Erhard Milch no longer saw eye to eye with Goering. When he implored the Commander-in-Chief of the Luftwaffe to order an increase in fighter production to protect the Reich, Goering flared up: "Who is running the German Air Force — you or I?" Milch henceforth got in touch with Hitler directly whenever it was possible. In his interrogation after the war ended, he blamed the failure of leadership — that is, Goering — for the loss of the war. No, he would not be made a scapegoat for Goering. While the Wehrmacht High Command deliberated about the defence of Festung Europa (Fortress Europe), Goering sent a parachute unit to capture Tito in Bosnia. They failed. When Hitler urged that a squadron of new type Messerschmitt 117's be made ready for action, Goering promised to have crews available within a fortnight. He asked Koller to organise their training rapidly. After three weeks, as Hitler pressed him, the men had not completed their training with the new machines: "What's delaying them, Koller?" Goering asked, and, when told that the men were just beginning to train for night operations, he exploded: "We don't need night fighters . . . send them to the front at once!" He would not listen to Koller, who explained that front-line pilots should be prepared for every kind of operation. The fear of Hitler's reproach drove him into a frenzy.

"That weakling is enjoying life at home, surrounded by his women!" Hitler kept saying within the hearing of a dozen generals. Goering had gathered his family and his friends around him, his wife and Edda, Else Sonnemann, his sisters, Paula and Olga. Frau Bouhler was with them. "Weiber! Weiber!" Hitler fumed. (Women, women.) "No wonder the Luftwaffe is such a Sauladen!" (Pig shop.) General Koller pleaded with the senior officers around Hitler: "If the Fuehrer is angry with the Reichsmarschall — that is no reason to insult and belittle the Luftwaffe!" The Bavarian air officer was perturbed: "What's the matter with the big chief?" he asked Goering's staff doctor, Ondarza. "Ask that Berlin Professor what's wrong with him — the one who feeds him all these drugs." Ondarza was trying to escape from this intolerable atmosphere. Frau Goering told me that he was one of the few members of her husband's entourage who refused to testify for him at Nuremberg.

It all seemed so futile now! There was Rosenberg, still writing memoranda about Russian agricultural produce. The Office of the Four-Year Plan sent documents about the dispersal of Russian workers. People were ravaging the proud German forests for wood, and he, the Reich Chief Forester, could do nothing about it. To the Obersalzberg, miners from the Hermann-Goering Works in Salzgitter were called to dig deep shafts into the mountain. "After the war they accused me of having employed slave workers and concentration camp inmates to dig the shelters under our house," Emmy Goering said to me, "as if we would risk having foreigners do such work!" She took them wine and food — it was later held against her. As Goering was digging in at Berchtesgaden, Field Marshals Rundstedt and Rommel were getting Fortress Europe ready for the inevitable Allied assault. Goering was in Potsdam when the dreaded signal flashed: "Invasion!"

He flew to join Hitler in Berchtesgaden. Bodenschatz told me that, with his particular flair, Hitler had pointed a dozen times to the Cherbourg peninsula, saying: "This is the spot." But he had been wrong too often. The generals were not taking any chances with his intuition. After twelve hours a message arrived: "The position is grave!" Bodenschatz told me Hitler was quite aware that, as far as the Luftwaffe was concerned, the superiority of the Allies in the air precluded successful intervention. Hitler was convinced, however, the Panzers would halt the invaders. Bodenschatz said: "After two days the issue was decided."

Goering looked grave, ill, almost paralysed in his helplessness. His staff officers were dealing with the requests for air support, which poured in from the West. Hitler, daringly, asked his pilot to fly him over the invasion front. "The Fuehrer has flown into grave danger!" Goering told his wife. "What if something should happen to him?" On the shores of France, the great battle was being fought out. In Germany, Goering pondered what to do if the Fuehrer should not return. "I asked him to make peace with the Church as his first measure!" Emmy recalled. "There is so much to do!" he replied. Goering knew there was no hope of the Luftwaffe beating off the invasion. "If things go wrong, I shall take my life!" he told Emmy.

The ring around Germany was closing. Only Hitler was undismayed. Jubilantly, he launched his "secret weapons" against Britain to accomplish what the Luftwaffe had failed to do. Side-stepping Goering and his production committees, he diverted technical experts, scientists, and labour to Peenemuende to step up the output of these trumps to win the war. Every fly-bomb which crossed the coast of the British Isles or hit the Western armies' continental supply post of Antwerp was, paradoxically, also aimed at Hermann Goering. Every hit on London drove another nail into the coffin of Goering's political career. In the West, Hitler withdrew Field Marshal Gerd von Rundstedt from the supreme command of the

Western Front (to prepare for the Ardennes offensive) and Field Marshal Kluge took over. Goering travelled to Venice. It was a last attempt to restore his health. To maintain appearances, he met Mussolini and conferred with Kesselring, the strong-minded, self-willed air strategist. If the fronts should break, Goering said, Kesselring, Commander-in-Chief in Italy, should withdraw his troops to the mountains of Austria and Bavaria and organise the defence of a redoubt. No Army general could be trusted with this project. In the mountains, if necessary, Goering was prepared to hold out—until death.

Death was nearer at hand than Goering thought. On July 20, 1944, the mobilisation of a new reserve army was scheduled for discussion at the Lagebesprechung in the Wolfschanze, Rastenburg. Kurfuerst, Goering's train, had taken the Reichsmarschall to Goldapp to be at hand if a call should come from Hitler. He had given up trying to mend his old friendship with the Fuehrer and was only waiting, waiting. . . . In the Wolfschanze, Hitler was due any moment. Staff Colonel Werner von Stauffenberg came into the conference room—Hitler had called to hear whether there was any news from his chief, General Fromm. Stauffenberg put his heavy briefcase at the foot of the conference table's marble support and went to make a telephone call. Hitler arrived, took his seat, with General Rudolf Schmundt by his side. Next to Schmundt was General Korten, next to Korten the chief stenographer. Bodenschatz was standing behind him.

Hitler was studying a document when the place went up in smoke and fire. Stauffenberg, the long arm of an Army conspiracy against Hitler, had smuggled a bomb into the room in his briefcase. When it exploded, it killed General Korten outright; the stenographer's legs were torn off; General Schmundt was so gravely wounded that he died soon after. General Bodenschatz told me that he only vaguely remembers the crash. His hands were severely injured, his ears burnt, his eardrums pierced by the blast. Hitler received only a slight injury on his arm; one of his eardrums went. He was badly shaken, but never lost consciousness and was able to greet Mussolini, who arrived at Rastenburg later in the day. Had Stauffenberg placed the bomb on the other side of the marble support, the full blast of the explosion would have hit Hitler. Half an hour later, Hermann Goering was on the scene. Martin Bormann looked at him grimly, did not let him out of his sight.

Having heard the crash, Stauffenberg telephoned Berlin to tell his fellow conspirators of the Army High Command that his operation had been successful. He did not imagine that Hitler could have escaped with his life. At the War Office in the Bendlerstrasse, Berlin, the generals made plans to take over. I spoke to Colonel Otto Remer, the Nazi officer in charge of the guards in the Berlin Government district, whose refusal to obey orders from his superior officer, General Haase, foiled the plot. Suspecting Haase, Colonel Remer, as soon as he noticed that something extraordinary was afoot, got in touch with Goebbels in his capacity as Defence Commissar for Berlin. Had Remer not sided with Goebbels, the putsch would have succeeded in spite of Hitler's escape. "I only did my duty!" Remer said to me. His troops cut off the Bendlerstrasse building and caught the conspirators red-handed. They remained on guard as, on Goebbels' orders, the first executions took place inside. Himmler arrived only later to throw the Gestapo net around thousands of suspects, whether they were involved in the plot or innocent. He started a massacre comparable only with the Roehm purge of June 30, 1934.

Hitler swept away the old Army organisation. He appointed Heinrich Himmler as Chief of the Home Army — General Fritz Fromm, who ordered the immediate execution of Colonel Stauffenberg to camouflage his own part in the plot, did not escape, and was hanged. Panzer General Heinz Guderian was made Army Chief of Staff. Hermann Goering was officially pushed aside and Goebbels became Trustee for General Mobilisation — which Goering had failed to organise. The Reichsmarschall only just managed to reach a microphone for a "proclamation." But not even his old oratorical gifts could turn his speech into anything but a half-hearted appeal to the people to support Himmler. Over his head Hitler called on Colonel-General Stumpff to take over command of the Luftflotte Reich to defend Germany. As Hitler tightened the reins inside Germany, the Nazi Empire around the Reich was crumbling away.

Field Marshal Kluge, in the West, took his life when he was suspected of having been a party to the plot. To Field Marshal Erwin Rommel, the rebels' nominee as Commander-in-Chief, the

Fuehrer sent two henchmen to offer his erstwhile favourite a choice of committing suicide or facing the People's Court as a traitor. General von Witzleben, one of the instigators of the putsch, was tried, convicted, and hanged. Dr. Goerdeler, the Mayor of Leipzig, who was to become Hitler's successor as German Chancellor, went into hiding, but was recognised and betrayed by Frau Schwaerzel, a Nazi woman who collected the million-mark prize which Hitler had put on his head: "I only did my duty," she told me when I questioned her in the "Alex" (the Alexanderplatz Prison in Berlin) in 1945.

Hitler trusted nobody except Martin Bormann, who cunningly kept Goering away as much as possible. Goering still had friends, but they were only embarrassing now. When Goebbels ordered a scorched-earth policy inside Germany, harassed industrialists implored Goering to intervene. The men who had accused him of wasting the economic substance of Germany with his Four-Year Plan measures now asked him to save it. Goebbels was not even prepared to discuss the matter. Hitler pinned his hopes on Rundstedt's Ardennes offensive and the "V" weapons. ("We could have built thirty or forty fighter planes for every V weapon," Milch complained.) Goering, in seclusion, gave birth to a new idea. He knew he was risking his head, but he approached the generals with a plan to withdraw in the West and turn all German armies against the Russians. No doubt, he said, the Western Allies would make common cause with Germany, even at this late hour, or else — they could not prevent an eventual Russian domination of the Continent!

The generals did not listen, and the Russians, although the Wehrmacht continued to resist, moved westward: they were already at the gate of Prussia. In the middle of October, Goering arrived at Karinhall with bad news for Emmy: "You must arrange for the evacuation of Rominten," he told her. "Get all our stuff away! The Russians may reach the district any day!" Emmy lost no time ordering the removal. Fifteen lorries took Goering's priceless furniture to Karinhall. Friends and relatives were waiting — most of them had lost their own belongings in the Blitz on Berlin. Emmy freely distributed the consignment from Rominten. A few hours

Frau Emmy Goering in Munich, November 1950.

The scene at the Courthouse in Nuremberg where the major Nazi wa
criminals were tried and convicted b
the International Military Tribuna
Goering, Defendant Number One, i

Left: Goering argues with Rudo
Hess, who occupied the seat in th
dock next to him.

his corner seat "of honour," as he
ıdly imagined. Beside him is Ru-
lf Hess, and behind, Grand Admiral
enitz. For the military police
ering always had a friendly word.

ght: Most of the time Goering dis-
yed an expression of studied ennui;
v vital turns in the trial escaped his
ention. Sometimes, to make a
w of his contempt for a witness, he
uld discard his earphones and sit in
dock glum, and apparently disin-
ested.

"HAUS GOERING" TODAY. Goering's Villa near Hitler's house in Berchtesgaden remains as it was after the Anglo-American bomber raid in April 1945. The bomb hit the swimming pool of which a corner is visible at the extreme lower left. Goering's study used to be just left of centre of the wreck.

GOERING'S GRAVE. An ashcan in Dachau (site of the former German concentration and extermination camp).

after it had arrived, it was gone with the wind. That evening, Goering was in a happier frame of mind: "News is better, Emmy," he said. "I think we can postpone the move from Rominten." Emmy did not have the courage to tell him that his beloved furniture had gone: "I stupidly hoped that the Russians would advance, after all, and rescue me from my embarrassing position, so that Hermann would never know what I had done!"

The Russians obliged. Goering never found time to inquire after the things. There were still one or two Luftwaffe problems to which he was forced to attend. To replace the late General Korten as Air Force Chief of Staff, Bruno Loerzer suggested the appointment of General Kreipe, a young staff officer with much fighting experience. He was a slim, effeminate-looking man with an unfortunate manner, one of his war comrades told me. At the Fuehrer Headquarters he was nicknamed "Fraeulein Kreipe," and the whispering tongues soon reached Hitler's ears. The result was as expected. Hitler refused to deal with the unfortunate Kreipe. He was not going to "have any woman around the place," he said contemptuously. Goering was forced to look for another Chief of Staff. Loerzer suggested that Ritter von Greim should be called from the Eastern Front to take on the job. But Greim felt that he could only undertake the assignment with the help of Karl Koller, the Chief of Operations. For a second time Koller felt excluded from a promotion for which he was clearly in line. He retired to a hospital and when Greim came to recruit his help, he reluctantly refused. Greim would not take over without the support of the last remaining qualified staff expert. He declined the appointment.

There were not many officers anxious to be put in charge of the remnants of the once mighty Luftwaffe, fewer still with the technical experience. With a heavy heart Goering called General der Flieger, Karl Koller: "Come and see me at Karinhall," he asked the general. Karinhall was guarded by a company of Goering's reconstituted division. Only a privileged few were allowed to pass the gates and approach the house at the end of the long drive. General Koller told me that he went to the interview with the greatest reluctance. It was the first of three interminable conversations with the Reichsmarschall. "I knew I should have to tell him many unpleasant things before I could even consider accepting the appointment," he said. Goering frankly opened the conversation: "Koller," he said, "you are cross because I have not appointed you Chief of Staff." Koller was cross, but there were other matters of greater urgency to be discussed. He asked Goering whether he could speak freely. For so long had Goering shut himself off from all criticism or even intelligent discussion of urgent problems that Koller was uncertain. He asked again: "I can assure you," came the reply, "that I welcome an honest word. Tell me what's on your mind!"

"Herr Reichsmarschall," Koller started, "the first thing is that you must be available for consultation with me. It's no good sending your adjutant to the phone whenever I call!"

"But I am always here!"

"You have not visited us at the Headquarters of Operations for almost a year."

"Haven't I . . . ?"

"We only know you over the telephone . . ."

"Not really . . . !"

"And when I ask for your decision, you must please make it at once!"

"Have I not always done that?"

He urged Koller to mention an occasion on which he had failed: "Remember, Herr Reichsmarschall, when I asked you to approve a change in the disposition of Luftflotte Reich? I waited one week, ten days — bombs were dropping and there was no word from you. And you had given strict orders that no change should be made without your personal permission. You know, Herr Reichsmarschall, I made that change without your permission, but to protect myself, I had to lodge copies of my unanswered telegrams in the War Diary!"

Goering, Koller said, no longer seemed to appreciate the seriousness and the implications of this incident. His neglect of duty as a Commander-in-Chief was on record in the most important document of State. He only buried his head in his hands and moaned: "Koller, you must help me," he pleaded. "You must become my Chief of Staff. I'll be a good boy, I promise!" "In that vein,"

Koller said, "Goering was irresistible!" Koller received a free hand. He was just the man to carry on with, or without, Goering's orders. His task was a melancholy one. There was not much need for him to refer matters back to his chief. But, once more, he crossed his path in the most fateful final convulsion of Goering's fortunes as a Nazi leader.

19

MEETING WITH DESTINY

AT THE beginning of 1945, one of the Luftwaffe staff headquarters was housed in the lunatic asylum at Wasserburg-Gabersee in Bavaria: "There was never a more fitting choice," noted the British Air Ministry's News Service casually in a release about the German Air Force. Goering's fifty-second birthday was celebrated at Karinhall, much as had been done in previous years. The guests tried to be jolly, were profuse in their felicitations. Goering was dejected. With Emmy he escaped the well-wishers into a quiet corner. "Emmy, the situation is hopeless," he said. "The war is lost. If I decide to make an end — will you go with me?" Emmy did not recognise her husband. To her, he had always seemed so strong, so confident, so optimistic. If he gave up hope, she thought, the end must be very near. "Of course, Hermann," she answered, "I shall follow you wherever you go!" But before she had finished the sentence, Goering broke in: "It's cowardly to run away . . . I shall see it through!" Thank God for that! Emmy felt relieved. While he lived, there was still hope.

Was there any hope left? Paris had long been liberated, but the Luftwaffe had rallied once more for an attack on Belgium and had raided Brussels which was in the hands of the British Army. Koller worked hard to keep the Luftwaffe moving and Goering signed an accumulation of papers which he had neglected for many weeks: "It's impossible — he can't have read them all!" Koller commented. Hitler, with a speech, celebrated the twelfth anniversary of the Machtergreifung (his ascent to power). Goering took to his bed in Karinhall. He was not now looking back into the past. It was impossible to keep out the pounding of events from his secluded, heavily guarded retreat. He might drown his fears with wine, deaden his senses and steady his nerves with drugs, but, as the weeks went by, the world of Hermann Goering was shrinking and the enemies were closing in. Warsaw was liberated and the Russians were deep in Pomerania, from whence his ancestors came. The Western Allies were crossing the Rhine and clearing Cologne (where a British Military Government Officer peremptorily sacked Dr. Konrad Adenauer, the anti-Nazi Catholic who had resumed his post as Mayor, from which the Nazis had driven him). Two German Army groups were encircled in the Ruhr, where Franz von Papen was one of the first German leaders to be captured by the Allies.

Extraordinary things were happening inside Germany, though Goering had no more than an inkling of them. Heinrich Himmler, the Police and Gestapo Chief, whose S.S. Death-Head Brigade had committed unspeakable cruelties against the Jews, started peace negotiations with Sweden's Count Folke Bernadotte, the President of the International Red Cross; and to store up good will for Himmler with the Allies, S.S. Upper Group Leader Walter Schellenberg, his principal aide, was releasing a few Jews from the horror camps of Auschwitz and Buchenwald, providing them with money and helping them to escape abroad. The wolf was donning sheep's clothing. Hitler was in the ruins of Berlin leading the life of a troglodyte. Only for a few moments every day did he emerge from the spacious deep shelter in the garden behind the Wilhelmstrasse Chancellery, which was the seat of his phantom government. Here he lived in a dream world, moving nonexistent armies on a map, ordering nonexistent Luftwaffe squadrons to the attack, calling up nonexistent reserves to mount a counter-offensive and to break the ring of two formidable Russian armies around Berlin. He shouted that the Russians would suffer their greatest defeat of the war at the gates of the capital. His girl friend, Eva Braun — "a nice, inoffensive, unfortunate young woman," Bodenschatz called her — was with him, so was his staff of adjutants, secretaries, and liaison officers — among them S.S. Group Leader Hermann Fegelein, Eva Braun's brother-in-law, representing Himmler. Staff officers from the three services came to report whenever possible. Liaison with

Luftwaffe Headquarters, now at Wildpark-Werder, was maintained by General Eckart Christian, the husband of Hitler's principal secretary, Gerda Daranovski-Christian.

Hitler, aged, ash-grey, stooping and his right foot dragging, as all surviving eye-witnesses confirmed, keeping awake only with the aid of Dr. Morell's injections, watched his environment with suspicious eyes. He hated the generals; he wished destruction on the German people who had proved themselves, he said, "unworthy of my genius." He was contemptuous of Goering, and he no longer trusted Himmler or the S.S. Black Guards. Vienna, defended by an S.S. Army under his old friend and guards commander, S.S. General Sepp Dietrich, fell to the Russians: "The cowardly S.S. have let me down!" he railed. "As a punishment I order them to be stripped of their S.S. badges of honour and their Swastika armlets!" "Whoever retreats one inch is to be shot!" he screamed. "Send the troops from Karinhall to the front!" he ordered next: "Goering does not need a private army!" When Koller came for consultation, Hitler had a new idea:

> HITLER: All jet-fighter-bombers are to be given to Rudel [an Air General], who is to concentrate them under his command. Has he taken over his new duties?
>
> KOLLER: I only heard about this yesterday . . . and not as an order.
>
> HITLER: The Luftwaffe works slowly, takes its time. I expect immediate action, not after weeks. Rudel is a brilliant officer . . . no other officer like him is left.

He disregarded Koller's explanations about the technical difficulties, and his remark that Rudel had not the special qualifications needed for the job: "Makes no difference whatsoever," Hitler shouted. "The Luftwaffe has no better qualified officer. None of the generals will go to the front. . . . Rudel is a fine fellow . . . all the others in the Luftwaffe are only clowns — they are actors, showmen, that's all they are. . . ."

Goering had decided to evacuate Karinhall and move to the Obersalzberg. Berlin as a headquarters for operations was clearly untenable. Communications with the rest of the Reich were interrupted. For weeks a large staff, under his personal supervision, packed up his art treasures. One by one he emptied the vitrines, helped to take down priceless paintings, watched the experts putting them into cases. They were sent to Berchtesgaden to be stored in the network of shafts under the mountain, or to Salzburg to be held in the cool temperature of the salt mines. Now the remaining furniture, his and Emmy's personal belongings, the trunks of Edda and the staff, of Else Sonnemann and all the others, were loaded onto a fleet of big lorries. Goering's plan was to persuade Hitler to accompany him to Berchtesgaden. There, in the inaccessible mountain redoubt, the leaders could hold out. Gathering the remnants of the Wehrmacht around them, they could make a stand until the tide should change.

In his Bunker, Hitler still stuck to a futile routine. There was to be a Lagebesprechung on April 20, his birthday, as on previous days. At noon everybody lined up to congratulate the Fuehrer. Koller disturbed the festive atmosphere by reminding the gentlemen that headquarters should be moved as quickly as possible. The last chance for a large-scale evacuation was fast disappearing — in a few hours it may be too late! Hitler was past making decisions; at best he had always delayed them until the last possible moment. Now his brain did not seem to function normally any more. Goering paid his respects, Hitler coldly shook hands with him. The Reichsmarschall was ready to leave. "I am staying!" Hitler insisted, like an obstinate child: "I shall defend Berlin to the last!"

Goering was driving through Berlin on his trip south when Allied bombers arrived in strength over the city. Dr. Ondarza, who was with him, told Koller that Goering at once decided to go to a public shelter. It would be an opportunity to talk to the people. His aides warned him not to show his face too freely, but Goering's instinct was correct. Dr. Ondarza was surprised at the friendly reception which people under a hail of bombs gave the man who had promised them immunity: "May I introduce myself," Goering said amid general laughter: "My name is Meier!" The people roared. Requests arrived from nearby shelters — would the Reichsmarschall please come and visit them, too! "Quite true," Emmy Goering told me, "when we later drove south, they gave him a great welcome, even in Pilsen. . . ." Koller wanted to see Goering for a last talk before his departure. He asked Colonel von Brauchitsch on the telephone: "Would the Reichsmarschall stop at my headquarters?

He must pass it, anyway. It is very important!"

"My watch showed 3 A.M.," Koller noted in his diary. "At this moment Goering, at the head of a column of cars, passes my house at great speed. . . . He has driven off without a word or even farewell!" Koller remained in touch with Hitler's Bunker. On April 22 he was on the telephone to General Christian, his liaison officer: "I can come and take over from you for a while," Koller offered. "That's no longer necessary," was the reply. "Historical events are taking place. I am coming to see you." Koller records that Christian arrived at 8.45 P.M. and reported: "The Fuehrer is in a state of collapse. He now regards the struggle as hopeless. He wants to stay in the Bunker and defend Berlin. His documents and corespondence are being burned in the courtyard. Goebbels, Frau Goebbels, and their six children are with him." "What for?" Koller asked. "They will kill the children and the grown-ups will commit suicide."

Brauchitsch called Koller on the telephone from the Obersalzberg where Goering had arrived with his family and entourage. The connection was bad; it seemed possible that the Russians were listening in. "The fellow to whom we must always report," Koller said, thus describing Hitler, "does not want to leave. I must get out of here."

"Exactly," answered Brauchitsch. "The Reichsmarschall wants you to come here at once!"

General Karl Koller, who is the principal, perhaps the only reliable, witness of events in these momentous days, told me how he went to see General Alfred Jodl, Hitler's intimate adviser, to discuss Christian's information. "What Christian has said is true," Jodl confirmed. "Hitler said that he is staying and will shoot himself in the last moment. He is not physically fit to fight, he says; also he is afraid of being wounded and taken prisoner by the Russians. When we suggested to him to turn all the troops from the West against the East, he said he could not do that, let the Reichsmarschall do it. Somebody remarked that no soldier would fight for the Reichsmarschall and Hitler retorted there was no question of fighting. When it came to negotiations, the Reichsmarschall could do that better . . . !"

It was obvious to Koller that this vital news would have to be conveyed to Goering at the earliest moment. He was also anxious to transfer the Luftwaffe command to Berchtesgaden, where the last dispositions could be made. Berlin was under heavy Russian fire.

With the remaining staff of the High Command of the Luftwaffe in fifteen Junker 52's, he flew from Gatow Aerodrome to Bavaria. At noon on April 23, he drove up the mountain to Goering's house. "With Goering," Koller told me, "apart from Brauchitsch, was Philip Bouhler, the Party Leader, one of his last remaining friends." Pointedly Koller told him he had a decisive report to make, to which Goering replied: "Bouhler can stay here; he can hear everything!"

Let Koller take up the story:

"I told Goering," he said, "about Christian's report and repeated my conversation with Jodl, verbatim. Goering seemed touched, but I gained the impression that he had expected something of the sort. Both he and Bouhler commented very adversely on Hitler. They regarded his behaviour as eine abgrundtiefe Gemeinheit [abysmal infamy]. Goering felt in a difficult position. He wanted a report on the military situation which I gave him with the help of maps. Then he asked me whether I thought that Hitler was still alive or whether he had, perhaps, appointed Martin Bormann as his successor. I told him that Hitler was alive when I left Berlin. There were still one or two escape routes from the city. The Russians had advanced to the Alexanderplatz. But ten hours had passed since then. . . . Personally, I thought that Berlin would hold out for another seven or eight days. . . . Maybe, too, Hitler had changed his plans . . .

" 'Anyway,' [Koller concluded] 'it is now up to you to act, Herr Reichsmarschall!' Through his action yesterday, Hitler had made himself commander of Berlin and excluded himself, for all practical purposes, from the political leadership of the State and the command of the Wehrmacht."

Bouhler supported Koller's contention. Goering agreed, but hesitated. As their relations were so strained, he said again, "Might not Hitler have appointed Bormann as his successor? Bormann is my deadly enemy; he is only waiting to get at me. If I act, he will call me a traitor; if I don't, he will accuse me of having failed at the most difficult hour!" From a steel case he took the decree of June 29, 1941, the law of succession as revised by Hitler after the flight of Rudolf Hess: "If I should be restricted in my freedom of action" — Goering read the operative sentence aloud — "or if I should be otherwise incapacitated, Reichsmarschall Goering is to be my deputy or successor in all offices of State, Party, and Wehrmacht."

Still doubtful about the full implication of the situation, Goering called Minister Hans Heinrich Lammers, the Chief of Hitler's Chancellery, who was staying in Berchtesgaden. After a new debate, Lammers said: "The law of June 29, 1941, is in force and legally binding. No new publication is required. The Fuehrer has made no other order. If he had, I would have to know. Without me, he could not have changed the decree legally."

Goering was still doubtful. Finally, he devised a wireless communication to Hitler, flowery, full of assurances of his loyalty. Koller cut him short. Only a brief message could be effective. Koller and Brauchitsch each worked on a draft. The text which Koller wrote read as follows: "Mein Fuehrer, since you have decided to stay in Berlin, do you agree that I shall take over the leadership of the Reich as your deputy in accordance with the law of 29.6.1941?" Goering asked that Koller should add: "With full powers internally and in external affairs." A further sentence was added to make sure: "If I should receive no reply by 10 P.M., I shall assume that you have been deprived of your freedom of action and shall act in the best interests of our country and people." There would have to be one more sentence, Goering insisted: "What I feel in this most difficult hour of my life, I cannot express. May God protect you and may you yet leave Berlin to come here, in spite of all! Your loyal Hermann Goering." Goering was afraid that Bormann might intercept this message and in another wire to Berlin advised Colonel von Below that it had been dispatched and should be put before Hitler personally.

Stimulated by the emergency, Goering took a hurried lunch with Bouhler and Koller. If there should be no reply, he would act quickly and decisively. He would never give in to the Russians, but offer capitulation to the Western Powers. Next morning, he would fly at once to General Eisenhower. In a man-to-man talk, he would soon reach an understanding. He asked Koller to make all necessary preparation for the flight at the shortest notice. "Unlike Hitler," Koller commented, "Goering was ready to take personal action." He also asked Koller to write a proclamation to the Wehrmacht which would make the Russians think that Germany was carrying on the war. It would have to imply to the British and Americans that he did not dream of continuing the war against them. It would convey to the German troops that they would have to fight on, but that the outcome would be favourable. "That's a diplomatic masterpiece," Koller answered, "which I cannot achieve." Goering was lively and active. Koller noted the change which had come over the man whom he used to call "His Master's Voice." Now he was looking forward to his new tasks. Excitedly, he told Emmy about the developments. The war was lost, but his hour had struck. He was the leader now. He had no time to remain with her.

What, in the meantime, had happened in Berlin was later told by Armaments Minister Albert Speer. As Goering had feared, Bormann had intervened. Maliciously he had pointed Hitler's attention to the time limit which Goering had set. "It's an ultimatum!" he insisted. Albert Speer recorded Hitler's reaction. According to him, Hitler was furious, and shouted: "I have known for some time that Goering is corrupt, a failure, a drug addict . . . !" Bormann raised his voice: "He must be shot." "No, no, not that!" Hitler replied. "I dismiss him from all his offices and from his right to succession." He asked Bormann to send a telegram to that effect. Bormann drafted it:

HERMANN GOERING OBERSALZBERG YOUR ACTION REPRESENTS HIGH TREASON AGAINST THE FUEHRER AND NATIONAL SOCIALISM THE PENALTY FOR TREASON IS DEATH BUT IN VIEW OF YOUR EARLIER SERVICES TO THE PARTY THE FUEHRER WILL NOT INFLICT THIS SUPREME PENALTY IF YOU RESIGN ALL YOUR OFFICES ANSWER YES OR NO

H. R. Trevor Roper [1] states that Bormann at the same time sent a telegram to S.S. Obersturmbannfuehrer (Upper Storm Leaders) Frank and von Bredow, the Commanders of the S.S. at Obersalzberg, ordering them to arrest Goering for high treason: "You will be responsible for this with your lives," he wired them. Goering also received the following message:

DECREE OF 29.6.41 IS RESCINDED BY MY SPECIAL INSTRUCTION MY FREEDOM OF ACTION UNDISPUTED I FORBID ANY MOVE BY YOU IN THE INDICATED DIRECTION ADOLF HITLER

[1] H. R. Trevor Roper, *The Last Days of Hitler.*

Goering, who had informed Himmler, Jodl, and Ribbentrop of his earlier telegram to Hitler, hastened to send them a second message

> FUEHRER INFORMS ME THAT HE STILL HAS FREEDOM OF ACTION REVOKING TELEGRAM OF TODAY NOON HEIL HITLER HERMANN GOERING

Goering was in his study on the first floor of his villa when the two S.S. leaders demanded to see him. Robert Kropp showed them up the stairs. As they were carrying revolvers in their hands, he followed them into the room, but Goering waved him off: "It's all right, Robert, I shall deal with this alone!" He knew Robert was prepared to defend him with his life. The conversation lasted an hour. Entering the room twice to keep an eye on his chief and his two uncanny visitors, both officers of Hitler's own Leibstandarte, Robert noticed their revolvers on the table in front of them. They had come to implement Bormann's threat, put Goering under arrest, and force him to resign.

Koller, who had returned to Villa Geiger, Headquarters of the Luftwaffe at the foot of the mountain, tried in vain to get in touch with Goering. Whenever he telephoned, Frank was on the telephone to say that the Reichsmarschall was not available. He sent two air force orderlies up the mountain. Neither of them returned. A little later his own orderly announced that von Bredow wanted to see him. "Shall I let him in?" asked the orderly; "he has two armed S.S. men with him!" Koller beckoned von Bredow into the room.

"I am sorry, General," said the S.S. officer, "but the Fuehrer has ordered me to arrest you!"

"Do you know why?"

"No."

"Where is the Reichsmarschall?"

"Under arrest."

"And Brauchitsch, Lammers, Bouhler . . . ?"

"Under arrest."

Koller calmly submitted. At Haus Goering a hundred S.S. men of the Leibstandarte were guarding Goering, his staff, and his family. One S.S. man remained with him in his room. "I am sure," Emmy Goering told me, "that Bormann had ordered them to kill my husband!" Everybody else was under the same impression. But it was obvious that even the S.S. were loath to put a hand on the Reichsmarschall. Koller, who had been told that he was under "honorary detention" only, was waiting for the arrival of Ernst Kaltenbrunner, Chief of Police and the Gestapo since the death of "Killer" Heydrich. Bodenschatz came to inquire after Goering. He was still convalescing. "I shall try and see the Reichsmarschall," he promised, but his attempt to reach Goering's house failed. The S.S. turned him back; only with difficulty did he escape arrest. Bruno Loerzer came to the Villa Geiger along a mountain path. Koller said this about his visit: "Gently, and in civilian clothes, he sneaked in by the kitchen entrance. He asked what he could do for Goering. Then he left the house again by the same route and hurriedly left Berchtesgaden. I never saw him again. And Goering regarded him as his best friend!"

His next visitor was von Greim, whom Hitler had summoned to Berlin. Koller gave him an account of the events, but Greim maintained that Goering should have stayed in Berlin. "That Goering left Berlin was absolutely correct," Koller retorted. "He had not a single friend there, only enemies who have fought him and the Luftwaffe for two years. Where should we get if every responsible leader buried himself in a shelter? I am not defending Goering," Koller added; "he has made too many mistakes for that. He has made my life miserable, has threatened me with erschiessen and court martial . . . but I cannot alter the facts of the last two days. Goering has done nothing that could be called treason. On the contrary, he has done the only correct thing . . . for once he does the right thing and they put him under arrest!"

Up on the mountain Haus Goering was like a prison. S.S. men stood guard in the corridors and on the stairs. Goering was not allowed to see his wife or his daughter. All were confined to their rooms. There were little Edda and her nurse; Goering's sister, who had arrived for a short visit, and was detained with him. Bouhler and his wife, Else Sonnemann, Christa Gormanns the nurse, Robert, and Cilli the maid, the other servants — all in a weird, precarious situation. For "security reasons" Frank had cut all communications, even the installation for air-raid warnings. Night fell and the uneasy company, so much like the dramatis personae in *Petrified Forest* under the guns of gangsters, went to bed, even if they could not find sleep. At nine the next morning, without warning, through a gap in the mountains and from an unexpected direction, came the drone of aircraft engines. Moving in for an attack on the Obersalzberg, Lancasters of the R.A.F. Bomber Command, escorted by Mustangs of the United States 8th Air Force and R.A.F. Fighter Command, appeared overhead. Goering was in his dressing gown; Emmy was still in bed. At Villa Geiger, General Koller was just shaving when the bombs began to drop — twelve-thousand-pound bombs, fused for deep penetration, some twelve-thousand-pounders, large numbers of four-thousand-pounders followed. *Crash!!* — and half of Hitler's Berghof was in ruins. *Crash!!* — and Martin Bormann's home went up in flames. *Crash!!* — and a stick of bombs hit the big S.S. barracks. Later, Flight-Lieutenant Jones, an R.A.F. navigator in one of the Lancasters, said: "This is the target we have been waiting for!" "I saw the flash right on Hitler's house," said Flight-Sergeant E. J. Cutting, a rear-gunner who comes from Ringwood. "The S.S. Barracks took terrific punishment," was the comment of Flying-Officer D. A. Coster from New Zealand. In their night clothes Goering, Emmy, the child, all the others, rushed down to the small shelter under the house. The S.S. guards followed. They were shaken by the impact of a bomb which dropped into the swimming pool only a few yards from the house, right under the window of Goering's study. As they huddled together in the cellar, the blast tore away Goering's study; the roof collapsed, the stairs caved in. Five years later, Robert showed me over the ruins which the bomb left behind. "That was my room," he said; "here was the kitchen — small, isn't it? Through this door we all went down — just in the nick of time!" But the atmosphere in the cellar soon became intolerable. Frank gave orders for everybody to move into the mountain shaft. Goering was brooding — they had no sooner settled down than he approached the commander of his jailers: "Send a message to the Fuehrer," he asked Frank. "Tell him that if he believes that I have betrayed him, I am prepared to be shot!" Frank turned to comply with the request. He was about to leave when Emmy ran after him: "Please don't send that message . . ." she pleaded. "My husband is excited . . . he does not mean what he says!" She knew that heads in Nazi Germany were not fixed very firmly on men's shoulders. Frank stared at her coldly. With tears in her eyes, she said: "All right, listen to me! The Fuehrer, on my wedding day, promised to grant me a wish. I want to remind him of his promise. If the Fuehrer orders my husband to be shot, I want him to have the child and me shot at the same time!" Frank agreed to send the message. An hour later Hitler's reply arrived. It contained one word: "Yes."

Koller's "honorary detention" was lifted as soon as Greim arrived in Berlin — the Luftwaffe could not be left without a Chief of Staff. He decided to fly north to consult with the military leaders. Christian had established a liaison headquarters at Rechlin Aerodrome. The High Command of the Wehrmacht was in a forest near Fuerstenberg. There Koller met Jodl and Keitel. "When I mentioned Goering's arrest," Koller noted, "they were evasive." Keitel apologised. He was busy, he said, and disappeared. Later Himmler and Doenitz arrived. Doenitz had succeeded Raeder as Grand Admiral. Once more Koller tried to raise the subject of Goering, this time with Himmler. "That's an unfortunate affair, this business about the Reichsmarschall," Himmler said. He would talk to Keitel about it later. Koller had been mistaken if he thought that Goering's arrest was the chief topic of interest. These people were no longer concerned about anybody but themselves. They knew that their epoch was coming to a close. Only Bormann was still active in Hitler's Bunker. On April 26, at his instigation, there was an announcement from Radio Hamburg:

"Reichsmarschall Hermann Goering," it said, "is suffering from a heart disease which has now entered an acute stage. He has, therefore, asked to be relieved of the command of the Luftwaffe and all duties connected therewith, because, at this moment, the full harnessing of all strength is need. The Fuehrer has granted his request. The Fuehrer has appointed Colonel-General Ritter von Greim to be the new Commander of the Luftwaffe, promoting him, at the same time, to the rank of Field Marshal."

Greim was with Hitler in the Berlin Bunker. General Wilhelm Burgdorf was there — one of Hitler's two emissaries who had presented Rommel with the fatal ultimatum. Other personnel were Admiral Voss, the naval liaison officer, General Krebs, Rattenhuber, chief of Hitler's S.S. Guard, Martin Bormann, Goebbels and his family, Eva Braun. Fegelein, who had no stomach for a hero's death in the Bunker death trap, had sneaked out to his private flat, but was brought back on Hitler's orders and shot "as a deserter." And there were the secretaries and officers of Hitler's staff, watching the sands running out. Koller, at Headquarters was warned not to fly to Berlin, which he might be unable ever to leave again.

The Goetterdaemmerung in the Chancellery Bunker has been recorded by H. R. Trevor Roper[2] in a description which will never be bettered. As a British Intelligence Officer, he interviewed most of the survivors, the eye-witnesses of the horrible end — when Goebbels and his wife poisoned their six children and themselves; when Adolf Hitler and Eva Braun were united in a death marriage. He described the sordid mediaeval burning of their bodies, the escape attempts of the staff, who split up into several parties for a dash through burning Berlin to meet either death or capture by the Russians. Bormann was with one of these groups. Though one witness believes that he was killed by a Russian bullet and claims to have seen his dead body, there is no definite confirmation of his death. "We are sure he is still alive and in Russia," high ranking German officers told me; "we should not be surprised if he turned up when Soviet plans for East Germany are complete. He has always been a National Bolshevist . . . "

Before his death Hitler appointed Grand Admiral Karl Doenitz as his successor. Doenitz was in Flensburg in Schleswig-Holstein, where most members of the Nazi Government were eventually captured. Ritter von Greim was one of the last men to leave Berlin by air, piloted by his friend Hanna Reitsch, a fanatical Nazi airwoman whose admiration for Hitler survived his death. Koller returned from Wildpark-Werder to the Villa Geiger in Berchtesgaden. When he inquired about Goering's fate, he was told that the Reichsmarschall was no longer at the Obersalzberg. Frau Goering herself is not quite sure how the train of events was set in motion. Hitler, or it may have been Bormann, had left orders that "all traitors should be shot," meaning Heinrich Himmler, of whose peace negotiations he had come to know, and Goering, who had "tried to usurp power" — as if there had been any power to usurp! After the bombing raids on the Obersalzberg, Goering and his party had

[2] H. R. Trevor Roper, *The Last Days of Hitler.*

been completely cut off from the world. "We were just waiting to see what would happen," Emmy Goering told me. As it was impossible to stay in the mountain holes any longer, S.S. Frank decided to move his prisoners. He discussed the move with Goering, who suggested that they might go to Mauterndorf, the castle of the Eppensteins, which he regarded as his own property. Frank consented and the move was made. For Goering it meant good-bye to his art treasures which remained in the mountain shafts where they were later found by the American Army.

Rapidly Fate was overtaking Goering's associates everywhere. Mussolini, with twelve of his ministers, was captured as he tried to escape to Switzerland and was shot by Italian partisans. Goering knew nothing of it. He was engaged in a battle of wits with Frank, the man with power to kill him at any moment. Subtly, with his old cunning, with his skill as a negotiator, with the determination of a man who fights for his life, Goering went to work on him. Frank, a thug, primitive, cruel, was himself out of touch with events. Himmler was not available; there was no word from Ernst Kaltenbrunner, the next S.S. leader in line. When it came to talking, he was no match for the Reichsmarshall. Goering's personality began to exert itself: "To Mauterndorf," he said to Frank; "We'll all be safe there!" At last Frank agreed to make the move, but he was still taking no chances. He insisted on separating Goering from his military staff. The Bouhlers, Paula Hueber, Goering's sister, Emmy, Robert, and Christa Gormanns were allowed to accompany him. Colonel von Brauchitsch, Lieutenant-Colonel Teske, Major Nuelle and Captain Klaas, the junior adjutants, were taken away by the S.S. guards and lodged in Salzburg Prison. Goering could manage Frank now. He wanted to send emissaries to Koller. Frank was unable to resist his prisoner's demand. On April 30 he agreed to allow two members of Goering's guards to take a message to the Luftwaffe Chief of Staff. Koller received them and made a careful note of what they said: "The Reichsmarschall," they declared, "feels that you have betrayed and sold him, Herr General. He says that he would not be in this position if you had stuck by the report you gave him on April 23 . . ."

Later in the day there was a telephone call from Mauterndorf to the Villa Geiger with a message from Goering: "If Koller is not a pig, he should come and see me tomorrow morning!" was what Koller's secretary heard and took down. "Calling me a pig — and to my secretary!" Koller noted. He was angry. But as a Luftwaffe general, he felt in duty bound to his chief and to every officer of his force. He was not going to allow the S.S. to humiliate the Luftwaffe. First he demanded the immediate release of the arrested officers of Goering's entourage. Then he sent a first-class mechanised Luftwaffe signal unit to Mauterndorf to protect Goering, who, by then, had won over another S.S. officer. Standarten Leader Brause came to see Koller. It was a tricky situation. Could he trust these S.S. fellows? There was murder in the air.

Brause plaintively said, "Don't you want to liberate Goering by force? You have more troops than I have!"

Koller replied, "I do not want to risk the danger of liberating a corpse!"

"I am grateful for that," Brause said. "In case of an attack, I could not guarantee for every one of my men. But if you hold your hand, Herr General, I promise that nothing will happen to Goering. But please see that his arrest is lifted soon!"

It was by now impossible to say who was on whose side. Fears, doubts, were the dominating emotions in every mind. Goering was desperately trying to get in touch with surviving leaders of the collapsing Reich. He studied a batch of documents which Koller sent him to show that he had neither sold nor betrayed him. Though he was now able to cope with the S.S., he suffered many grievous disappointments. One of his staff officers, he found out, had declared in the hour of his arrest, "The Reichsmarschall under arrest — my duty is to the Fuehrer," and had gone off, taking almost all the belongings of his fellow officers with him. In the turmoil of the move from the devastated Obersalzberg, a chauffeur had relieved Frau Goering's maid of her jewel case: "I'll hold it," he said politely. Next minute he was gone — and the jewels with him.

Robert for the time being saved Goering's own green leather jewel case, with the rings and cuff-links, the diamond studs and cigarette cases. It was probably worth a million. Heinecke, Goering's shadow, made off. "He was never caught," Robert said. "He went underground. Last I heard, he was living as a farm labourer under an assumed name somewhere in the North!" Koller's intervention on behalf of Goering's staff officers was successful. They were released and allowed to join their chief in Mauterndorf. Then Koller motored to see Field Marshall Kesselring: "Can't you order the release of the Reichsmarschall?" he asked. Kesselring was evasive; there was Kaltenbrunner to consider. From a distance, even, that sinister man spread fear. Kesselring promised to get in contact with him and Doenitz.

In the Austrian mountains, Luftwaffe and S.S. were playing cat and mouse. Goering in Mauterndorf was contemplating his fate. There was little he could do except to try and wriggle out of his detention. He was no longer clear whose prisoner he was. Could he trust Koller? Would Kaltenbrunner order his execution? Would the Americans arrive to take him prisoner? Or might not even the Russians advance from the East to find him — like a rat in a trap? Christa Gormanns tried to keep him fit enough to carry on. "He took one pill after another," Robert told me. Conversations were vague. Goering seemed ashamed, in his predicament, to face the people around him, even his wife and sister. I asked Emmy Goering what he did, what he said. "What was there to do?" she retorted. "What could he say?" She told me that his main worry was — Hitler: "When he heard of his death, he could no longer be angry with the Fuehrer!" He was driven nearly to despair: "He is dead, Emmy," he said. "I shall never be able to tell him that I have remained loyal to the end!"

While Goering was thus manoeuvring, history was being made elsewhere. Doenitz sent Admiral Friedenburg to Lueneburg Heath to offer Field Marshal Montgomery the surrender of the German armies. In Italy, behind the back of the Commander-in-Chief Kesselring, an S.S. General Wolf initiated negotiations for the surrender of the Southern Army Group. The Americans were approaching when, at last, an order came for Goering's release. General Pickard, whom Koller had sent south to make contact with Kesselring, was returning in his car when he passed Mauterndorf. He had no idea that Goering was there and was surprised, he later said, to see the Reichsmarschall standing at the gate.

"Pickard," Goering said — Koller, to whom Pickard reported, gave me this account of their conversation — "listen to my orders!" Goering was the boss again: "I want full protection," he demanded. "Tell Koller to act now! A general should be sent to Eisenhower to make it possible for me to have a man-to-man, soldier-to-soldier, talk: that's the way to deal with the situation." He was convinced that his name still had a good ring abroad: "The conversations need not be binding." Goering made it quite clear that he regarded himself still as the Fuehrer's rightful successor. "Anyway," he said, "I am the most popular of all leading Germans in the eyes of the outside world, particularly in the United States!"

He did not know that Eisenhower had different views about Nazi leaders and German generals. "As far as I was concerned," Eisenhower wrote later, [3] " . . . none of them would be allowed to call on me. I pursued this practice to the end of the war, and not until Field Marshal Jodl signed the surrender at Rheims . . . did I ever speak to a German general and, even then, my only words were that he would be held personally and completely responsible for the carrying out of his surrender terms. . . ." Goering was not aware how much his prestige had suffered, even inside Germany. When Koller tried to find alternative accommodation for him and his family, he selected a castle at Fischhorn in Austria belonging to a brother of Fegelein. "I would not live under the same roof with this traitor," was Fegelein's reply when Koller approached him. If he had only known that Hitler, whom Goering was supposed to have betrayed, had ordered his own brother to be shot! Koller requisitioned the castle and turned Fegelein out.

Still at Mauterndorf, Goering settled down to work on two long letters. He had made his plans. One letter was to the divisional commander of the approaching American Army, asking him for protection. The other was addressed to General Eisenhower. "General," it said, "I request the honour of a personal interview with you as man to man." He handed the letters to Brauchitsch with an order to go out and meet the Americans. Brauchitsch drove off. A few hours later he reported to Koller, asking for assistance in his attempt to cross the lines. Goering ordered his family and his staff to get ready for immediate departure. It was May 8. But time dragged, hours seemed eternity. When there was no word from Brauchitsch, Goering decided to approach the enemy personally. The American Army's 36th Division, under Brigadier-General Robert J. Stack, was in the meantime pushing in toward Mauterndorf. Goering was about to meet his destiny.

[3] General Dwight D. Eisenhower, *Crusade in Europe.*

20

"OH, EISENHOWER . . . !"

THERE were chaos and confusion on the roads when Goering tried to make contact with the Americans. He was relieved to have escaped from the S.S., a far greater menace than the American Army. Impatiently he set out from Mauterndorf, and an emissary, sent by Koller to tell him that an American general had been ordered to meet him, found the castle deserted. Goering at this moment was caught up in a maze of transport on the road to Radstadt. Wehrmacht men were making for home, civilians were moving in all directions. Tanks, lorries, motor cars, horsecarts, were interlocked in a hopeless tangle, through which footsore, aimless refugees weaved in frantic attempts to avoid the approaching enemy. Those who recognised Goering raised weary hands in a weak salute. Heading a column of cars with the thirty-odd members of his party and two big lorries carrying his luggage, neatly packed by Robert in monogrammed pigskin suitcases, Goering was lost in the chaos of defeat such as he had helped to inflict on many countries.

An American search party, under the command of First Lieutenant Jerome N. Shapiro, found him between Mauterndorf and Fischhorn. Open-eyed, young G.I.'s, thrilled by their most facinating assignment of the war, saluted smartly. Goering put a shaky hand to his cap. Lieutenant Shapiro noted that he wore his grey-blue uniform and only three medals—and, said Shapiro, badly needed a haircut. Headed by a jeep, whistles screaming, horns blowing, the cavalcade raced away as Germans, uniformed or civilians, on foot or in cars, hurriedly scampered for the ditches and out of the way. When Koller arrived at Fischhorn, the Reichsmarschall had been there and gone again.

Shapiro's impression of Goering was coloured by the mental picture which he had made for himself of the legendary figure of the Nazi leader. He expected to find a loud-mouthed, boisterous fellow. Goering was quiet. But Koller's emissary, Major Sandmann, who eventually caught up with Goering and talked to him, reported that he and his party were cheerful and relieved. When the Americans arrived, the women in the party fell round each other's necks, congratulating each other on their liberation. Capture by the Americans, indeed, meant security from the S.S. Goering soon smiled happily. He knew how to handle soldiers — of whatever nationality. With a few English words he made the Americans laugh with him.

Hermann Goering was now a prisoner of General Patch's Seventh United States Army. From Fischhorn he was first taken to divisional headquarters at Zell am See. When Koller came to Fischhorn, Philip Bouhler told him that Goering sent his best regards: "He has the greatest confidence in you," Bouhler said. Goering's message was that he had gone to see General Eisenhower. He would be back in a week. "Some hope!" commented Koller. No, he could not see Frau Goering, Bouhler told him. She was still resting. After lunch Koller drove off. "As I left," he recorded, "I saw Frau Goering at the window of the castle in a white dress and a huge sun hat!" I asked Emmy Goering about the incident: "You know," she said, "in the situation in which we were, one does not bother much about clothes." She told me that her husband was confident of coming to an arrangement with Eisenhower. "Anyway," she said, "he later sent word from Kitzbuehel that the Americans had promised protection for his family!"

"Shake!" said Brigadier-General Robert J. Stack, assistant commander of the 36th Division, who received Hermann Goering at Zell am See. Goering saluted. They shook hands. Later, Stack heard what his Supreme Commander thought of the "handshakers." He told Goering that he could have a bath — "And we'll have dinner later!" Such courtesies, due to his rank, which the Wehrmacht, the Nazi Party, the S.S., had denied him during the last oppressing fortnight, pleased Goering. It was probably only a lack of understanding which made a young United States officer knock at the door of his bathroom after three-quarters of an hour, asking him to hurry: "The photographers are waiting!" It was the old familiar routine. "Photographers, of course!" Goering posed patiently. He still appreciated the value of publicity. Robert gave him pills and they had the usual effect. Goering was buoyant, sparkling. Another Army officer asked him a few questions. Pure formality: Name, age, address, family . . . After lunch, Goering was driven to Kitzbuehl, Headquarters of the American Seventh Army, to meet General Spaatz. Koller received a report that "Goering had been seen on the balcony of the hotel headquarters, laughing, surrounded by high ranking American officers, a glass of champagne in his hand."

"Yes, the Chief was in high spirits," Robert Kropp told me. "At Zell am See, he personally organised the party to accompany him to Kitzbuhel. He went in an American car, but Willi Schulz, our driver, followed with his grey-blue, supercharged Mercedes 200, in which I travelled. Colonel Brauchitsch was with us and Captain Jansen of our staff." Before they left, Goering said to Robert: "Everything is fine, Robert. I am going to a conference with General Eisenhower . . ." At Kitzbuehl, Robert received orders to take charge of a lorry with Goering's luggage and to meet his chief at the airdrome. Goering went in his own car. "Five big American planes were waiting," Robert said, but Goering was perturbed: "There is something wrong," he said, "no American escort, no officer to accompany me?" Tactfully Goering did not ask where he would meet General Eisenhower. After all — he was a prisoner of war.

Robert was not there when the United States aircraft with Goering and his two aides landed in Augsburg: "When I eventually caught up with them, the Reichsmarschall was in a state of utter dejection!" There had been no welcome, no officer to greet him on arrival. Unceremoniously the party had been taken to a former workers' settlement of small houses on the outskirts of Augsburg, which had been adapted as a prison camp for high ranking officers. Robert looked at the Reichsmarschall in surprise. During the air trip his medals had been taken from him. How strange to see him without his Pour le Mérite, his Iron Cross, and his Golden Air Medal! The Marshal's baton was gone — it was later given to President Truman and is now lodged in the United States Army Museum in Washington. Two rooms were set aside for Goering's party. Outside in the corridor a six-foot United States Negro soldier, with fixed bayonet, stood guard.

"The Chief paced the tiny room for hours," Robert said. He was wondering, waiting . . . "Eisenhower," he murmured twice, three times. He was still hoping to meet the Supreme Commander of the victorious Allied armies. For a brief moment he cheered up when an American orderly arrived and asked him to join the camp commandant for a drink that evening. Goering pulled himself together. At such social gatherings he was still the old lion. At the "party" he met Bodenschatz again, for the first time after many months. "He had only been to see me once at hospital," Bodenschatz explained to me. "I had been disappointed, but it was good to see the familiar face of the Marshal again! Goering was upset about the delay of his meeting with Eisenhower," Bodenschatz recalled, "but very optimistic about the future." Two things, he told his old friend, were on his mind. After a successful conclusion of his talks with Eisenhower, he would start work on a proclamation to the German people. They were entitled to an explanation about the events which had led to the end of the war. They would have to be told that the mistake of waging a war on two fronts carried with it the seeds of inevitable disaster. He would not discredit the Fuehrer—loyalty forbade it: "But the German people must be told the truth!"

Robert thought that the Chief was enjoying himself at animated cocktail parties. Goering usually returned to his room around 2 A.M., a little flushed, still lively and talkative: "We are discussing the war, Robert," he told his valet. "What stories he must have told them!" Robert commented; "things of historical interest, tales of his encounters with the great of the world!" Goering was giving his listeners a few gems from the rich fount of his experiences. The American party was spellbound. But slowly he realised that this was not just a pleasant way of whiling away the time until General Eisenhower had returned from his travels, wherever he was, and was ready to receive him. This was the first stage of his interrogation, which experienced American Intelligence officers disguised as a happy get-together to "soften-up" a particularly tough customer. If there had been any doubt in his mind it was dispelled when, from among the uniformed Americans who looked so much alike to him emerged an officer who addressed him in perfect German: "Why, Kempner. . . . !" Goering exclaimed.

He was standing face to face with the former Oberregierungsrat (Upper Government Counsel) of the Prussian Ministry of the Interior, Dr. Robert M. Kempner, Chief of the Police Department, which used to deal with National Socialist affairs. Kempner! Kempner, the man whom Rudolf Diels had sacked in the hectic days of January, 1933, was now an officer of the United States Army, designated to join the team of American Prosecuting Counsel who would draw up the charges against the Nazi war criminals. Kempner was cool, correct; Goering showed signs of embarrassment. Clearly, Kempner, who had gone to America as a refugee from Nazism, was an expert with whom it would not be easy to argue about the rights and wrongs — particularly the wrongs — of Nazi policy!

But Goering was still able to turn his back on a difficult situation. There were other American officers whom he could impress. "Let me send Robert to get a few more clothes — and one or two other things!" he asked one of them. "I may have a surprise for you!" he added. The bulk of his luggage had been left at Kitzbuehl. The unfortunate American complied with Goering's request and Robert returned with a large package. "Here, my friend — with the compliments of the Marshal of the German Reich!" Goering handed the American a valuable landscape painting. He was still making presents, and Goering souvenirs were something worth while collecting in these days! "It was terrible," Robert said. Next day the poor Ami (as Germans call the Americans now) was led away in chains." He had been arrested for accepting gifts from his prisoner.

On May 20, Goering returned from his nightly conversations, the initial interrogations by United States Intelligence officers. "Robert," he said, "at long last . . . I am flying to meet General Eisenhower!" Excitedly he supervised the packing of a suitcase. "My pills . . ." he said. "Don't forget them, Robert!" Silently he slipped two capsules into his pocket. Every member of the Nazi Government had carried one or two of these capsules for many months past. In a metal container, nearly two inches long, was a thin glass phial with potassium-cyanide, enough poison to kill a regiment. Once or twice while they were prisoners of the S.S. in Berchtesgaden, Robert had seen his master fondling the capsules. He knew that Goering had been thinking of suicide — if the worst should happen. "Listen, Robert," Goering said now. "I have been given permision to take one member of my entourage with me — I do not need Brauchitsch on this mission, I have asked for you to accompany me!"

At the crack of dawn they took off — destination unknown. Goering, in spite of his old skill as an airman, was unable to gauge the direction. "Where are we going?" he asked the American pilot. "I am afraid — I am not allowed to tell!" Goering, Robert said, was anxious to know how he would be accommodated. The Augsburg arrangements had not been to his liking. "Am I going to stay at a hotel?" he asked. "Sure, sure. . . . ! " said the pilot in a slow, Southern American drawl. "All will be well, Robert," Goering said, but he sounded as if he was only trying to convince himself.

He peered out of the window as the plane circled to land. He did not know as yet, but he was coming down in Luxembourg. Heavily he raised himself from the seat. Robert was close behind him as the door of the aircraft swung down. He did not see Goering's face, but he noticed his shoulders droop, his body sag; trembling hands sought support. Looking over his shoulders, Robert took in the sight which had shaken his chief. Drawn up in a half-circle around the aircraft was a platoon of United States military policemen, light, multiple automatics under their arms, revolvers in their belts, staring into space with the devastating aloofness of trained police officers doing their job. "Come on!" a sergeant beckoned Goering. He pointed to a truck with a canvas cover. "You take charge of the luggage!" he told Robert. Pale, crestfallen, Goering heaved himself into the truck. Two young military police jumped in after him, pushed him into a corner. "Let's go!" they shouted to the driver. Goering's eyes seemed empty. Later, he said that all he remembered were the monotonous motions of the Americans' jaws chewing their gum.

The pilot had told him the truth. The truck stopped outside the entrance of the smart Palace Hotel at Bad Mondorf, eleven miles from Luxembourg. But Goering seemed not to care any longer.

Robert said that he did not bat an eyelid when he was shown into his room on the second floor. Room? It may have been an elegant apartment once — but now it hardly resembled any hotel room he had ever seen. The floor boards and the window frames had been ripped out and a thin meshed wire covered the space where there had once been a glass pane. There were no fixtures of any description. "A prison cell would have been better!" Robert commented. He was separated from Goering, but as the highest ranking servant he was put in charge of a staff of twenty German prisoners of war employed as cleaners. His red armlet, he told me, allowed him greater freedom than the others. Next day he sneaked up to Goering's room. "They have taken everything from me," Goering said. He looked ill. "I have given them one of my capsules — kept the other, you know!" he added, with a tired wink of his eye. "They confiscated a couple of thousand of his pills, too!" Robert told me — "and I knew he needed them!"

Goering complained because the American guards did not allow him a pillow. "I pinched one and took it up to him," Robert said, "the last favour I was able to do him. The next day they had taken it away again!" On June 2 was the last time Robert saw him. "Herr Reichsmarschall," he said, "I fear our times together are coming to an end. I shall not be able to come up here again!" "If I only knew what's become of my wife and child," Goering moaned. "I hope they are all right. Stack promised that he would look after them . . . !" He had tears in his eyes as Robert took his leave. "Take care of yourself, Robert, and thank you for everything." Two days later, on June 4, Robert and the rest of the German staff were ordered to assemble for removal to another camp. "As they marched us away," he told me, "I saw the Reichsmarschall standing at the window looking through the wire meshing . . . " He never saw him again.

A German prisoner-batman was allocated to Goering. He recognised him at once. It was the chauffeur who had driven the late General Jeschonneck for years. He told Goering that the hotel was filling up with new guests. On May 23 the members of the Flensburg Government of Grand Admiral Doenitz, having implemented the terms of surrender, were arrested. They were taken to Bad Mondorf. Heinrich Himmler, captured at Lunenburg, had swallowed poison and died within a minute. A few days later, Ribbentrop, arrested in Hamburg, joined the Mondorf assembly of fallen Nazi leaders. American medical officers consulted Dr. Karl Brandt, one of Hitler's doctors, about Goering's health. "He is a drug addict," Brandt said. "He cannot carry on without his pills very long! He has been taking twenty times the average dose!" Now the American doctor in charge permitted him eighteen pills per day.

Goering later told his wife that Mondorf was like a bad dream. Except for Kempner, the American interrogation officers were cyphers, known only by their code names. Their inquiries ranged over his whole life. Questions about his financial affairs exasperated him. In his prime he had not paid much attention to the details of his liabilities. He had bothered as little about his assets. It seemed all very vague.

During one session he was asked by a very nice American boy, obviously of German origin: "When you wanted money, or foreign exchange — was there a record made at the Ministry of Economics?"

"No," he replied, a little bored with questions which centred around the obvious. "If I wanted foreign exchange, I asked the Reich Bank. The Reich Bank was dealing with foreign exchange."

"And who gave permission — the Office of the Four-Year Plan or the Ministry of Economics?"

"In my case . . . the Ministry of Economics gave permission."

Was it necessary to mention that his word was equivalent to permission for everything? Was it necessary to question him about such a simple procedure? In Germany — in his Germany — not many questions were asked if the Reichsmarschall made a request or gave an order! Permission? Ridiculous!

"Who was dealing with these matters?"

"Details," Goering replied. "My secretary, my adjutants, scores of people were dealing with all this!"

Every sphere of his activities was reviewed. For six, eight hours every day, he was questioned until he was too tired. Occasionally he still felt ill and was absent-minded, bothered, irritated by the grinding questions, designed to throw light on one of the darkest chapters of recent European history. On such days he was tight-lipped and unresponsive. His memory was not as good as it used to be. But slowly, as his allocation of drugs was reduced and his health improved accordingly, he recovered his mental faculties, Goering, for the first time in his life, became patient. He was polite, helpful, anxious to please the interrogators who were dealing with subjects involving the fate of Germany, the conduct of the war, the destiny of nations. As time went on, he relaxed completely and seemed pleased to open a door into periods of his life to which he looked back with pride and satisfaction. But the questions probed ever deeper into the sordid aspects of German politics between 1933 and 1945, and he became aware of the measure of responsibility which he had taken on his shoulders. A signature, hurriedly committed to a document, an order casually made to one of his aides, began to assume frightening proportions.

At first, after his disappointment about Eisenhower's refusal to meet him, he regarded himself simply as a prisoner of war, but the longer the interrogations proceeded, the heavier grew the weight of the charges with which he knew he would be confronted. The slave workers of a dozen countries — they were really the responsibility of Labour Minister Fritz Sauckel. But was Sauckel not technically under his orders? The treatment of prisoners of war — he always had his own views about them. What happened in the Stalag Luft (Luftwaffe prisoner-of-war camps) — would he not be made to answer for the damning, criminal events? "Too much was put on my plate!" he told his interrogators. "I never really considered these details!"

Once more he enjoyed the privilege of his position. Allied newspaper correspondents were invited to interview the star prisoner, the highest ranking surviving leader of defeated Nazi Germany. They fired questions at him. He was never at a loss for an answer. It was the kind of shadow-boxing in which he knew how to dodge a blow, how to strike, and how to fight his way out of a corner. The apt phrase still came easily to his mind. "Death is the fate of the defeated," he said, with a superior gesture. "It cannot be avoided!" Few reporters believed that he really meant what he said.

Bodenschatz told me that he knew of Goering's rising apprehension about his ultimate fate. The conviction grew in his still alert mind that he and his fellow defendants would have to answer for terrible things. Whether or not they were aware of details and of every single act of the Nazi administration — they could not avoid responsibility. For Goering, it was no longer a question of a proclamation to the German people. He knew that he would be put in the dock like a common criminal. And he had little doubt what the verdict would be.

There were hours when he felt weak, lonely, deserted, in need of comfort. He could still plead like a little boy, arouse sympathy, compassion — even if he could no longer command respect. His American guards were wax in his hands. Now his parleys with the interrogators were only excursions of his mind from the narrowing circle of his fear. He was told early in August that the victorious Allies had agreed on a procedure to deal with him and the other prisoners; that they would implement their decision to try the war criminals, to hold them responsible for atrocities in Occupied Europe (as decided in Moscow in 1943) and punish them according to the verdict. A copy of the London Agreement between Britain, the United States, France, and Soviet Russia of August 8, 1945, incorporating this decision, was read to him.

By the time he was transferred to the old Palace of Justice in Nuremberg, Goering was thinner and healthier. He was lodged in cell number five of the prison annex at the back of the building. For a while he was gratified by the secret, if unmistakable, respect with which the American guards treated him until familiarity began to breed contempt. But he could not hide his dislike of Colonel B. C. Andrus, the commandant of the United States Military Police at the Nuremberg Palace, a stocky little man wearing a green steel helmet adorned with warpaint of his own design. So utterly was Goering divorced from his past that his hard bed, the mediocre food prepared from American Army rations, the tedious routine of prison life, hardly bothered him. One of his American guards, still a serving officer and reluctant to reveal his identity, told me: "Sometimes a serene smile played around Goering's lips. Then he looked like a man who has made peace with the world and with heaven." Emmy Goering, when she was eventually allowed to visit her husband, had the same impression. He was, she said, beyond caring. But that was many months later.

The charter of the International Military Tribunal provided that the four Great Powers — the United States, Great Britain, France, and the Soviet Union — would jointly conduct the trial. Rules of procedure were laid down. An indictment was prepared against the individual defendants and against the organisations responsible for the conduct of German affairs — the Reich Cabinet, the leadership corps of the Nazi Party, the S.S. and S.D. (Security Service), the S.A., the Gestapo, the General Staff and the High Command of the Wehrmacht (German Armed Forces). The indictment against Goering and the other leaders specified four counts — (1) The Common Plan or Conspiracy; (2) Crimes against Peace; (3) War crimes; and (4) Crimes against Humanity.

On October 19, 1945, at 2 P.M., the door of Goering's cell opened. In Nuremberg Prison, as in all other prisons, news miraculously penetrates the thickest walls, and Goering knew what to expect. At the head of a procession a young British officer, in service dress and Sam Browne belt, entered the door. It was thirty-year-old Royal Artillery officer, Major (later Lieutenant-Colonel) A. M. S. Neave. Mr. Neave, now a barrister in London, described the occasion to me. "I was a member of the staff of the General Secretary of the Tribunal," he said. Neave had been taken prisoner at Calais in 1940, had escaped from a German prison camp in 1942, and rejoined the Army to be decorated with the D.S.O. at Nijmegen. "I was accompanied by Colonel B. C. Andrus, the Commandant of the Guard; by Mr. Harold B. Willey, the General Secretary of the Tribunal, and a retinue of American soldiers," Mr. Neave said. He first entered the cell of Rudolf Hess to hand him the indictment. Hess did not seem interested, put the bulky document on his table, and reached for a novel. "Then I went to cell number five, next door," said Mr. Neave. It was at the end of a long corridor on the left-hand side. As the door opened, Goering rose from his iron bedstead and bowed. Major Neave said: "Hermann Goering, I am the officer appointed by the International Military Tribunal to serve upon you a copy of the indictment in which you are named as defendant." Goering took the document. "I must read the document," he said. "And I would like to have further information about it." Major Neave nodded, and Goering continued: "I attach very great importance to having my own interpreter," he added. "I am sure there will be the best of interpreters," Neave replied. "Goering seemed depressed and nervous," Mr. Neave told me, "but he was extremely polite and apologised because there was so little room in the cell. Unlike some of the other defendants, he was co-operative and intelligent in discussing his rights under the charter of the Tribunal. But he was obviously under a great strain. His mouth was twitching and he looked as if he was going to cry." As he left, Major Neave said: "Good-bye — I shall be seeing you in a day or two." It was his task to establish contact between the defendants and their counsel. Goering was already immersed in the study of a list giving the names of approved German counsel for the defence.

A United States military policeman was looking through the grille into Goering's cell shortly after and saw the former Reichsmarschall reading the indictment. Goering was thumbing through the pages and glancing over the headings, a relentless enumeration of his road to power, listing the activities of the Nazi Party since 1921; recalling how the Party plotted to overthrow the German Government by "legal" means supported by terrorism; how Nazi control was eventually utilised to prepare foreign aggression; how the aggressive war was planned and carried out. Murder, ill-treatment of civilian populations, the deportation of slave labour and prisoners of war, the killing of hostages, the plunder of public and private property, the wanton destruction of cities and villages, the Germanisation of occupied territories, the persecution on racial, political, and religious grounds — it was a frightening record.

> The defendant Goering [the indictment said], between 1932 and 1945, was a member of the Nazi Party, Supreme Leader of the S.A., General in the S.S., a member and President of the Reichstag, Minister of the Interior of Prussia, Chief of the Prussian Police and Prussian Secret State Police, Chief of the Prussian State Council, Trustee of the Four-Year Plan, Reich Minister for Air, Commander-in-Chief of the Air Force, President of the Council of Ministers for the Defence of the Reich, member of the Secret Cabinet Council, head of the Hermann-Goering Industrial Combine, and Successor-Designate to Hitler. The defendant Goering used the foregoing positions, his personal influence, and his intimate connection with the Fuehrer to promote the accession to power of the Nazi con-

> spirators and the consolidation of their control over Germany, the military and economic preparation for war set forth in Count One of the Indictment. He participated in the planning and preparation of the Nazi conspirators for Wars and Aggression and Wars in Violation of International Treaties, Agreements, and Assurances set forth in Counts One and Two of the Indictment; and he authorised, directed, and participated in the War Crimes set forth in Count Three of the Indictment, and the Crimes against Humanity set forth in Count Four of the Indictment, including a wide variety of crimes against persons and property.

There was nobody to record Goering's reaction. Major Neave went to see him again two days later. "I don't know any of these lawyers," Goering said. He was perturbed about his defence. Major Neave was under the impression that he doubted whether he would receive a fair trial. But at his next visit, Goering surprised him by saying that he recognised the name of Dr. Otto Stahmer, a well-known Kiel lawyer, on the list of admitted German counsel. He would like Stahmer to take charge of his defence. "I made arrangements accordingly," Mr. Neave told me, "but when Stahmer arrived, I could not have imagined a person more different from Goering." Stahmer was a seventy-year-old frail little man, but he proved an energetic, alert counsel for the chief defendant. Goering told Major Neave a few days later that he was glad Stahmer was his counsel. "We see eye to eye with each other," he said.

A week later he was told that his wife had been arrested at the porter's lodge of Veldenstein Castle, into which she had moved after his capture by the Americans. She was held in prison in Straubing. Her sister Else was taken into custody with her. Christa Gormanns, the nurse, was detained at the same time, and allowed to share Frau Emmy's cell. Goering was prostrate to think of his wife in prison, even if he did not know that she and Christa Gormanns had to sleep on the floor of their cell. Neither was he told when little Edda was taken to join her mother in prison a few weeks later. "Frau Goering demanded it," a Bavarian official told me.

"When Edda arrived," Frau Emmy told me, "I was hungry and

hoped there might be food in her little satchel, which was tightly packed." But Edda calmly unpacked — her doll and all its clothes. Emmy and the child stayed in prison until March, 1946.

In the meantime, Hermann Goering was discussing his defence with Dr. Stahmer and his assistant, Dr. Werner Bross. He was not an easy client to deal with. Unlike many other Nazi leaders, he had never kept a diary. Apart from official documents which were in the hands of the prosecution, there was little concrete evidence to go on. Goering's memory served him well; indeed, he remembered much more than was relevant to his defence and was liable to stray from the subject under discussion.

A few days after he had been served with the indictment, there was a commotion in the prison corridor. Dr. Robert Ley, the former leader of the Nazi Labour Front, had been found hanging from his window, dead. Goering realised that there might be a search of the cells. Soon he heard the military policemen walking down the corridor. He had nothing to hide — except his cyanide capsule for which he quickly found a safe place in the rim of his lavatory. But the guards did not visit him on this occasion. Goering, in spite of the stringent regulations, was never properly searched.

The study of the documents and material dealing with his activities and covering a span of twenty-five years was by no means an unpleasant chore. His lawyer realised that a last new ambition had taken shape in Goering's mind. Though he was determined to plead "Not Guilty" to every one of the four counts of the indictment, he would not shirk his responsibility for the policy of the Third Reich. He had known everything, he insisted, though it was clear that he had signed a thousand documents without reading them. He was determined to admit his share in every decision which Hitler had made, though Hitler had rarely listened to him after 1942, and he had known of many vital decisions only after they had been taken. He had run away from the Hitler trial in 1924 after the Munich putsch. But this would he *his* trial; he was going to make a success of it. The worry about his wife and child weighed heavily on him — but he did not let it weigh him down. The former Marshal of the Reich, the Fuehrer's deputy and successor, the last exponent of National Socialist policy, would show the world his mettle.

21

GUILT UNIQUE

THE big Nuremberg trial started in November, 1945, but Hermann Goering was not called to the witness stand until five months later. The passive rôle of a silent number in the dock, even if he was Number One, did not suit his temperament. Behind the scenes of the trial his world, which once stretched from the gates of Moscow to the Channel coast, from the north of Norway to the African shores, was now enclosed by the bare walls of his small cell or prison corridors, The lord of many manors with exquisite furniture was left with a field bed and two blankets, a chair, a lavatory, a cardboard table too frail to carry a man who might want to hang himself, as Dr. Ley had done, from the small high window. His eyes, which used to rest fondly on a unique art gallery, had only one picture to behold—a photograph of his wife and daughter. The master of many servants was handed his food on a tin plate through a hatch in the heavily bolted door. Later the prisoners took their lunch at tables for four in common rooms. Every evening Goering's braces were collected—he wore riding boots or he would also have had to part with his bootlaces.

Sometimes depression overcame him in his cell. The guards would see him lying on his bed, staring into space with half-open eyes, mumbling to himself, his mouth twitching. They often watched him, chewing the stem of his big Austrian pipe, sitting at his table, nervously scribbling notes to his lawyers, writing letters to his wife, tearing them up and starting again. The prison officials found him sometimes childish and petulant and deeply concerned about the impression which he made on others. They might have known that it had always been the same in the privacy of his home, in the intimate circle of his friends, while he still enjoyed the prestige and the power of a Reichsmarschall.

Like any other prisoner, he welcomed every distraction and visit which broke the monotony of the prison routine. One of his regular visitors was the prison chaplain, Henry F. Gereke. The pastor said that all attempts to convert Goering to real Christianity failed, although he was always anxious to observe religious formalities. He took part in the Sunday Chapel Service, but only because it enabled him to leave his cell for an extra half-hour. He boomed carols at the Christmas Service — not with much religious conviction, but like a little boy who loves to roar and shout and to hear his voice rising above those of others.

The prison psychiatrists, determined to find out what made the Nazi leader tick, came to ask him a hundred questions and submitted him to many tests. He co-operated willingly. One of them, Captain G. M. Gilbert of the United States Army, has written an account of his experiences with the imprisoned Nazi leaders.[1] It makes very interesting reading. But it was as difficult for Gilbert to penetrate Goering's mentality as it is to gauge a tiger's behaviour in the jungle from observation of his antics in a zoo. Yet there was much of the old Goering in the deflated figure of cell five whom Dr. Millar, the patient prison physician, had completely weaned of his paracodeine drug.

When he emerged from his cell, he made a vigorous bid to establish his position in the prison community. Relations of the prisoners among themselves reflected, of course, their previous attitude toward each other — only they were now more honest, less restrained and removed from the commanding influence of Hitler. But tension produced many changes as the trial went on. The shock of defeat, arrest, confinement, the unfolding of the grave charges, the damning testimony of witnesses and the incontrovertible documentary evidence began to tell on them. The hammer blows of Fate, however well deserved, left their mark. Goering in the presence of the others, seemed undaunted. His one aim was to retain his leadership, even behind bars. As he had done in his heyday, he freely meted out approval or disapproval, criticised, intervened, interfered at every opportunity. When he met resentment, he was offended or

[1] G. M. Gilbert, *Nuremberg Diary*.

angry in turn, but he never gave up trying. It did not enhance his popularity with the harassed prisoners of Nuremberg Jail.

The common fate did not temper his contempt for Ribbentrop. Only gradually could he bring himself to talk to the former Foreign Minister, whom he regarded as architect of Germany's diplomatic isolation. Some of his irrepressible remarks were at the expense of Rudolf Hess and his amnesia. On other occasions he sought him out, called "Rudi!" across the prison yard, and engaged him in lengthy conversations. He despised Hans Frank, the former Governor-General of Poland, who was gripped by religious mania and beat his breast in tearful bouts of repentance. As did almost every other prisoner, he kept away from the uncouth Julius Streicher. Like many people, Goering did not realise what a nuisance uninvited advice can be, and he could not desist from pursuing his fellow prisoners with suggestions, information, and ideas about their own cases and defence. On Keitel and Jodl, particularly, although they were least friendlily inclined toward him, he showered his free gifts of advice. When Keitel, under the merciless cross-examination of the British Prosecutor, Sir David Maxwell Fyfe, was cornered into grave admissions, Goering pulled him up. "Be a man!" he told him. "There is no need to prostrate yourself!" During another recess, he challenged him again. "You must not allow yourself to be badgered. There is no need to bare your breast before them" — meaning the Tribunal.

He regarded it as his duty to back up his fellow defendants whenever they took a stand against Allied authority. Though he had little contact with Dr. Schacht, he was loud in his approval of the economist's righteous anger at "being treated like a criminal." Schacht was eventually acquitted. Every piece of evidence which was submitted to him for comment, Goering scrutinised suspiciously. Speaking to his lawyer, he angrily disassociated himself from the mass murder of European Jews, but he was sceptical of the evidence. He demanded technical information about the gas chambers and wanted to know how it was physically possible to exterminate two and a half million Jews. And when he spotted a group of Jews in the public gallery listening to the proceedings, he could not suppress a quip. "Look at them," he whispered; "nobody can say we have exterminated them all!" His mouth was still as big as it had ever been. A film showing the bodies of thousands of Poles in a mass grave at Katyn was produced as evidence. Goebbels, in a wild propaganda campaign during the war, had accused the Russians of this mass murder, but the trial elicited German responsibility for the crime: "The film proves nothing," Goering said, "it could just as well be the bodies of German prisoners put into Polish uniforms!"

When there was difficulty in tracking down a witness for his defence or delay in bringing him to Nuremberg, Goering was as impatient as ever. He wanted to call Karl Koller, but the former Luftwaffe Chief of Staff could not be quickly located: "Ridiculous!" he stormed. "The British or Americans must know where he is." Koller was a prisoner of war in Britain and his evidence was eventually produced. A woman secretary refused to appear in court as a witness: "Obviously," Goering commented. "Why should a woman want to go through this? . . ." He did not show his disappointment.

However skilfully he chose the arguments for his defence, nothing would induce him, even by implication, to stab the dead Hitler in the back. Dr. Stahmer, with the help of the psychologists, tried to dissuade him from his insistence on posthumous loyalty. After all, they explained, Hitler had dropped him and treated him shamefully. "I am guided by my oath of allegiance, from which even Hitler's death cannot free me," he answered. "It is a question of principle with me and it does not matter what Hitler did. It would be contemptible of me to betray him now!" He was openly rude to Speer when it was shown in the course of the trial that he had plotted to eliminate Hitler. Such "disloyalty" exasperated him. Admission of it in court was even worse.

To prevent similar admissions which might damage the prestige of Hitler, Goering was prepared to go to any length. A complaint reached the prison authorities that he had threatened his fellow prisoners with the Feme (revenge murder organisation) if they persisted in compromising National Socialism. It was one of those idle threats which he often made. Just as, in 1923, he had threatened to murder hostages which he did not hold, so he now conjured up a Feme which did not exist. To shield the other prisoners from his persistent interference and to prevent the trial from being used as a Nazi propaganda platform, Goering had to be separated from the others at mealtimes. The seating order of prisoners was so arranged that the sensible elements should have an opportunity of subtly converting the radical Nazis. Indeed, Albert Speer completely undermined Baldur von Schirach's faith in Hitler.

The psychiatrists were extremely suspicious of Goering's motives and intentions. They doubted his show of realism. But he had always been a "realist," as he saw it, and if he had often avoided facing unpleasant facts in the past, he knew he could not escape them now. The picture which he presented was of a man who, with utter fatalism, had decided to stand manfully by his lost and wicked cause rather than to make a show of regrets or an admission of mistakes. Whether he consciously intended to plant a political time-bomb in the minds of the German people, whether he acted from a genuine sense of loyalty or was simply motivated by exhibitionism (of which, except for the proverbially introvert English, few public men are free) who can say?

Goering knew that he would not leave Nuremberg alive, but, after talking to his closest associates, I cannot believe that his attitude in Nuremberg was only a pose. It needed more than vanity, even in the face of certain death, to act in the way which moved a generous opponent, Sir Archibald Sinclair, to tell me that in his view "Goering deserved credit for the indomitable spirit and the courage which he displayed during his final ordeal at Nuremberg." However clearly the flaws of his character appeared in captivity, nobody questioned his courage when he faced the Tribunal.

On March 8, a few days before he was due to be called to the witness stand, press photographers were admitted to the prison to take pictures of Goering in his cell. The procedure made him painfully aware of his decline and fall. It was probably the first time that he did not enjoy having his picture taken. Next day he received the news that his wife and daughter had been released from prison in Straubing. They moved to a small lodge at Sackdilling, not far from Veldenstein Castle, which had been handed over as a billet to a hundred Sudeten German refugees.

In her letters Emmy Goering tried to hide from him all details of her predicament. She was plagued by sciatica, suffering from a weak heart. She had no clothes except the dress and coat she was wearing, little to eat and hardly a penny in the world. "A day after I was released," Frau Emmy told me, "American Army investigators came to search my house." They had heard a village rumour that Martin Bormann had been seen in the neighborhood and was hiding in her cottage. "I could not make them understand," Frau Goering said, "that Bormann was the last person in the world whom I would wish to hide or to protect." Frau Emmy could not bear the thought of her husband being confined in a small cell. "To think of him in prison," she said, "was agony. He needed the open spaces and fresh air like his life blood." She underestimated Hermann Goering. He was more concerned about her than about himself. He sent Dr. Stahmer to see his wife and child and nervously waited for a report. Dr. Gilbert wrote that Goering received a letter from Frau Emmy and a postcard from Edda, but did not want to read them in his presence. Later Goering returned little Edda's postcard to Emmy, who gave it to me. On the back of her photograph the child had scribbled with the typical effort of a schoolgirl: "Dear Papa, come back to me again soon. I have such longing (Heimweh) for you. Many thousand kisses, from your Edda!!!"

Every morning the prisoners were marched into court, Goering leading the procession. Ponderously he moved to his corner seat in the dock, adjusted his earphones over which the German translation of the proceedings reached him, put on dark glasses to protect his eyes from the glare of arc lights, installed for the benefit of the photographers. Every day he had a greeting or a joke for the tall, impassive American guards around the dock. He whispered to Rudolf Hess, who sat next to him, or turned to Doenitz behind him — the "weekend Fuehrer" as he called the man who had supplanted him as Hitler's successor. In open court Goering was alert, observant. Studiously he watched the Allied pressmen — he still appreciated the value of publicity — noted their peculiarities, had a nickname for many of them. Maurice Fagence, of the London *Daily Herald*, who used to tiptoe silently to his seat, he dubbed "the ballet dancer" — a very apt description.

From the dock he accompanied the questions of counsel, the answers of witnesses, the reading of documents, with a display of animated facial expressions, registering agreement or disagreement, hurt innocence or rage. "Scoundrel!" he would call out, or "Fool!" he could be heard mumbling. Incriminating evidence was given by

General Erwin Lahousen of the German Army Abwehr espionage organisation which claimed anti-Nazi leanings and a part in the plot against Hitler. Goering blurted out: "That's one we have forgotten to knock off after July 20, 1944"—the day of the attempt on Hitler's life. Goering kept up a running commentary on the proceeedings, whether anybody listened or not. His eyes rested fondly on his old friend and Secretary of State, Paul Koerner, and he beamed when his "Pilli" described him as "the last surviving Renaissance figure." Erhard Milch he watched anxiously, with signs of apprehension, but he nodded assent to every word Karl Bodenschatz said in his testimony. Of his entourage or immediate collaborators, none had a bad word to say about him.

On March 13, 1946, he was up early, paced his cell nervously, did not touch his breakfast. This was his day in court when he would take the stand to speak, not only for himself, but for Adolf Hitler, for the Party, for National Socialist Germany—which was no more. An hour later he was in his corner seat as usual, waiting for the great moment. Lord Justice Lawrence, President of the Court, representing Britain, was in the chair. He was flanked by the United States, French, and Soviet members of the Tribunal. The other twenty "major war criminals" in the dock were as tense as Goering was. (Twenty-four Nazi leaders had originally been indicted, but three were missing—Martin Bormann who was tried in absentia; Gustav Krupp von Bohlen und Halbach, the Ruhr armaments king, who was too ill to be present; and Dr. Ley who—to use a literal translation of the German expression—had "judged himself" by committing suicide.)

The former Field Marshal Albert Kesselring had just left the witness stand when Dr. Otto Stahmer rose to say: "If the High Tribunal agree, I wish to call the former Reischmarschall, defendant Hermann Goering, to the witness stand." Now that his turn had come, the star turn of the trial, Goering was calm and very sure of himself. With a few strides he walked to the witness stand a sheaf of papers in his hand. Looking straight at the President and speaking in German, he repeated the oath in his clear, metallic voice: "Ich schwoere—I swear by God the Almighty and Omniscient that I will speak the pure truth—and will withhold and add nothing." He looked around the court, a slight smile on his lips. It was obvious that he enjoyed being the centre of attention once more. For three days he spoke in his own defence. His cross-examination by the prosecutors and the counsel of the other defendants lasted until March 22. He was the key-witness of twenty-five years of political developments in Germany, the only man who knew the whole — well, almost the whole — truth about National Socialism.

Representatives of all nations were impressed when they watched him. He may not have spoken the truth, but he was never flustered or lost for an explanation. It was remarkable how he could reconstruct and interpret his actions over a period of many years past. He elucidated the policy and the plans for the Nazi Government with clarity — however confused or wrong-headed they had been. His defence was based on his favourite theory that acts of war or a country's political affairs cannot be measured by standards of morality applicable to individuals. "I should like to say the same words," he concluded his testimony, "which one of our greatest, most important, and toughest opponents, the British Prime Minister, Winston Churchill, used: 'In the struggle for life and death, there is, in the end, no legality.' "

Goering was given great latitude to describe political developments beyond those covered by the four counts of the indictment. He was flattered by the decision of the Tribunal not to hear the others on the generalities of which he had given an expression. Goering's testimony produced few high-lights. A dozen times Goering countred questions by saying that he had not been aware of certain facts at the time. "But, of course," he always added, "I accept full responsibility." He disputed many depositions of witnesses or documentary evidence, but when told that he had signed a decree or a letter or an order, he concurred quickly: "Then I am responsible!"

There were a few heated interchanges during his cross-examination by the United States Prosecutor Justice Robert H. Jackson, but it was usually Justice Jackson who lost his temper. When asked to answer simply "yes" or "no," Goering bided his time until the prosecutor gave him an opening: "Excuse me," he said, "you have just asked me a number of questions at the same time and it is impossible to answer 'yes' or 'no.' " Justice Jackson asked him about German war preparations "of a character which had to be kept entirely secret from foreign powers." Immediately Goering's reply came: "I do not believe I can recall the publication of the preparations of the United States for mobilisation." Justice Jackson protested, but the President of the Court did not intervene. The American press sportingly recorded: "Goering wins first round." He did not win the fight. He continued to score a few points, but Justice Jackson triumphed in the end with the help of hard facts which proved Goering's guilt.

On behalf of Britain, Sir David Maxwell Fyfe took up the cross-examination and concentrated on the murder of fifty British airmen who had taken part in the mass escape from Stalag Luft III, a prisoner-of-war camp. "It was the one accusation which deeply hurt my husband," Emmy Goering told me when I asked her about his comments on the trial. "He was stunned that he, an airman, should be connected with such an outrage against men of his own profession. And you know," she added, "I supplied the missing link of these events for him. He did not remember where he had been on the critical day. It was my birthday — and he spent it with me. He only knew about it much later. . . ." But if it was not proved that Goering had issued the criminal order, he was guilty of having tolerated the crime, had been too weak or even unwilling to prevent the massacre.

To General R. A. Rudenko, the Chief Soviet Prosecutor, Goering was often outright rude. Here, he was short, to the point, as if he wanted to limit to the barest possible minimum the verbal exchanges with the representative of the hated Russians. "I have already explained that!" he said, with a show of short temper. "I do not understand the meaning of that question!" was another retort. "Just a moment!" he would interrupt the Soviet general. When Rudenko tried to make a point, Goering flared up: "What you say proves nothing!" His curt demeanour could not gloss over the grim facts which the question suggested. Goering seemed not to care, seemed content to show his contempt for the Soviet Union. In that he succeeded.

Goering left the witness stand on March 22 and the trial dragged on until, by the end of August, the time came for each defendant to make his final statement. On Saturday, August 31, 1946, it was Goering's turn: "The prosecution," he said, ". . . has treated the defendants and their testimony as completely worthless. . . . One seems to forget that Germany was a sovereign State and that her legislation within the German nation was not subject to the jurisdiction of foreign countries. . . . If we, the leaders, as individuals, are called to account and condemned — very well! But you cannot punish the German people at the same time . . . the German people are free of guilt." Then Hermann Goering pulled himself up and spoke his credo, confident, he said later, that it would find its way into the books of history. Certain that the verdict of the Court would be "Guilty" and the sentence would he Death, he said his last piece in public:

> I did not want a war, nor did I bring it about. I did everything to prevent it by negotiations. After it had broken out, I did everything to assure victory. Since the three greatest Powers on earth, together with many other nations, were fighting against us, we finally succumbed to their tremendous superiority.
>
> I stand up for the things that I have done, but I deny most emphatically that my actions were dictated by the desire to subjugate foreign peoples by wars, to murder them, to rob them, or to enslave them, or to commit atrocities or crimes.
>
> The only motive which guided me was my ardent love for my people, its happiness, its freedom, and its life. And for this I call on the Almighty and my German people to witness.

Goering looked around the court as if waiting for a round of applause. But all he heard was the voice of the President saying: "I now call on the Defendant Hess . . . " The Goering chapter was closed. Had he been told, he would have been unable to understand, that the German people to whom he addressed himself for the last time were hardly listening or even reading the reports of the trial. If the Allies ever intended the trial to have any propaganda purpose, it had long lost all news value. Germans who glanced at the short accounts in the newspapers quickly turned over the pages to study the latest announcement about food rations. The rising prices, the black market, the intolerable housing conditions were, at the moment, of greater interest to them than the heroics of the man whom they were inclined to judge by the monument he left behind — the ruins of their country.

After hearing the final speeches, the Tribunal adjourned. There was no doubt in anybody's mind what the verdict against Hermann Goering would be when judgment should be read at the resumption one month later. Emmy Goering, in the meantime, obtained at last permission to see her husband. It was eighteen months since they had been parted at Fischhorn. From mid-September onward the wives of the imprisoned men were allowed to visit them daily for half an hour. Dr. Stahmer offered Emmy Goering hospitality in Nuremberg — she could not have made the trip from Sackdilling very often.

Though ill and weak, she girded herself for the brief reunion. Emmy Goering was not going to show any sign of weakness. And Hermann, she told me, received her, composed, almost cheerful, as if his American guard was just a shadow, as if there was no wire grille between them as they spoke, as if he did not notice the difference in her appearance, her face, her coat, her only hat. Only those who have visited a prison and watched the tortuous, embarrassing contact between two worlds which have so little in common can understand how Hermann and Emmy Goering felt. Emmy talked about the child, about the little house in which she was living. And Goering assured her that he felt well and fit. The half-hour was almost over before a reference was made to the trial: "Don't worry, Emmy!" he smiled; "they will not hang me!"

He remained strong and unbowed during the following visits until Frau Goering obtained permission to take Edda to see her father. When he set eyes on his child, Goering broke down for the first time. He could not restrain the flow of tears. Emmy hurried away long before the allotted time. There were so few practical things to discuss even the next day. She would not allow him to mention financial affairs — how could she make him understand that but for the charity of a friend she and the child would be starving and that there was often not enough money for bread in the house? Robert Kropp had a request — would the Reichsmarschall give him a testimonal and confirm that he was never a member of the Party? In his firm handwriting, Goering wrote it out: "I, the former Reichsmarschall . . . declare . . . that Robert Kropp was never a member of the Party and has never engaged in politics. . . ." Robert Kropp, he stated in a second note, was "beyond praise as regards his character and his ability . . ." signed: "Hermann Goering." It did not occur to him that probably never before had a prisoner under the shadow of a death sentence been asked to write a testimonial.

The encounters with Emmy became an unbearable strain. Both were almost relieved when told that no further visits would be permitted after Sunday, September 29. They thought it was farewell forever, though Frau Emmy was eventually allowed to see him again on October 7. But from that last meeting Goering returned to his cell a broken man. He was shaken by convulsions and cried like a child. To a prison guard he said that he was not afraid of death; now he was afraid of living another day. Monday, September 30, the sittings of the Tribunal were resumed. The whole day was taken up with the reading of the general terms of the judgment. In the morning session of the following day, the two hundred and eighteenth day of the proceedings, the quiet, sonorous voice of the President of the Court came over the communication system: "Goering," said the voice, "is convicted on all four counts. The evidence shows that, after Hitler, he was the most prominent man in the Nazi régime. . . ."

In English, French, Russian, and German simultaneously the whole grim record of his life was being read — concentration camps . . . Gestapo . . . Roehm purge . . . sordid removal of Fritsch and Blomberg . . . the Anschluss . . . Poland . . . "Even if he opposed Hitler's plans against the Soviet Union," continued the voice, "he did so only for strategic reasons." And the recital continued — aggressive wars . . . slave labour . . . spoliation of conquered countries . . . the persecution of Jews . . . "There is nothing to be said in mitigation," the voice concluded, "for Goering was often, indeed almost always, the moving force, second only to his leader. . . . His own admissions are more than sufficiently wide to be conclusive of his guilt. His guilt is unique in its enormity. The record discloses no excuse for this man. The Tribunal finds the Defendant Goering guilty on all four counts. . . ."

Late in the afternoon, standing still and upright in the dock, this man heard Lord Justice Lawrence pronounce sentence: "Defendant Hermann Wilhelm Goering, on the counts of the indictment on which you have been convicted, the International Military Tribunal sentences you to death by hanging."

22

DEATH WITH A SMILE

There were tears in her eyes when I talked to Frau Emmy Goering about her husband four years after his death. From Sackdilling she had moved to Haus 52 of the tiny village of Etzelwang. Haus 52 is a small wooden shed which the villagers call "The Barrack." The lines of the railway which connects Etzelwang with nearby Nuremberg pass four feet behind the Barrack and fifty-two times during the day, sixty-four times during the night, the shed shakes as the trains rumble by. Here, Frau Emmy, when I saw her, lived with her faithful sister, Fraeulein Else Sonnemann, and with Cilli Wachowiak — Cilli died in the summer of 1950. Frau Goering, suffering from sciatica and a severe heart complaint, occupied a tiny room. Over her bed was a picture of Goering lifting up his baby daughter Edda, with the happy smile of a proud father. On the other wall was a picture of the Reichsmarschall in full regalia, and by the door a drawing of the young Goering with his sharp, clear, blue eyes. From the Barrack Edda went to school by train every morning at the crack of dawn, to return late in the afternoon — just one of the village children. Many of her little schoolmates hardly knew the meaning of the name of Goering.

About her husband's last days in Nuremberg Jail, Emmy Goering knew as little as the rest of the world. She knew nothing of the sound of hammering which faintly reached his cell when an American Army execution squad began to erect four gallows frames to hang Hermann Goering and the ten other Nazi leaders who were condemned to death with him. She has never read the interview which the boisterous American hangman, Sergeant John Wood, gave to the press and in which he said that he was particularly looking forward to hanging the fat Hermann; nor has she seen the picture of Wood displaying the strong rope with which he would do the job.

Hermann Goering spent his last days writing and rewriting three long letters. One was a manifesto addressed to the German people, one a letter to the prison authorities, another a farewell note to his wife. These documents were eventually confiscated by the prison authorities and suppressed. He tried to persuade Chaplain Gereke to administer the last rites to him, but the pastor was not satisfied that Goering was genuinely repentant and refused. Some of the prisoners said that the last few days before their death passed as if they were in a dream. Goering's eye rested critically on the two generals, Jodl and Keitel, to see how they bore their fate. He had kind words even for Ribbentrop and Kaltenbrunner. What did it matter now that S.S. Chief Kaltenbrunner only eighteen months earlier had wanted to have him executed? He was considerate to Rosenberg and Streicher, although they had become almost strangers to him. With Frick, Sauckel, and Seyss-Inquart he exchanged a few polite, but meaningless, phrases now and then.

Eventually, a four-power commission was appointed to investigate the circumstances of Hermann Goering's death. The conclusion at which they arrived was that Hermann Goering, at around 20.45 P.M. on October 15, took his life by swallowing potassium cyanide poison. At a press conference Major Frederic Teich, prison operations officer, explained that Goering very likely had the poison with him during the whole course of his imprisonment. He had probably hidden it in the inside rim of his cell's lavatory. At one time or another he may have concealed it on his body. But rumors of a surgical operation which he was supposed to have undergone to bury the capsule in his flesh were discounted. As often happens in death, the scar of his war wound had broken open. This gave rise to the rumour. Franz von Papen, one of three acquitted men, said later that he regarded it as unlikely that Goering could have hidden the poison for any length of time. He, Papen, had been searched carefully several times. But Goering was never properly searched.

He could not have concealed the capsule in his clothes because the uniform he wore during the trial was taken from him every evening. It was, however, handled by a German prisoner of war who performed the duties of a prison tailor. For a time the tailor was under suspicion of having given Goering the poison. Among twenty-six people similarly suspected were a number of S.S. prisoners who were engaged in reconstruction work on a building overlooking the prison yard. The prison chaplain was mentioned in connection with the affair, but Mr. Gereke's statement after Goering's death clearly excluded him as a suspect. The chaplain was very emphatic in his condemnation of Goering, who had demanded the last rites while he was already planning to commit the supreme sin of taking his own life. Gereke would not have been the accessory to what he considered a deadly sin.

On the eve of Goering's death, a man in an American uniform visited Frau Goering at Sackdilling. "I have good news for you," he said. "Hermann Goering has been reprieved!" "I was so overjoyed," Frau Goering told me, "that I gave him my last piece of jewellery, my ruby engagement ring!" Next morning she was told that her husband had committed suicide. She broke down, but to me she said that she was happy that he had died by his own hand. "If he had been hanged, I could not have believed in God any more!" Emmy Goering was high on the list of suspects who had, however remotely, contact with Hermann Goering in the days before his death. "It is insane to suspect me," she replied when questioned. "I was never allowed to touch my husband!" To me she added: "He would not have taken the poison from me; he would not have put me in a position where I might be accused of a crime!" Dr. Kempner was convinced of Frau Goering's innocence. He ridiculed another rumour that she had transmitted the phial to her husband with her parting kiss — there was no parting kiss. "Are you not glad now," Kempner asked her, "that you were not allowed to touch him?" She shrugged her shoulders. Robert Kropp would not say much, but he knew that his master had the capsule when he last saw him.

One of ten American prison guards has since boasted that he had given Goering the poison, but he was in his cups when he said it. He was one of the guards outside the prison who never met Goering. To get the credit for having helped the Nazi leader to "cock a snook" at Allied Justice, a number of Germans have also "admitted" that they were the culprits. Their stories were checked and dismissed as the fairy tales of cranks.

Among people who might have had an opportunity of passing the poison to Goering was Dr. Otto Stahmer, his lawyer, and a number of American guards in the courtroom. They have all been cleared by the investigating commission. Hints have been made that an American diplomat had a hand in the plot to rescue Hermann Goering from the gallows. But those who know Goering best are convinced that he needed little help. There is no mystery behind his death except the neglect of the American authorities who accorded him the privileges of an extraordinary prisoner.

The bare facts of his death are simple. At 10.30 P.M. on October 15, a guard saw Goering apparently asleep in his cell. Regulations provided that the condemned men should at all times keep their hands clearly visible outside their blankets, but, although Goering was completely covered, the guard did not interfere. There was excitement in the prison because, in spite of orders to keep the date and the time of the executions secret, it was known that they would begin at 1 A.M. on October 16. The guard went to look through the windows of the other cells. At 10.45 P.M. he was back outside Goering's door and noticed that the right hand of his prisoner was hanging limp from the bed. Entering the cell, he found a small metal container on the floor. It was similar to the one found after Himmler's suicide. Goering was dead. He looked peaceful, with a sardonic smile around his lips.

The cremation was carried out at Dachau concentration camp, where hundreds of thousands of Jews and Anti-Nazis had been imprisoned and had met their death. The last remaining incinerator of original Nazi design was used. At the Tribunal's orders, the ashes of Hermann Goering, originator of concentration camps, former Prime Minister of Prussia, President of the Reichstag, Field Marshal, Creator and Commander in Chief of the Luftwaffe, were thrown onto the trash heap.

THE END

BIBLIOGRAPHY

Bleibtreu, Peter M. *Ich Werde nichts Verschweigen.* A pamphlet based largely on Hermann Goering's testimony at Nuremberg. 1950.

Bodenschatz, Karl. *Jagd in Flanderns Himmel.* Munich, Verlag Knorr & Hirth. An account of the First World War exploits of the Richthofen Squadron by its adjutant.

Bongartz, Heinz. *Luftmacht Deutschland.* Essen, Essener Verlagsanstalt. A Nazi propagandist's account of the creation, development, and activities of the Luftwaffe until the conclusion of the campaign against Poland.

Brickhill, Paul and Conrad Norton. *Escape to Danger.* London, Faber & Faber, 1946. The story of escape adventures of R.A.F. pilots captured by the Germans.

Bross, Werner. *Gesprache mit Hermann Goering.* Flensburg und Hamburg, Verlagshaus Christian Wolff, 1950. The annotated diary of the assistant to Goering's Defence Counsel at Nuremberg, incorporating conversations with Goering at Nuremberg Jail.

Dahlerus, Birger. *The Last Attempt.* London, Hutchinson, 1948. The description of the Swedish businessman, of his bid to mediate between Britain and Germany on the eve of the last war.

Diels, Rudolf. *Lucifer ante Portas.* Zurich, Interverlag A. G. The first chief of the Gestapo explains his activities.

Documents Concerning German-Polish Relations. London, His Majesty's Stationery Office, 1939. The official publication setting out in documents the diplomatic developments which led to the German war against Poland.

Dodd, Martha. *Through Embassy Eyes.* London, Gollancz, 1940. The daughter of the former American Ambassador in Berlin writes about her encounters with Nazi leaders in the years before the war.

Dodd, William E. *Ambassador Dodd's Diary.* London, Gollancz, 1941. The notes of the American Ambassador in Berlin, who watched the early activities of the Nazi Government and was one of the few Western diplomats to raise his voice in warning.

Dungern, Professor Dr. Otto von. *Ahnentafeln Beruehmter Deutscher.* Leipzig, Zentralstelle fuer Deutsche Personen und Familiengeschichte, 1937. A study of Goering's family tree, one of a series of family histories of well-known Germans.

Eisenhower, Dwight D. *Crusade in Europe.* New York, Doubleday, 1949. The Supreme Commander of the Allied Armies' own story.

Emessen, T. R. *Aus Goering's Schreibtisch.* Berlin, Historisches Kabinett, 1946. A collection of papers which were found in Goering's desk after the Allied occupation of Berlin in 1945.

Frischauer, Willi. *The Nazis at War.* London, Gollancz, 1940. The author's own record of conditions inside Germany during the first year of the war.

Frischauer, Willi. *Twilight in Vienna.* Boston, Houghton Mifflin, 1938. The author's book dealing with the political and social conditions prevailing in Austria in the interwar years.

Gedye, G. E. R. *Fallen Bastions.* London, Gollancz, 1939. The incisive record of a British foreign correspondent who observed the Austrian scene before the Anschluss.

Gilbert, G. M., Ph.D. *Nuremberg Diary.* New York, Farrar, Straus, 1947. The American prison psychiatrist at Nuremberg Jail recalls his experiences and meetings with the major war criminals during their period of confinement.

Goebbels, Joseph. *The Goebbels Diaries* (tr. by Louis Lochner). New York, Doubleday, 1948. Extracts from Goebbels' diaries which were found in the ruins of Berlin in 1945.

Goering, Hermann. *Germany Reborn.* London, Elkin, Mathews & Marrott. A book dictated by Hermann Goering in forty-eight hours for the purpose of publication in Britain.

Grey, C. G. *The Luftwaffe.* London, Faber & Faber. A record of the Luftwaffe's origin, development, personnel, and activities by a British journalist.

Gritzbach, Erich. *Hermann Goering.* Munich, Zentralverlag der N.S.D.A.P., Franz Eher Verlag. The official biography of Hermann Goering produced under his supervision by the chief of his secretariat.

Gritzbach, Dr. Erich. *Hermann Goering, Reden und Aufsatze.* Munich, Zentralverlag der N.S.D.A.P., Franz Eher Rachs. A collection of Hermann Goering's speeches and newspaper articles, edited by the chief of his secretariat in the Prussian Ministry, one of his closest collaborators.

Gunther, John. *Inside Europe.* New York, Harper, 1940. An American reporter's survey of personalities and politics in pre-war Europe.

Halder, Franz. *Hitler als Feldherr.* Munich, Dem-Verlag, 1949. A short treatise by the former Chief of the General Staff of the German Army about Hitler as a war leader.

Hart, W. E. *Hitler's Generals.* London, Cresset Press. Character sketches of the outstanding leaders of the German war machine.

Heiden, Konrad. *Hitler das Leben eines Diktators.* Zurich, Europa Verlag, 1936. The original German version of Heiden's Hitler biography.

Heiden, Konrad. *One Man Against Europe.* London, Penguin (English version), 1939. One of the outstanding Hitler biographies written before the war.

Henderson, Sir Nevile. *Failure of a Mission.* New York, Putnam, 1940. An account of the pre-war British Ambassador in Berlin of his attempt to avert the war.

Hitler, Adolf. *Mein Kampf.* London, Hurst & Blackett, 1939. Written in Landsberg Prison in 1924, *Mein Kampf* was the bible of National Socialism, a verbose account of Hitler's own development, experiences and theories.

Holldack, Heinz. *Was Wirklich Geschah.* Munich, Nymphenburger Verlagshandlung. A German writer's collection of official documents, dealing with vital years of Nazi diplomacy, with a commentary on the events.

International Military Tribunal of Nuremberg. The official record of the proceedings of the ten months' trial of the major Nazi war criminals in Nuremberg and a collection of documents produced at the trial.

Kehrberg, Arno. *Das NS-Fliegerkorps.* Berlin, Verlag Bild und Buch Anton Schuhmacher. An account of the Nazi Party Air Force Organization.

Koller, Karl. *Der Letzte Monat.* Mannheim, Norbert Wohlgemuth Verlag. An account of the last few months of the war by the last Chief of the General Staff of the Luftwaffe.

Kunckel, Ernst-Ewald. *Der Preussische Staatstrat.* Berlin, Mittler & Sohn. The official history of the establishment and organization of the Prussian State Council, a model for dictatorship.

Lee, Wing-Commander Asher, O. B. E. *The German Air Force.* London, Duckworth, 1946. The authoritative book of an R.A.F. Intelligence Officer, describing Luftwaffe history, organisation, activity, achievement, and decline.

Lennhogg, Eugen. *The Last Five Hours of Austria.* London, Rich & Cowan, 1938. An Austrian editor's review of events in Vienna immediately preceding the Anschluss.

Lockhart, Bruce. *Guns or Butter.* London, Putnam, 1938. The famous British journalist's study of political events which led up to the war.

Ludecke, Kurt G. W. *I Knew Hitler.* New York, Scribner, 1931. The description of his relations with Hitler and other Nazi leaders by one who was close to them.

Matthias, Tschersich. *Goering, Soldat und Flieger.* Denpitas Ville, Berlin, 1936. A number of stories about Goering's First World War activities in the German infantry and air force by his platoon sergeant.

Mihan, George. *Looted Treasure.* London, Alliance Press. A short description of some of the art deals and art looting for which the Nazi Government was responsible.

Moellendorf, Graefin Fanny von Wilamowitz. *Karin Goering.* Berlin, 1935, Verlag Martin Warneck. The story written by her sister of the life of Goering's first wife.

Muggeridge, Malcolm, editor. *Ciano's Diplomatic Papers.* London, Odham's Press, 1948. Notes and records of Mussolini's son-in-law and erstwhile Foreign Minister.

Price, G. W. *I Know These Dictators.* London, Harrap, 1938. The famous British correspondent describes his encounters with the leaders of the Fascist countries before the war.

Rave, Paul Ortwin. *Kunstdiktatur im Dritten Reich.* Hamburg, Verlag Gebr. Mann. An outline of the dictatorship which the Nazi Government established over art and cultural activities.

Riess, Curt. *Goebbels.* New York, Doubleday & Co., 1948. A biography of the Nazi Propaganda Minister by an American author of German origin.

Royal Institute of International Affairs. *Chronology of the Second World War.* A detailed chronicle of the recent war.

Sievers, Max. *Unser Kampf gegen das Dritte Reich.* Stockholm, Axel Holmstroms Forlag, 1939. The account by an anti-Nazi of his battle against the Third Reich.

Sommerfeldt, Martin H. *Hermann Goering.* Berlin, Mittler & Sohn. A short biography of Goering by his former Press Chief.

Supf, Peter. *Luftwaffe von Sieg zu Sieg.* Berlin, Im Deutsches Verlag. The record written from a personal angle of an eye-witness of the Luftwaffe's initial victorious campaigns in Eastern and Western Europe.

Trevor Roper, H. R. *The Last Days of Hitler.* New York, Macmillan, 1947. The most authoritative account of the Nazi Goetterdaemmerung by an Oxford don and former British Intelligence Officer.

Vox Populi. *Gefluestertes.* Heidelberg, Freiheit Verlag, 1946. A collection of "whispered jokes" about the Nazi leaders.

Welles, Sumner. *The Time for Decision.* New York, Harper & Brothers, 1944. The former American Under-Secretary of State describes his experiences during a mission to Europe which he undertook on the instructions of President Roosevelt in 1940.

Werner, Max. *Battle for the World.* London, Gollancz, 1941. A well-known military expert's analysis of the Nazi plan to conquer the world.

Wetzler-Muhlens, P. R. *How They Did It (Field Marshal Goering).* London, Pallas. A short biography of Hermann Goering.

Willenbacher, Jorg. *Deutsche Fluesterwitze.* Karlsbad, Verlagsanstalt Graphia, 1936. Another volume of "whispered jokes" which were popular in Germany during the years of the Nazi régime.

World Committee Victims of German Fascism. *The Brown Book of the Hitler Terror.* London, Gollancz, 1933. An exposition of the Nazi plot to burn the Reichstag and a well-authenticated enumeration of the terror acts preceding and following the crime.

Young, Desmond. *Rommel, The Desert Fox.* New York, Harper, 1950. A biography by a British Brigadier of the most popular German General of the last war.

INDEX